THE UNIVERSITY OF KNOWLEDGE
WONDER BOOKS

GLENN FRANK, EDITOR-IN-CHIEF

ART IN THE MIDDLE AGES

EUROPE—ISLAM—FAR EAST
AMERICAN INDIANS

BY

JOSEPH PIJOAN
Lecturer on Art
University of Chicago

●

UNIVERSITY OF KNOWLEDGE, INCORPORATED
CHICAGO - 1940

XXII—1

TABLE OF CONTENTS

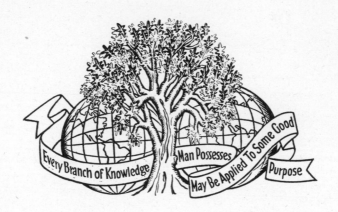

Every Branch of Knowledge Man Possesses May Be Applied To Some Good Purpose

ART OF THE MIDDLE AGES

IN EUROPE, OF ISLAM,

IN THE FAR EAST, AND

OF THE AMERICAN INDIANS

Joshua and a Prophet. Frescoes in the synagogue of Dura-Europos, Mesopotamia.
Painted before 262 A.D., when the city was destroyed.

ART OF THE CATACOMBS

IT HAS GENERALLY been believed that the first Christian art was
that of the Roman catacombs and that it began during the persecution
of the early Christian church. We shall see in another chapter the part
played by the Orient. The churches of Syria and especially of Egypt
were a most important factor in the colossal task of producing a complete
artistic repertory suited to the needs of the new religion. To facilitate our
study we shall, for the time being, accept provisionally the supposition that
here in the bosom of the Roman church the pious sculptors and painters who
decorated the early Christian cemeteries were the first to attempt a portrayal of the Evangelical themes and of the symbolic figures which were
later to represent the Savior, the Virgin, the apostles, and the saints of the
religious traditions. Even though we later come to recognize the fact that

Alcove in a Roman catacomb. On the left of the arch, Moses striking the Rock; on the right, Noah coming out of the Ark.

some of the painters of the catacombs were Orientals who had come to Rome with artistic ideas already formed, nevertheless these cemeteries will always be the principal source of the material for the study of the origin of the new art. The subterranean galleries of which the catacombs are composed are long tortuous passages and contain a complete series of pictorial representations of Christian society during the first four centuries of our era.

These underground cemeteries are all outside the city walls. The laws of the Empire prohibited the burial of the dead within the city, and pagan tombs are also found along the highways which radiate from the capital across the plains of Latium. Like many of the pagan tombs, these Christian cemeteries were probably at first communal sepulchers designed to contain all the dead of a certain congregation. We know that at first worship was carried on in private houses in chapels which differed from the other rooms of the dwelling only in the absence of paintings or other objects which were too suggestive of the pagan religion. In the house of John and Paul, discovered beneath the church later erected in their honor, we find that erotic pictures were substituted in places by others of a religious character. Indeed, the subject matter of the paintings often found on the walls of houses of ancient Rome was obviously unsuitable. On the other hand there could be no lack of a place of worship; "For where two or three are gathered together in My name, there am I in the midst of them." Here the Master would bring peace to the souls of the faithful and fortify their spirit with His love. A secluded room in the house of one of the faithful, therefore, was sufficient for their religious gatherings; here their devotional exercises could be carried on undisturbed. The Epistles of St. Paul give us a clear idea of the character of the Christian societies of the first century. There were probably two or more flocks in a large city, each with its own pastor; and in Rome each community must have had its own common burying ground outside the walls, to which it held a legal title like the pagan *collegium*.

As persecutions increased in number, it was natural that the fraternities of true believers should feel still more strongly the necessity of possessing a safe place where they could deposit the last relics of their many martyrs, the confessors of a new faith. For this purpose they utilized the subterranean galleries in the outskirts of Rome from which the porous limestone called *puzzolana* had been taken to manufacture cement. The volcanic rock of the country contained veins of this material, and innumerable galleries of this sort existed in which the Christians could easily bury their dead without fear of being molested. To convert these quarries into underground cemeteries, it was necessary only to straighten their walls somewhat and support

Arch in a Roman catacomb, with fresco decoration. On the left, a Prophet; on the right, the Three Hebrews in the Fiery Furnace.

Decoration with Good Shepherds, orantes, Cupids, and heads of nymphs. Dome over
a room in the Catacomb of Lucina.

the roof with light brick walls where the excavations had made it unsafe.
Sometimes the dead were buried along the passages in niches extending
lengthwise and closed by a slab of stone or terra cotta which was covered
with cement and duly inscribed. They also utilized the chambers where a
number of galleries intersected and enlarged these spaces into small halls
with chapels adjoining them. Here they deposited the bodies of elders
and of those who had held some office of importance in the church. In
the walls of these cubicula they often hollowed out hemispherical recesses
which formed a sort of shrine above the tombs of the martyrs. Here was
set the marble urn containing the precious relics. In early times these

recesses may have been used as altars. For a long time, indeed well into the Middle Ages, priests from the various churches of Rome went out on certain days to celebrate mass over the tombs of the martyrs in the catacombs. The very long passages are so narrow as to allow people to walk only

A nymph. Fresco in a Roman catacomb.

in single file, and they are all undecorated except some rooms at intersections of galleries. In rare cases the larger rooms are lighted from the outside by means of a shaft, but in general there is no light whatever. Their damp close air makes a visit to the catacombs far from agreeable.

The work of enlarging and decorating the interior of the catacombs went on until after the recognition of the church. In the fourth century the great Spanish Pope, Damasus I, zealously devoted himself to the work of beautifying the tombs of the martyrs. Filled with affection for his sainted predecessors, he embellished the sepulchers of the *Episcopi Romani* with epitaphs in verse which help to solve the problem of determining the topography of the catacombs. A number of the inscriptions of St. Damasus have been discovered *in situ*.

The veneration inspired by these souvenirs of the days of the persecutions brought many visitors after the conversion of Constantine and during the first centuries of the Middle Ages. Hence, we have a number of lists of these cemeteries in the manuscripts which describe the itineraries of the pilgrims, who visited the catacombs in a regular order, beginning with certain ones and proceeding to those lying nearest. They also made careful note of the names of the various crypts and the principal martyrs interred in each. These lists have been of the utmost value in identifying the various portions of the catacombs, for the location of a known crypt

Orantes. Fresco in a Roman catacomb.

Above, Jonah and the Whale; below, Jonah under the gourd-vine. Frescoes in a Roman catacomb.

indicated the identity of those lying adjacent. The pious workmen of early Christian times left nothing in the catacombs to reveal the creation of a new architectural type, no new style of capital or any other form to become traditional in later Christian architecture.

To the paintings on the walls of these burial places we must ascribe the honor of being the first artistic manifestations of the new religion in Rome. At first the decorative themes were those of pagan art. During the first century the painters of the catacombs reproduced the familiar little Cupids weaving garlands, birds, grapevines, flowers, and other motives of an ornamental character. A writer so little open to suspicion as St. Augustine could still give the advice: *"Profani si quid bene dixerunt, non aspernandum,"* which is to say that Christians could profitably learn from profane authors if their writings were in accordance with the truth. And Christian artists had all the more reason for making use of a pagan repertory, lacking as they did any rules or traditions for their own religious pictures. We see, for example, in the catacombs of the first century, representations of the sun, of Cupid and Psyche, symbolizing the union of the soul with God, of the winds, and of the seasons. Sometimes the compartments of the vaults contain decorations of semi-nude figures of languid nymphs, lovely personifications of the woods and springs. Yet, in these earliest frescoes we note a certain reserve and sweetness, prophesying the noble creations of a purely Christian character, which the new era was to bring forth.

Now we are beginning to believe that the Jews had a very old repertory of illustrations of the biblical text. At Dura Europos was found a synagogue whose walls were decorated with frescoes representing scenes from the history of the Jews. Since Dura Europos was destroyed in 262, before many of the Roman catacomb frescoes were painted, and since no other synagogue with frescoes has been found anywhere else, it seems logical to believe that the Dura Europos frescoes are indigenous to Mesopotamia. They, however, reveal a profound knowledge of the writings of Philo of Alexandria, so much so,

Above, Jonah thrown into the sea; below, Jonah and the whale under the gourdvine. Frescoes in a Roman catacomb.

Frescoes in Roman catacombs. Above, frieze with orantes, Three Hebrews in the Fiery Furnace, and Daniel in the Lions' Den. Below, Moses striking the Rock, the Three Magi, and Noah, Daniel, and Jonah.

that it can be said that the Dura Europos frescoes illustrate Philo's commentary on the Bible. This would seem to prove that the origin of the Dura Europos frescoes was in Alexandria. After all this is not really so strange, because Alexandria for centuries was the center of Jewish learning. Up to the present, there has been a reluctance to acknowledge any contribution of Jewish subjects to Christian art, because the notion has been taken too seriously that the Law forbade the representation of sacred scenes. But, as a matter of fact, this prohibition was never enforced. The Jews today use many texts illustrated with very old iconography.

The first biblical personages to be represented in the catacombs appear without the involved symbolism of Philo that saturates the frescoes of the Dura Europos synagogue. Nevertheless, even in the catacombs are found frescoes which we call "parallelisms." Moses bringing forth water from the rock is a symbol of the baptism; the sacrifice of Isaac alludes to the more recent sacrifice on the cross; and Jonah and the whale represent the burial and resurrection. Likewise, the three young Hebrews in the fiery furnace recall the purification; and Susannah shows the fidelity of Christ's love. Tobias, Job, and David all represent the rebirth through love, the new man created within us by the Word.

Moses at Horeb. Detail of a fresco in a   Marriage scene. Fresco in a Roman
          Roman catacomb.   catacomb.

At first the artists presented the biblical themes strictly as the Old
Testament tells them; later they entered whole-heartedly into the undertaking of creating a genuine Christian repertory. Whenever it was possible, they availed themselves of the elements already existing in Classical
art. For example, Noah, with the ark and dove, is taken from old Classical
models: Noah is dressed like a philosopher; the ark is represented as a small
chest similar to the one in which Perseus was placed with Danaë in ancient
paintings; the flying dove is like the one associated with Venus.

Classical themes still persisted in the second century. Orpheus, surrounded by the wild beasts which had been tamed by the music of his lyre,
was too plain an allusion to Christ to be completely forgotten. To many
of the early Christians, Orpheus seemed to be a figure prophetic of the
coming of the Savior. With his songs he had raised the walls of the ideal
city; impelled by love he had descended into Hades in search of his wife;
and his fateful end was easily interpreted as a prophecy of the tragedy on
Calvary. But at the same time Christian themes also began to appear illus-
trating the Gospel texts. This repertory was not a large one; the same representations were constantly repeated with little variation; the reproductions
of a given type, so characteristic of ancient art, continued to a distinctive
feature of Christian art.

But Christian life had brought into being a sentiment which demanded
something more than these allegorical illustrations of the Gospels. Repre-

sentations of the two protagon-
ists of the new faith were
needed; one a figure showing
the soul in prayer; the other a
mediator, the Christ who
brings the soul to God. These
have been the two principal
characters in the Christian life
in every period that mystic
feeling has dominated. The de
vout soul and Christ are bride
and bridegroom, the sheep and
the Good Shepherd. This mysterious relationship has never
been rendered with more delicate feeling than in the catacombs of Rome.

The Christian soul commu-
nicating with God through
prayer is shown as the Bride of
the mystic Christian marriage;
and it is also represented in the
catacombs as a man or woman
praying with raised arms, a
custom derived from the East
and still followed by orthodox
Jews even today. Tertullian, an
African writer, tells us that
kneeling to pray is reserved for
early morning prayer, the *pos-
tulatio* for the dead. We call

Three representations of the Eucharist.
Frescoes in the Roman catacombs.

these praying figures *orantes*. They are the most typical and expressive
figures in the whole iconography of early Christian art. The female *orantes*
are dressed in long tunics and veils which cover the hair falling over the
shoulders. The males wear short mantles. The apparel of both is very
simple. Beside each is an inscription with the name of the deceased and
the words *"in pace,"* for the praying figure was intended to symbolize the
Christian both here on earth and in the world to come. Sometimes the
members of a family were all represented as *orantes* in the same scene. As
time went on, however, the artists became more explicit and even portrayed
the Lord's Supper, showing people seated about a table in the manner of
the first eucharistic feasts.

Representations of the Bridegroom necessarily succeeded those of the
Brides. This, of course, involved enormous difficulties for the painters, who
knew only the idealized figure of the Christ as revealed in the words of the

Two sarcophagus reliefs. Above, vintage scenes with Good Shepherds. Below, the story of Jonah. Lateran Museum, Rome.

of the catacombs. In the provinces we know of at least one center, that at Arles, which had a factory for making sarcophagi for the whole of Gaul. Other makers of marble sarcophagi seem to have been established at Salona on the Dalmatian coast.

The Christian sarcophagi contained a tremendous quantity of iconographic material for the study of early Christian life. Many of them were made after Constantine, when there was no longer any need for hiding the ideas of the faith beneath an allegorical cloak. Besides the themes of the catacombs there gradually appear on the sarcophagi new subjects that might be termed ecclesiastical. On some, Christ is shown as bearded but still dressed as a philosopher, seated on a throne and passing to the Apostles the roll of the Scriptures. The Apostles are in two groups, six on each side of the Master, exalted to the dignity of divine doctors of the church. This scene which we call *"Dominus legem dat,"* or "The Lord gives the Law," was repeated with very few variations. As time passed, the Apostles were given definite characteristics; Peter was well provided with curly hair, and Paul had a bald head. On occasions the faithful buried in the sarcophagi were introduced into the scene as small figures kissing the feet of Christ.

The sarcophagi made after the beginning of the fourth century preserve

Statue of the Good Shepherd. Found in the catacombs. Lateran Museum, Rome.

Two sarcophagi. Above, representation of the three Magi. Ravenna. Below, Christ giving the Law, *Dominus legem dat*. On sarcophagus containing the bones of St. Gorgonius. Cathedral, Ancona.

for us a precious series of portraits of early Christians. The sculptors, who carved the reliefs and finished them to the smallest detail, left the portraits unfinished until the sarcophagus was bought for a definite individual, and then the facial features were filled in. There are some sarcophagi on which the portraits were left merely sketched; but on others it is charming to see husband and wife united in death, as they were in life, by the same faith. When there is space enough these figures carry the roll of the Scriptures, perhaps the Epistles of Paul, which were more popular during the first centuries than the Gospels themselves.

Four examples of gilded glass in a pictorial style resembling that of the frescoes in the catacombs. Above, two Christian portraits. Below, the crowning of Peter and Paul by Christ. Metropolitan Museum of Art, New York.

Very few bronze and ivory artifacts have been found in the catacombs. Most of the objects left with the bodies were carried away as holy relics. A few beautiful pieces of broken glass have been found among the ashes, most of them the round bases of cups, perhaps used for the Eucharist. These fragments of glass are decorated with designs painted with black enamel and then covered over with gold leaf and protected with a second layer of glass. On looking into the cup the little picture could be seen at the bottom. These cup bases repeat over and over again in their single color of black, the subjects of the frescoes of the catacombs, such as the *orantes* and the heads of the Apostles crowned by the Lord. Besides, there are a great number of delightful portraits of Christian men and women of the time, perhaps the owners of these vessels.

They reveal a new spirit and confirm the impression received from the portraits on the sarcophagi. As it is expressed by Paul in the Epistles, the believers are of different kinds and classes, but they all bear testimony that they are revived and motivated by the one common faith.

Portraits on glass, with gilded background and painted shadows. Brescia Museum.

Exterior of the Basilica of San Lorenzo, Rome.

EARLY CHRISTIAN ART IN THE WEST

WE HAVE already noted that the first places of Christian worship must have been in private houses. We read in the Acts of the Apostles: "And when the day of Pentecost was fully come, they were all with one accord in one place." This was the "upper room" where they usually met together. The religious service probably consisted of prayers and breaking bread and drinking wine in the manner the Master had taught them. We are told further, "And all that believed were together and had all things in common." Although they sometimes met in the shelter of the Portico of Solomon, St. Stephen made it plain in his speech before the Sanhedrin that the Christians did not recognize the peculiar sanctity of the Temple of Jerusalem. Indeed, he quoted the words of Isaiah: "Heaven is my throne, and the earth is my footstool: what house will ye build me? saith the Lord: or what is the place of my rest? Hath not my hand made all things?"

Systematic exploration of the older churches of Rome has shown us that generally the remains of a private house lie under the ground floor of the church. A private palace originally occupied the site of the Lateran; a house

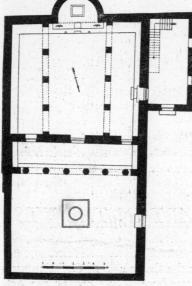

Cross section and plan of the synagogue
of Beth Alpha, Palestine. By Sukenik,
the discoverer of the synagogue.

lies underneath S. Clemente, and the same is true of S. Maria Maggiore, S. Pudenziana, the Basilica of SS. John and Paul and most of the churches discussed in this chapter. The religious service probably took place in the principal hall of the house of some prominent member of the congregation. The records of the martyrdom of St. Cecilia say she was beheaded in her own home which was a meeting place of the Christians. This lady was of noble family, and the remains of her house still lie beneath the church which was later erected upon the sacred spot. We can readily understand how centuries later the faithful would still hold in devout veneration the places where in the great days of the new religion the Fathers had gathered together "in spirit and in truth," and where they had shed their blood for the sake of Christ. After a time, it is probable that in the rooms used for their unassuming worship a special place was set aside for the pastor and the deacons, and possibly there were separate divisions for the men and women.

Besides the tombs of the martyrs and the homes where Christian groups gathered, there were other meeting places of the Christians, very seldom mentioned. That the first Christians were Jews is a fact that has usually been ignored. In the Epistle of James the church is still referred to as the synagogue. During the first centuries there must have been some congregations of Christians who could hardly be distinguished from Jews. The gap between the Christian church and the synagogue did not become impassable until the dogma of the Trinity was a matter of discussion. In remote places like Spain it was quite possible that Jews and Christians met in the same room, but perhaps on different days. There are buildings in the Balearic Islands and southern Spain which have not yet been identified definitely as churches or synagogues. It is important to understand this fact because it helps us to explain why the shape of the Christian church building became fixed upon a rectangular plan. We have a curious case in Gerash, Transjordania, where a synagogue of rectangular plan was made over into a Christian church. The synagogue, of the same plan as the church, lies beneath, its orientation reversed. The Jews traditionally faced Jerusalem, which, in Transjordania, meant facing west; while the Christian churches of the first centuries were required to face east.

The search for the origin of the Christian building everywhere except in the Jewish places of worship seemed perfectly justifiable before anything was known about early synagogues. During the last ten years, however, excavations of a number of synagogues in Palestine and Arabia have been made. In addition, at the Greek sanctuary of Delos, a synagogue of the first century, in a fairly good state of preservation, has been brought to light. Therefore, we no longer have reason for ignoring the possibility that some Christian churches were derived from the Jewish synagogue. Those synagogues of Transjordania and Palestine are rectangular in shape, with side galleries in the second story for the women. A chapter of the CONSTITUTION OF THE APOSTLES, a very early text of the Christian Church, much read in the fourth century when many of the first Christian buildings were being erected, contains this paragraph: "See that the building is long, its head toward the orient, and vestries on each side at this end. There in the center is to be put the bishop's throne, and on each side the benches for the presbyters. The deacons are to be nearby; the laymen to sit at the west end. The women shall sit apart and always be silent." The CONSTITUTION does not say that the women must be upstairs, but since the men were to occupy the west end, the logical solution of the problem was to build galleries for the women.

Another explanation of the rectangular plan, the one until recently most generally accepted, is that the first Christian basilicas were pagan buildings which Constantine turned over to the Christians to use as temples for the new religion. Evidence is found in the similarity of the Christian basilicas to those ancient structures which served as places for assembly and for making business contracts. Such a theory becomes quite acceptable when we consider that there were many basilicas in

Exterior and Interior of the synagogue at Tell-Um, Palestine.

Interior of the Basilica of Santa Maria Maggiore, Rome.

Rome and other great cities of the Empire which were no longer in use during the centuries of business depression.

Many of these buildings, although long abandoned, required only slight restoration to be converted into churches. An excellent example is the palace of the Lateran, which was the residence of the popes until the fifteenth century, when they moved to the Vatican. The Lateran originally belonged to the family of Sextius Lateranus, whose descendants lived in affluence until their wealth, including the beautiful palace, was confiscated by Nero. Later it was included in the dowry of Fausta, the sister of the Emperor Maxentius, when she married Constantine. In 323 A.D. Constantine gave it to Pope Sylvester, as a token of his good will toward the new religion, and it became the ecclesiastical center of the Roman Church. In its final form, after many alterations, the Lateran included a palace, a basilica, a baptistery, and a large number of smaller buildings.

In general, however, the popes preferred, whenever possible, to erect new structures to vie with the great monuments of Imperial Rome. Whenever the early *Episcopi Romani* had sufficient resources at their disposal they wished to commemorate their pontificate with buildings either new or elaborately rebuilt. Baptisteries became resplendent with mosaics, and the triclinia of their palaces and the crypts of martyrs beautiful with paintings. The papal chronicle of these first centuries, the LIBER PONTIFICALIS, is filled with accounts of the new structures which the Apostolic Church erected in every quarter of the city.

Interior of the Basilica of St. Paul's Outside the Walls, Rome.

In 324, at the time the basilica of the Lateran was in process of transformation, Constantine ordered two churches to be constructed over the tombs of the Apostles Peter and Paul. The building to St. Paul at first was the smaller of the two, for the site of the martyr's tomb was only a hundred feet from the eastern side of the highway between Rome and Ostia. Since the altar had to be placed at the eastern end of the church and also had to be set directly above the sepulcher, the size of the building was very much limited. In 386, however, a change in the orientation of the building was decided on, and the church was made to extend in the opposite direction from the road, without however moving the altar above the tomb. The later building, much larger and composed of a nave and four aisles, was preserved until early in the last century, when it was destroyed by fire. The present Church of St. Paul is its restoration.

No such limitations existed in the case of the church erected over the tomb of St. Peter, and the original structure was built with all the magnificence befitting the memory of the "Prince of Apostles." The body of St. Peter has always been greatly venerated by the popes; it was at first buried in the catacombs of the Vatican and was probably removed for safety from there to another cemetery on the Appian Way. But forty years later it was returned to its original place of burial close to the spot where the saint suf-

Interior of the Basilica of St. Agnes, showing *gyneceum,* or gallery for women. Rome.

fered martyrdom. The sepulcher is in a chamber beneath the altar and has never been opened since the saint's remains were placed there.

The basilica constructed by Constantine is somewhat larger than that of St. Paul. It had, also, four rows of twenty-three columns each. These shafts of granite and marble were surmounted by Corinthian capitals and supported

Interior of the Basilica of Santa Maria in Cosmedin, Rome.

an entablature. The columns in the Church of St. Paul, we may note, supported a series of arches. The great arch and the apse at the eastern end were bright with mosaic decoration depicting the Savior in the center with St. Peter and St. Paul on either side. At one side of the basilica were two baptisteries, with tombs placed in the niches formed by buttresses. A cloistered atrium in front of the sanctuary served as a gathering place for the faithful. At its center was a magnificent antique bronze pine cone, which is still preserved in the Garden della Pigna in the Vatican.

When it was decided to replace it with the present Renaissance church, the old basilica of the Vatican was in very poor condition. The walls on one side deviated about three feet from the vertical, and many of the timbers were worm-eaten and rotten. Its destruction, nevertheless, was one of the greatest misfortunes ever suffered by art. The loss of the ancient frescoes and mosaics that lined its walls is irreparable.

The Church of S. Maria Maggiore gives us a better

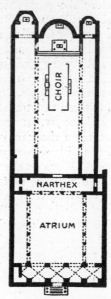

Plan of a Roman basilica.

Mosaic in the apse of the Basilica of Santa Pudenziana, Rome.

idea of the early basilicas than any other church of Rome. It is certainly the best preserved, and many believe it to be the most ancient. It appears to have been an ordinary pagan basilica and not a Christian place of worship before the recognition of the Church by Constantine. Its well matched columns support a horizontal architrave, giving the building the appearance of a purely Classical monument. According to modern scholars, the mosaics of this building cannot be later than the fourth century, proving that before that time the structure must have been a church in a private house. It is believed to have been the residence of a family by the name of Sicinini; and it seems likely that one of the patrician members of this family, converted to Christianity, transformed the great hall of his palace into a church.

We know, however, the precise date of erection of another of the Constantinian churches of Rome. This is S. Agnèse, a partly subterranean basilica, which was constructed in 324 above the catacombs where the saint was buried. Much smaller than the churches of St. Paul, S. Maria, or St. Peter, it has an unusual, almost effeminate grace, well suited to its purpose of commemorating the modest virgin saint who is still the beloved patron of the shepherds in the hills around Rome. It consists of a nave and two aisles, with galleries over the aisles reserved for women, in conformance with a custom still in force in orthodox synagogues today. The antique columns are made of beautiful marble of many colors, red, green, yellow, black, and white. In the apse can still be seen mosaics of the seventh century.

Not nearly so beautiful, but much less restored, is the basilica of S. Clemente, accidentally discovered in 1857 beneath the present church. It was well known that the church of S. Clemente was originally built over the house of the saint on the Caelian Hill, for St. Jerome mentions it in a letter

Detail of the head of Christ in the apse mosaic of San.a Pudenziana, Rome.

written in 392. About the end of the eleventh century the old church was
destroyed by fire and was subsequently rebuilt. As by this time the level
of the city had risen considerably, the new edifice was constructed above
the old one which thus became the foundation of the present church. Nevertheless the old plan was preserved, and the movable furnishings were
transferred to the new building, among them the altar, the marble screens
which enclosed the choir in the center of the nave, and the pulpits for the
Gospels and the Epistles. As it stands today, of all of the religious edifices

Jeweled cross in mosaic decorating the apse of a basilica at Ravenna.

of Rome, the Church of S. Clemente gives us the best idea of what a small Christian basilica was in ancient times. We still find the court, or narthex, in front of the main façade, and the priest faces the worshipers in the nave, choir, and aisles. Behind the altar is the antique marble seat intended for the pastor of the little Christian flock, and the mosaics of the apse are also very old.

The early Christian basilicas were usually supplemented by a court, or cloister, in front. Here stood the catechumens and penitents who were not permitted to enter the church proper. At the back of the court was a lobby, called the narthex, which led to the interior of the basilica. This was reserved for those who were allowed to view the ceremonies from a distance. It was still in use in the churches of the Middle Ages, although by that time it often served merely as a vestibule where meetings which were not purely

"Casket of Brescia." Of the fourth century. Above, Jonah under the gourdvine, with an orans and Moses at the sides. Below, the judgment of Ananias and Sapphira, as related in Acts V. At the bottom, the story of Moses.

of a religious character were held. Here officers were elected, and discussions regarding church finances took place. Beyond the court and narthex was the basilica which extended lengthwise, a nave flanked by aisles. There were no chapels or altars except those in the apses.

The central nave was higher than the aisles, permitting the church to be lighted by means of large windows in the walls above the roofs of the aisles. The walls were covered with mosaics and paintings representing scenes from the Old and New Testaments. St. Paulinus of Nola called them the "Bible of the Illiterate," for it was from these colored pictures that the ignorant were able to learn much regarding the principles of the new faith. Between nave and aisles were the columns and arches which separated the various divisions of the church, and it is this feature that still gives the Roman basilicas a certain artistic grandeur. Their diversified colors are reflected on the floor of the nave and aisles, which are paved with flags of hard polished stone. The roof was of wood and followed the lines of the façade. From the court could be seen the outline of the roof sloping on either side; while the façade, like the interior, was decorated with colored paintings and mosaics. The ceilings were flat. The apse projected beyond the rear wall through an opening at the far end of the nave which formed a triumphal arch. This was ornamented with mosaics or paintings, as was

One end of the Casket of Brescia. Above, Moses; the men in the Fiery Furnace. Center, Christ restoring sight to the blind; Christ raising Lazarus. Below, Moses and the Egyptian woman; the killing of the Egyptian.

the apse itself; and here we find the most important pictorial art of the Christian basilicas.

Nearby were the baptisteries where, as the name indicates, the ordinance of baptism was administered by immersion, cleansing the neophyte of the sins of the flesh. A central *piscina,* sufficiently large to immerse the convert, was required. A circular or octagonal plan was most often employed.

The mosaic compositions of the basilicas are the most artistic of any that have come down to us from the period following the official recognition of Christianity. We find in them work by artists with sufficient resourcefulness to produce new themes of undeniable aesthetic interest. It must be recognized that the mosaics of the basilicas are a continuation of the art of the catacombs. They draw their inspiration from the same sources that gave birth to the art of the first Christian cemeteries; but we find a new magnificence in these pictures, since they were meant to be seen from a nave much larger and brighter than the dark and narrow cubicula of the catacombs.

The earliest of these mosaic decorations is the famous one in S. Pudenziana on the Esquiline. According to tradition this basilica was built on the site where formerly stood the house of that Senator Pudens who is reputed to have received St. Peter as his guest when he first arrived in Rome. The level of the city is about ten feet higher than it was in ancient times; and, in consequence, we find the basilica today that much below the street. It is a low building with a single restored nave, which would have little interest for us if it were not for the beautiful mosaics which decorate its apse.

Ivory pyxis (or box) with pastoral scenes and a nymph. Louvre.

The composition possesses the serenity and balance so characteristic of Classical art. A hemicycle of columns in the background of the picture frames a group of persons in friendly conversation, while in the center, Christ is seated upon a cathedra, in an attitude of majesty. He wears a beard and holds in his hand a book. This is a new type, one very different from that of the beardless Christ of the catacombs. The artist may have intended to represent the blessed estate of the Elect, Pudens and his daughters, in heaven with Christ and his Apostles. The buildings and the great jeweled cross dominating the background of the picture lead us to believe that Jerusalem is intended, although perhaps only as a symbol of the New Jerusalem, the Heavenly City. The curved portico represented in the background was very

Ivory pyxides (or boxes) for wafers, with the scenes of Christ giving the Law and of the Sacrifice of Abraham. Abbey of Reichenau, and Museum of Berlin.

Statue of St. Peter. Probably a Renaissance bronze copy of a marble original of the fourth century. St. Peter's, Rome.

likely meant to be the round building in the Holy Sepulcher at Jerusalem. The cross set upon the hill seems to be a faithful reproduction of the famous one set up on Mount Calvary by Constantine and his mother Helena. The jeweled cross was to remain a characteristic feature of mosaic art, as was the majestic figure of the seated Christ, seen for the first time in the apses of S. Pudenziana. In the upper part of a mosaic in the Lateran basilica we also find the bearded Christ surrounded by nine angels and in an attitude of benediction, just as the legend assures us he appeared at the dedication of the church. Below the vault of the apse stand two groups of saints composed of Mary, Peter, Paul, John the Baptist, and John the Evangelist. In the last zone is the monumental gemmed cross set upon a hill from which a spring gushes forth, a symbol of the baptism. Two flocks of sheep come to drink from it and move toward two miniature cities, *Jerusalem ecclesia circumcisione* and *Bethlehem ecclesia gentis.* In this mosaic in the Lateran we have an entirely new repertory, much richer than that of the isolated scenes in the catacombs, representing the miracles of the Gospels and the love-feasts of the early Christians. The whole conception is purely Christian; the souls, some of them refreshed by the water which flows from the foot of the cross on Calvary, find their home in the two cities which symbolize Heaven. Below the appearance of the Lord and his angels to Abraham on the plains of Mamre, we see angels surrounding the Christ child, the new apparition adored by the Magi.

The guise in which the Savior should be represented became a question which gave rise to much heated discussion throughout the fourth century. Some authorities like Tertullian believed that Christ should be pictured in

The so-called "Barberini Ivory," representing a Byzantine emperor to whom Earth offers fruits. The squire carries a statue of Victory. Below, barbarians bear offerings. Louvre.

an unattractive manner, that he should even inspire terror, that we might not fall into temptation through his physical beauty. Others agreed with the gentle St. John Chrysostomus that Jesus should be presented with a grace and charm that would supplement His divine precepts in drawing souls to

Diptych representing the Consul Boetius on both leaves. He carries the consul's scepter and a handkerchief with which he signals for the games to start.

His service. The latter view finally triumphed, and the artist was permitted to produce the beautiful works of the Middle Ages. The Christ of S. Pudenziana was to become that of the Byzantine mosaics and the Gothic cathedrals, ever the same figure dressed in Classical robes, a book in His hand and wearing the flowing beard that gives to His face the thoughtful expression of mature years.

Interesting examples of early Christian sculpture are the wooden and ivory reliefs which have been preserved in the museums and treasuries of the older churches. We find on a rectangular casket in Brescia the same themes that we have already noted in the catacombs. One side is carved with the story of the healing of the man blind from birth and of the raising of Lazarus, the figures being very similar to those found on the sarcophagi and frescoes of the catacombs. On another side is a representation of the punishment of Ananias and Sapphira, who were miraculously struck dead for concealing their wealth from the Christian community, a story related in the Acts of the Apostles. There are other ivory caskets cylindrical in form, which may have been used to hold the bread in the Eucharistic ritual, rather than for relics like the casket of which we have just spoken.

But perhaps the most artistic Christian ivories are the little reliefs used as book covers or given as mementos by the consuls on the day they took possession of their offices. Some must have been diptychs, opening like books, the inside surfaces being covered with wax and used as notebooks. Sometimes as many as five were joined, and probably used for pure decoration. Such, for example, is the book cover known as the Barberini Ivory, which glorifies Constantine as the Defender of the Faith.

We have no large Christian statues or images dating from the time imme-

Consular diptych, representing the apotheosis of an emperor. Below, the image of the emperor in a funeral chariot drawn by elephants. Above, his soul is carried to heaven by two genii. British Museum.

diately following the official recognition of the church. True, we find in the catacombs the figure of the Good Shepherd carved in the full round, and it is probable that other similar statues also existed in the early Christian basilicas. But almost all of these have disappeared. Only one statue of life-size has been preserved in the Christian Museum of the Lateran. It appears to be a figure of St. Hippolytus seated upon the ancient consular throne and dressed in a Classical toga, like the figures of the mosaics in S. Pudenziana. The famous Vatican statue of St. Peter, whose foot pilgrims still kiss in pious veneration, portrays the saint, like S. Hippolytus, seated upon a chair; and his garment is of the Classical period.

Enameled cross of the fifth century. From the Sanctum Sanctorum,
Vatican.

Façade of the church facing the main court of the Monastery of St. Simeon, Kalaat-Seman, in the Syrian desert. Princeton University Expedition.

EARLY CHRISTIAN ART IN THE EAST

A DISCUSSION has arisen in the last thirty years which seems likely to modify greatly the generally accepted ideas regarding early Christian art. A number of German critics and younger archaeologists of the Russian school began to question the belief that Christian art had its beginning in the Roman catacombs and was exclusively of Latin origin. They contradicted the traditional idea held until recent times, that when Constantine founded his new capital at Constantinople Byzantine art continued to be motivated by the impulse it had received from Rome and to develop the types which had been created in the Occident. Just as Rome had governed the ancient world with her laws, so she was supposed to have imposed upon the Eastern provinces her new art, the iconography of which already existed in a rudimentary state in the frescoes of the catacombs and the mosaics of the early basilicas.

Those who held the Roman origin theory of Christian architecture put great stress on the fact that the Christians adopted the Roman type of closed basilica for their churches. When the Christians wished to build churches with vaults or round buildings for baptisteries, they could find no better masters than the Romans who, if they were not the originators of the vault,

Miniature in a Genesis manuscript of the fifth century, representing Rebecca at the Well.
The well is personified by a nymph. Hofbibliothek, Vienna.

possessed unsurpassed skill in its construction. At the time the discussion
concerning the origin of these Christian buildings started, no Jewish buildings of the first centuries were known; for Syria and Asia Minor were
practically unexplored.

Let us mention now the arguments against that Roman origin of
Christian and Byzantine art, as stated by later German and Slavic archaeologists. First, they pointed out the anomaly, that the Christian church should
have taken their liturgy, dogma, music, and traditions from the Jews and
the rest of the East, while they took their art and architecture from the
Roman pagans.

We have already called attention to the mosaics of S. Pudenziana at
Rome, the first Christian composition to decorate the apse of a basilica, and
have shown with an analysis of the porticoes and domes of its background
that the picture was intended to suggest Jerusalem. This was further con-
firmed by the presence of a great jeweled cross which resembled the one
Constantine set up on Mount Calvary. In spite of the fact that close relations
were still maintained between Rome and the Orient and that pilgrims had
begun to visit the Holy Land, we still must admit that it seems rather
strange for a Roman artist to be so well acquainted with the sky line and
details of the distant Judean city. We detected a certain Oriental character
also in the ornamentation of the doors of S. Sabina; the grapevine reliefs

carved on the moldings resemble those of the Orient, rather than the traditional themes of Roman decorative art.

In fact, Oriental motifs occur so frequently in the Christian monuments of the first centuries that critics formulated a theory very different from the idea already current as to the part played by Rome in the formation of the new art. Just as Christianity had come already formed to Rome from the Orient, so were its artistic themes also brought from Asia and Egypt by the artists who decorated the catacombs. Furthermore, later Christian art originated at the imperial court of Constantinople in the Orient, and Roman influences were at best but negligible factors in its formation. We shall cite some examples of this Oriental origin to show how carefully these modern critics have analyzed, one by one, the elements of the most important Christian monuments before they ascribed them to the Orient.

In the field of pictorial art, we might mention two of the most famous early Christian codices containing miniatures. One of these is the handsome manuscript of the BOOK OF GENESIS now in the Imperial Library at Vienna. It is profusely illustrated and probably dates from the fourth century. Modern critics have produced an entire literature of commentaries on this codex. Wickhoff, who was the most pro-Roman, devoted a voluminous work to this manuscript, in which he seeks to demonstrate that the style of its miniatures,

Entry into Jerusalem. Miniature in the EVANGELISTARY of Rossano. Calabria.

Miniature from the Gospels illuminated by the monk Rabula at the monastery of Zagba, Mesopotamia, in 586 A.D. It represents the Crucifixion, the Women at the Sepulcher, and Noli me tangere. Laurentian Library, Florence.

the manner of presenting picturesque features, the atmosphere, and the perspective were still the same as in the ancient Roman art. He calls attention to the *continuous style,* which is the style of the reliefs of Trajan's Column. To refute Wickhoff's arguments, the anti-Roman critics had only to point out that the flora and fauna represented in the miniatures of the Vienna GENESIS were found nowhere except in the Orient. In the "Meeting of Eleazer with Rebecca at the Well," the camels of the former are of a desert variety unknown to Roman art.

The Ascension of Christ. Below, the Virgin as an orans, the Apostles, and two angels. GOSPELS of Rabula.

In the Cathedral of Rossano in Calabria is another very famous Christian manuscript containing the Gospels illustrated with miniatures. This, too, seems to be of Oriental origin because in it are found pictures of goats with long horns and tails, a species found only in Syria. The importance of the GOSPELS of Rossano is due to the fact that it contains many representations unlike anything found in the catacombs. On the frontispiece preceding each GOSPEL is the seated figure of an Evangelist writing, similar to those of

Doors of Santa Sabina. Fifth century. Rome.

Byzantine art in the East and to later manuscripts in the West. The evidence, therefore, goes to prove that Syria was the cradle of some most important themes of Christian art.

The GENESIS of Vienna, and the GOSPELS of Rossano are written in Greek, which was the official language of the early Christian Church at Rome as well as in the Orient; so the language of the text hardly indicates their origin. But there are also a number of codices written in Syriac, the vernacular of the Christian Near East, and some of the miniatures found in

Detail from the doors of Santa Sabina, with the Crucifixion represented for the first time. Rome.

these are worthy of mention. One of the most interesting is a manuscript of Gospel stories compiled and illuminated by a monk named Rabula, in 586. Among its text illustrations are large miniatures of the Crucifixion and the Ascension of Christ, the appearance of which in this manuscript proves these subjects to have been executed in Syria before they were treated in the West.

Elements proving Oriental origin have also been observed in sarcophagi. Strzygowski, leader of the anti-Roman school of Christian art origins, noticed that the first time the halo of Christ appears with a cross within it, is in a series of sarcophagi certainly imported from the East. The proof of this importation is based upon an analysis of the marble showing it to be the kind used in Syria and Asia Minor.

Many ivory reliefs among the treasures of Western churches quite certainly have an Oriental origin also. Some show depictions of the group of buildings of the Holy Sepulcher at Jerusalem, too near the church itself to have been done only from hearsay. Others, the "Baptism of Christ," for example, introduce a personification of the River Jordan as a river-god coming out of the water to bear witness that Jesus is the Messiah. Since

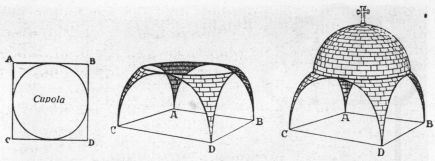

Spherical pendentives connecting the angles of a square area with a dome.

the Romans were unfamiliar with this local tradition, it is easy to believe that these ivories were brought from Syria or Palestine.

The controversy about Roman and Oriental origins in Christian art has been discussed so much in detail here because of its importance in the history of art. For a century scholars have been plagued by the problem. Those who held the pro-Oriental theory seem to have been able to produce the more convincing proof. It is important, however, not to lose sight of the fact that although large numbers of Western Christians were converted by those who had come from the East, these converts were thoroughly Roman. The supremacy of Latin culture in the West was undisputed; but the art remained Oriental in flavor, and in this the influence of the East was paramount. It was only much later, after the time of Charlemagne, that the art expression of the Church became entirely Roman. This it did to such an extent that we can truthfully call the Catholic Church the direct descendant of the Roman Empire.

Let us now turn to the cradle of Christianity: Syria and Palestine. Greek taste prevailed in these Eastern lands. The Antiochi and Seleucidae, kings, re-Hellenized the people and superimposed a culture of great magnificence. Antioch was then the third city in the world, surpassed only by Rome and Alexandria in monumental grandeur and extent. St. John Chrysostom, a bishop and a man of letters, in the fifth century describes in very poetical language the Antioch of his time. He relates the devotion of the faithful and how their religion led them to build great hospices to shelter the widows and orphans. The chief church building of Antioch, called the "Gilded Church" because of its gold mosaics, was

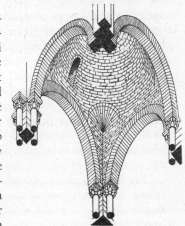

Example of pendentive (inside view), with squinch.

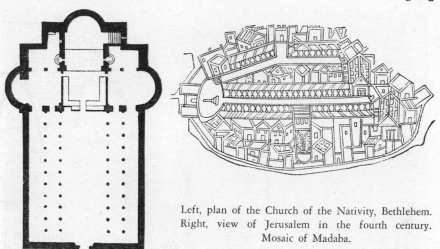

Left, plan of the Church of the Nativity, Bethlehem.
Right, view of Jerusalem in the fourth century.
Mosaic of Madaba.

built by Constantine. The plan did not follow that of the Roman basilica, but was of octagonal shape, with galleries for the women. These people turned to Christianity with a joy and youthful enthusiasm of which the Romans were incapable, wearied as they were by the decline of their decadent empire.

Little remains in the city of Antioch itself today to bear witness to the greatness of its Christian community; but in the extensive suburbs are many half-destroyed monuments, and further inland are entire cities, as well as monasteries and innumerable country churches, which offer material for our study of Eastern Christian edifices. This region, colonized by Alexander's successors, had flourished throughout its Roman period. But from the seventh century this portion of Syria seems to have remained uninhabited; for the Christians at that time, fleeing before the Persians and Saracens, took refuge in the great cities of the coast. Their cities, almost intact on the bare, rocky desert, still stand and reveal the life and customs of their early inhabitants. The fact that these buildings were constructed of limestone has been largely responsible for their preservation. Syria abounds in deposits from which large blocks of building stone could be easily quarried, and timber has always been very scarce. Consequently, almost every kind of structure was vaulted and thus stimulated the invention of new roofing systems.

The great innovation was a vault made by erecting a series of parallel arches and filling the spaces between with large stones to form a roof. The weight of the roof was thus distributed over a number of arches, and its lateral thrust was sustained by adding to the thickness of the walls. In many of these Syrian structures the dome is supported by octagonal walls, and the angles are closed with triangular, curved surfaces, called pendentives.

The Monastery of St. Simeon Stylites, Kalaat-Seman, in the Syrian desert.

Although this type of dome may have been employed previously by the Romans, it was used only in small structures. It could hardly be said they had solved problems such as were involved in the great monuments of Syria and later of Constantinople.

Most important of the monasteries found in Syria is that of St. Simeon Stylites, which still forms an imposing mass of ruins in the desert. The Arabs called it *Kalaat-Seman,* or the Castle of Simeon, for the memory of the famous anchorite, who lived on the top of a pillar, still persists among the Bedouin tribes of Syria. When this holy man died, his disciples dedicated to his memory a fine monastery with four spacious churches facing the court, in which stood the precious column on which he sat so long.

In the fourth century the entire Roman Orient, from the shores of the Black Sea to the Euphrates, and from the tablelands of Asia Minor to Egypt, was profoundly stirred by the discovery of the True Cross and the Holy Sepulcher. The interest of the Christian world was concentrated on Jerusalem. Pilgrims went from distant places, not only to visit the place sacred to Christ's memory, but to stay and die there as well. The church, which was built by Constantine, over the Grotto in Bethlehem, where Christ was said to have been born, is still miraculously preserved. It is a strictly Roman type of building, with nave, two aisles, and a flat ceiling.

For our knowledge of the buildings Constantine erected in Jerusalem, we have to depend on descriptions by pilgrims. All agree that the Church of the Holy Sepulcher covered an extensive area and was comprised of many buildings. A portico, decorated with mosaics, was approached through magnificent gates. At the center of the enclosure were two great monuments: the *Anastasis,* built above the place where Christ was thought to be buried, and the *Martyrium* on the supposed spot of His crucifixion. These two locations were situated conveniently near each other. The Anastasis, a circular church, had a dome supported on twelve columns, its style probably resembling the Gilded Church of Antioch. The Martyrium, on the other hand, retained the rectangular plan of the basilica at Bethlehem. Constantine built still another church on the Mount of Olives; but whether it was of Roman or Oriental plan we do not know. What we have observed in connection with the style of the buildings erected by Constantine in Palestine, shows either that the architects were eclectic, taking their ideas from different styles, or else they came from different schools of architecture.

The personal interest of the Emperor in carrying out this building program in Palestine seems well proved. Eusebius, his biographer, tells how he gave orders as to the manner in which workmen were to be assembled and materials secured. He was eager to hear of the progress on the work; and, we are told by Eusebius, that he asked the architects whether "the ceilings were to be decorated with panels, because in that case they could be covered with gold." He demanded reports on the number of columns and marble slabs needed, in order that he might arrange to have the necessary material sent from distant lands.

One of the dormitories for pilgrims at Kalaat-Seman.

Fresco on a dome of the church in the Oasis of El Kargue, near Thebes, Egypt. Above, the Israelites leaving Egypt. Below, *parthenoi,* or virgins, going to the sepulcher; the sacrifice of Abraham; and Jonah.

In the ruins of Madaba, a city in Palestine of this period, there still exists on the floor of a church a map in mosaic which shows the entire country in perspective. In the center is Jerusalem, with its walls, gates, arcaded streets, and principal buildings. The city appears to be elliptical in shape and surrounded by turreted walls. A wide street lined with porticoes, probably the *Via Recta* of the pilgrims, extends from the Gate of Damascus straight across the city. On this street is a building with three doors set up on a terraced platform; this is undoubtedly the Church of the Holy Sepulcher. The other long street, arcaded on one side only, is probably the *Via Dolorosa.*

Of the part played in the formation of Christian art by the churches of Mesopotamia and Persia we are still in ignorance. Christianity was very early established in these lands; and since they were beyond the borders of the Roman Empire, they were free from persecution. When further study is made they should have valuable information to offer. There is a tradition that Jesus corresponded with a certain Abgar, king of Emesa on the Tigris. This is an unlikely story, but there are ruins of Christian buildings of the first centuries at Emesa. This city boasted of having a cloth with a contemporary, authentic portrait of Christ. Quite likely it was the model for the bearded Christ, which, as we mentioned before,

Fresco in a chapel of the Coptic Monastery of Bawit, Egypt. Above, the Lord, with the symbols of the Gospels on either side. Below, virgins and Apostles.

came to replace the beardless figure of the young shepherd. The tradition is that the portrait of Emesa resulted from the actual contact of the face of Jesus with the cloth. It was copied innumerable times because of its presumed miraculous qualities. It was finally taken to Constantinople, and from there copies of it reached the West.

Another image which had a strange origin was the supposed *Akeizopoietos,* or autographed portrait of the Virgin Mary. Of more recent date perhaps than the cloth portrait of Jesus, this *Akeizopoietos* was revered as an icon at Jerusalem. It was supposed to have been painted by the Virgin herself, who was said to be endowed with knowledge of the art of painting. In the ancient world there were many Madonnas which the pious thought had been painted by St. Lucas; but this was the only one made by the very hands of the Mother of God. This autographed portrait of Mary was finally taken to Constantinople by the Empress Eudocia, who built a church for it near the Golden Gate of the great metropolis. The icon was probably copied and used as the model for images of the Madonna still to be seen in other churches.

In Egypt there were other art centers during the first centuries of Christianity. The city of Alexandria maintained closer relations with Rome, perhaps, than did any of the Near Eastern capitals. We have already referred

Miniature from a manuscript of the Christian COSMOGRAPHY by Cosmas, a monk of Alexandria. Vatican.

to the fact that many modern critics believe certain ritual objects of the early Christian Church to have been produced in Alexandria, where Hellenistic art so long had its center. If we wish, however, to find architecture of any importance in Egypt, we must study the so-called Coptic art of the famous monks of Thebaid.

The idea of monastic life originated in Egypt and thence spread rapidly to Asia Minor. At first Anthony, then Paul and his disciple Macarius, and later the great founders of the Coptic monasteries, in particular that of Shenûdah, prepared the way for St. Benedict and St. Basil, who established the first monastic orders. The communities of Egyptian monks grew extremely large, but they lost their fervor early and contributed little to the development of the Christian doctrine. Their contributions to art were

Miniature from the COSMOGRAPHY of Cosmas, with four scenes: Paul on the way to Damascus, Paul falling on the ground, Paul walking, and Paul meeting Peter at Antioch. Vatican.

more important. They had more of terror for the devil than they had of love for God. They spoke of temptations and visions of demons who were often half goat and half man, creatures of evil, of whom Mephistopheles may be considered a late descendant. The monks believed that sometimes the devil took the form of a beautiful maiden who was changed into her real form through the prayers and penance of her victims. In time these terrors of the monks came to be recorded in pictures. In addition, the Apocalypse offered a text which could be illustrated with the forms of devils and monsters; and it is quite probable that we owe to Egypt the first illustrations of this work.

The "Trivulzio Ivory," representing the Holy Sepulcher building, and The Women at the Tomb. Milan.

Because the Egyptian Christians embraced beliefs considered heretical, after the Council of Chalcedon they became completely isolated from the rest of the Christian world. Thus Coptic art, thrown on its own resources, was obliged to seek themes in the symbolism of the old Egyptian religion. The Copts Christianized the mythologies of Egypt and the Orient, giving them a strange interpretation of their own.

But before this isolation the great monasteries of Thebaid were constructed. They were all built on a similar plan, having a great rectangular enclosure ornamented with Egyptian moldings, and within, a cruciform church with domes over transept and apses. The architectural decorations are geometrical in appearance, being composed of angular leaves which fill the entire field of the relief, as in Byzantine art.

The earliest pictorial manifestation of Egyptian Christian art was found in the catacombs of Alexandria in 1863, near the so-called Column of Pompey. But the frescoes had faded so much that they did not offer sufficient evidence on which to base conclusions. Next in time are the frescoes in the monastic city of El Kargue in the desert of Thebes. This city must have been a great center of Christian Egypt if we can judge by the large number of ruins of churches and tombs still found there. It was at El Kargue that the heretic Nestorius finished his life in confinement. Two buildings still preserve domes painted with frescoes of the fifth century. The scenes represented are more com-

The cathedra, or official chair, of Bishop Maximianus. Museum of Ravenna.

plicated with theological allegories than are those usually found in the
West. Later frescoes, seen in the churches of the Convents of Bawit and
Sakkara, represent scenes from the Gospels together with pictures of local
saints.

Coptic painting can be characterized generally by its austerity, its for-
malism, and its grotesque exaggeration, all of which relate to the Orient
and to Byzantium. But there are exceptions to this style in some of the
miniatures, which seem to be more Hellenistic than Oriental. Produced
in Alexandria, they seem to establish a connection between ancient Classical
civilization and the element that may be called classical in later works
of art. Our best impression of Coptic art is gained from the textiles. Thanks
to the dry Egyptian climate, many are preserved in all their splendid color-
ing. In addition, we still have a considerable number of embroidered tunics
and *sudaria* which date from early Christian times.

Red porphyry sculptures representing two pairs of emperors
embracing. St. Mark's, Venice.

Byzantine capitals, with wind-blown acanthus leaves. Characteristic style of the time of
Theodosius. St. Mark's, Venice.

THE GOLDEN AGE OF BYZANTINE ART
(500-800 A.D.)

IT WAS GENERALLY BELIEVED in the past that when Constantine founded his new capital on the Bosporus, he simply brought with him the architecture and plan of the Eternal City, Rome. To substantiate that belief, it was pointed out that many old patrician families migrated to Byzantium (or Constantinople, as it was later called), that it was divided into seven parts, like the seven hills of Rome, and, finally, that an edict named it New Rome. For a long time it was believed that Constantinople was little more than an ambitious Latin colony founded at the whim of an emperor, on the straits between Europe and Asia.

But the contrary is the fact. As we have already noted, Rome had for some time before ceased to be the cultural center of the world, and the East had come again to life, rejecting the tutelage of the once powerful city and recovering its Hellenistic traditions. When Constantine recognized the necessity for a capital in the East, he first considered rebuilding Troy in Asia Minor; there was also some reason for considering Spalato and Nicomedia, where the Emperor Diocletian had sometime before established headquarters; but the small Greek city of Byzantium was finally decided upon. Little is known of its origin, for it played an insignificant part in Greek history. One advantage was its location not far from the marble quarries

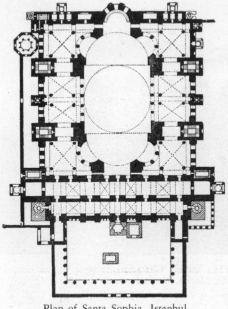

Plan of Santa Sophia, Istanbul
(Constantinople).

of the Proconnesus on the Sea of Marmora. Here Byzantine marble workers flourished, and from here many columns and other carvings were exported to the most distant cities of the Empire.

A fourth-century historian tells us that Constantine himself traced the line of the walls of his new capital. The work was carried on rapidly, and in March, 330 A.D., the ceremony of consecrating the new metropolis took place. Without analyzing the accuracy of these statements, we know positively that Constantine practically completed the project before his death. The water system had been installed, the walls and gates constructed, and the city already possessed the nuclei of the great monumental structures which, though they were rebuilt from time to time, were the pride of the city all through the Middle Ages.

An arcaded street similar to the Jerusalem thoroughfare shown in the Madaba mosaic traversed the city from the westernmost gate to the shore of the Golden Horn. This was called the *Mesé,* or Central Street; and it started from the square called the *Augustaion,* around which were grouped the principal buildings of Constantinople.

All during the Middle Ages the Augustaion retained much the same form that it assumed in the time of Constantine. Around all four sides was a colonnade, and the square was adorned with statues of the Savior and other figures connected with the Christian faith, set side by side with celebrated works of pagan art. The ancient cities of the Orient had been despoiled of their sculptures in order to embellish the new capital. Great quantities of statues were brought from Athens, Rhodes, Antioch, and Seleucia; even from Rome a wealthy matron sent a number of shafts of marble to assist the first Christian emperor in carrying out his project. Throughout the Middle Ages

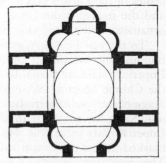

Plan showing structural scheme
of Santa Sophia, Istanbul
(Constantinople).

Exterior of Santa Sophia, Istanbul (Constantinople).

Constantinople never lost its dual character of a Hellenistic city and a Christian capital. When the Crusaders captured the city in 1202, a gigantic bronze statue of Hercules by Lysippus still stood in one of the colonnades of the Augustaion, where it was destroyed by these fanatics. But in the center of the Forum was a monumental cross adorned with precious stones; and the figure of the Good Shepherd was everywhere present, the special ornament of the fountains of the city.

To the east of the Augustaion was the Senate House, one of the finest buildings of the capital; but we know little about it. Behind it was the Imperial Palace, and opposite was the Hippodrome. At the northern end was the Church of Holy Wisdom, Santa Sophia, founded by Constantine and magnificently rebuilt by Justinian. Of all the buildings of the Augustaion only Santa Sophia still stands. No trace remains of the Senate House or the Imperial Palace; of the Hippodrome only the three monuments which marked the spina are still in place. These are: the Egyptian obelisk which Theodosius brought to Constantinople, still resting upon its sculptured base; the three-headed serpent column from Delphi; and another monument somewhat resembling an obelisk. Today the site of the great Circus is

Interior of Santa Sophia, Istanbul (Constantinople).

occupied by the square of At-Meidan. It is only by means of these monuments and the Church of Santa Sophia that we can determine the sites of the other buildings which formerly lay about this square. We know their relative position from the descriptions that have come down to us.

Constantine's project was supported by the rich patricians of Rome who transferred their families and possessions to the new city. Like the higher nobility of the Middle Ages and the cardinals of the Renaissance, some of these early Byzantine magnates possessed residences which almost rivaled that of the Emperor. One which belonged to a certain Lausus was of enormous size; the palace together with its subsidiary buildings occupied an entire district on one side of the main street called the Mesé.

If some of the patricians were reluctant to leave their old homes at Rome, Constantine found means to persuade them. We are told how the Emperor sent twelve of his wealthiest generals on a campaign against the Persians and in the meantime transported their families to Constantinople, where he had reproduced their Roman palaces even to the very doors and windows.

But all these buildings constructed in the reign of Constantine have

long since disappeared. Probably the only examples of fourth-century construction still remaining in Constantinople are the famous cisterns. Their
arrangement has no precedent in Roman architecture. They are divided
into squares by rows of parallel columns supporting shallow domes, which
recall the roofs of the Orient.

We are still very doubtful about the style of the buildings put up by
Constantine at Byzantium. Descriptions of the original church of Santa
Sophia, afterwards reconstructed by Justinian, seem to point to the fact
that it was more like a Roman basilica with a flat ceiling than an Oriental
building covered with domes. To add to the difficulty, there remain very
few fragments of architecture from the time of Theodosius, a period of great
building activity throughout the Empire. Some capitals used again in later
buildings probably date from this time and certainly could be called Byzantine. But a great building recently discovered in Egypt and dating from
the time of Theodosius still has the plan of a Roman basilica. During the
long reign of Justinian the hesitation between the old and the new ceased;
and from that time on, architecture consistently followed the new style
which we call Byzantine.

The most famous structure of the Justinian period and, for that matter,
of all Byzantine architecture, is the great Church of Santa Sophia. According to tradition, the original church had been burned by the wrath of Heaven
when Arcadius demoted John Chrysostom from the Patriarch's throne for
censoring the conduct of the Empress and the ladies of the court. When

Detail of interior of Santa Sophia, Istanbul (Constantinople).

Exterior of the Mausoleum of Galla Placidia, Ravenna.

Justinian rebuilt the church, he employed all the structural methods and ingenious devices of the new school of architecture. So interested was he in the project that he supervised the work himself. He erected temporary quarters near the building and watched the progress from day to day. The populace ascribed the plan and all the details of the church to the inspiration of an angel who often visited the Emperor. Procopius, the official historian of the reign, who wrote a book on the buildings of Justinian, tells us of the active part taken by the Emperor and his daily consultations with the directors in charge of the work. "To carry out his ideas," says this writer, "he appointed Anthemius of Thralles, who was without exception the greatest architect, not only of his own time, but of all succeeding generations. Although he was chief in authority, with him was associated Isidorus, born in Miletus, a man of unusual intelligence and truly worthy of being called to the execution of the work conceived by Justinian Augustus. We must do justice to the great perspicacity of the Emperor," continues Procopius, "who was able to select from among the men of this profession those who were most capable of interpreting his lofty conceptions. He succeeded in making the church a work of incomparable beauty, extraordinary to those who know it by report only."

These words of the Byzantine historian reflect the same consciousness

Interior of the Mausoleum of Galla Placidia, Ravenna.

of beauty which Phidias and Pericles felt when the Parthenon was built ten centuries earlier. But what a difference in their conceptions of beauty!

The very plan of the building reveals the fact that it developed in obedience to a new artistic feeling. The briefest examination makes it evident that it was arranged with the problem in mind, of supporting the great

XXII—5

Exterior of the Church of Sant' Apollinare in Classe, Ravenna.

central dome. One hundred and seven feet in diameter, this dome forms a circle inscribed in a large square and is upheld by four curvilinear triangles, called pendentives. This is the plan we have already noted in earlier Christian buildings of Syria. Each pendentive rests on a lofty pier built of massive cut stones; and instead of mortar, lead is poured in the joints. The cupola rests only upon these four supports and not on a broad circular wall, as in the Pantheon and the Baths at Rome, many of which have a greater spread than the dome of Santa Sophia. Through the medium of the wall the Roman dome really rests upon the ground, while that of Santa Sophia is an airy structure supported by arches and piers and buttressed by semi-domes on two sides. On the other two sides the lateral pressure is resisted by two arches which also act as counterforts. To lessen the weight of the dome as much as possible, the ingenious architects of Santa Sophia constructed it of the spongy bricks manufactured on the Island of Rhodes. These are so light that five of them scarcely equal the weight of an ordinary brick.

The exterior of the great central dome is disappointing. It is masked for a third of its height by a drum which is pierced by a line of windows encircling the great hemisphere and illuminating the church. But nothing could be more striking than the interior. The eye is lost in the vast space overhead.

We do not receive the impression of repose and solidity produced by the Pantheon. The large dome of Santa Sophia seems to float as if suspended

Interior of Sant' Apollinare, Nuovo, Ravenna.

from on high. The brilliant mosaics which once decorated it must have heightened this illusion of ethereal lightness.

The two sides have galleries from which the ladies of the court could look down upon the ceremonies taking place below. Procopius praises the magnificence of the decoration of those galleries: "Who could describe," he asks, "the upper story of the gyneceum? Who can tell of the splendor of the columns and the marbles with which it is adorned? One would think that one had come upon a flowery meadow; one marvels at the purple hues of some, and the green of others!"

Surely the galleries of Santa Sophia are numbered among the most precious gems in the treasury of mankind. The church is enriched by its two vestibules. The outer one, like a closed porch, formerly opened upon a rectangular court; and the broad narthex, which adjoins the main body of the church, is still almost intact with its beautiful columns and mosaics.

The building was begun in 532 and completed in December, 537, when it was consecrated. Restorations soon became necessary. Procopius writes that even during the lifetime of Anthemius and Isidorus faults developed in the arches which supported the great dome. A few years later the dome itself fell in, as the result of an earthquake, and it was necessary to rebuild it. This was accomplished under the direction of a nephew of Isidorus, who had inherited the ability as well as the office of the master.

Detail of the mosaic showing the Procession of the Virgins. Sant' Apollinare
Nuovo, Ravenna.

Of all the monuments built at the time of Justinian at Byzantium, the
most often mentioned by the Byzantine writers was the Church of the
Holy Apostles, which served as a mausoleum for the imperial family. It
was built on a high spot with a fine view over the Golden Horn. But,
perhaps because of its magnificent situation, it was demolished to make way
for the Mosque of Mohammed II. The
emperors used to go to the Church of the
Holy Apostles in their processions on
feast days. Therein was a group of
civil buildings besides the church, the
hospital, and the monastery. In a palace
there the Emperor used to take a bath
before visiting the tombs of his predecessors. The great saints of the Greek
Church, Basil and John Chrysostom,
were also buried in the Church of the
Holy Apostles. As the church has entirely disappeared we have to rely upon
written descriptions. Procopius praises

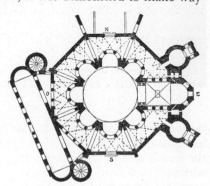

Plan of the Church of San Vitale,
Ravenna.

Interior of San Vitale, Ravenna.

the building of Justinian in these words: "Its nave and transept form a cross; like Santa Sophia's, the roof is domed, but here the domes are smaller. Above the four arches at the intersection rises a hemispherical cupola, pierced with windows, and so lofty that it seems to float in the air. There is a similar dome over each arm of the cross, but without windows." Later descriptions of the Church of the Holy Apostles give the details of the mosaics decorating the

Christ being presented with a model of the Church by St. Eclesius and passing a crown to Saint Vitale. Mosaic in the apse of San Vitale, Ravenna.

walls. But we are still in great doubt about the relative position of its five domes. This seems a trifling detail, but it is important because with this datum we might be able to trace the plan of that church in St. Mark's Church at Venice. The Turks whitewashed the walls and stripped the furnishings from the churches of Constantinople in order to make them suitable for mosques. The Christian buildings, however, are being restored as far as is possible, and Santa Sophia has been turned into a Christian museum. An American Byzantine Institute, with Turkish co-operation, is cleaning away the paint that covered the mosaics, and eventually we shall be able to see Santa Sophia with the mosaics restored. But in the meantime, in order to gain the sensation of the best mosaics of the Golden Age of Byzantine art, we must go to other cities—to Salonika or Ravenna.

A small Roman city on the Adriatic Sea, Ravenna became important at the time of Honorius. When the Emperor of the West saw the Italian provinces threatened by the barbarians, he began to fear even for Rome itself and moved his court to Ravenna. This city was defended by the malarial lagoons and was a most favorable site from which, in a last resort, he might take ship and flee for safety to Constantinople, where his brother, Arcadius, reigned as co-emperor with him. A number of important buildings were erected in Ravenna during Honorius' time, and by good fortune a splendid mausoleum erected by his sister, Galla Placidia, has been preserved intact. It is a cruciform building, the arms of which are barrel-vaulted, and above the crossing is a dome. This small structure has a charm which once seen can never be forgotten. The blues and greens of the

Two clerestory windows in the Church of San Vitale, Ravenna.

Justinian and two courtiers. Detail of a mosaic at San Vitale, Ravenna.

ceiling are strewn with golden stars; on the wall is depicted the Good
Shepherd surrounded by his lambs, all in the finest mosaic; and beyond,
behind the altar, is the great sarcophagus of Galla Placidia. In the transepts are the sarcophagi of her brother Honorius and her husband Con-
stantius. As of all the buildings of Ravenna, the exterior is of modest
brickwork, ornamented only with the arcaded panels so characteristic of
Byzantine and early Romanesque architecture.

Four large basilicas of Ravenna date from the time when that city was
the capital of the West. But only two have retained their original appearance. The other two were entirely remodeled during the Renaissance.
The two basilicas which have preserved their Byzantine character are dedicated to St. Apollinare, the patron of Ravenna. According to tradition,
this Saint was sent to Ravenna by St. Peter to preach the Gospel; he lived
in a cave outside the city and preached until he was martyred. Nevertheless, he was considered the first bishop of Ravenna, and was dressed in a
bishop's robe. The tomb of St. Apollinare was in a basilica in the suburb,
Classis. It has a nave and two aisles with Byzantine mosaics in the apse,
still well preserved. Because of fear that the bones of the bishop-saint were
not safe in that maritime suburb, they were removed to another basilica
inside the city, dedicated to St. Martin. The church had a ceiling of gold, and

Theodora and two attendants. Detail of a mosaic in San Vitale, Ravenna.

was called St. Martin of the Gilded Roof. When the bones of St. Apollinare were placed there, the name was changed to St. Apollinare Nuovo.

Its plan is genuinely Latin, consisting of a nave and two aisles separated by rows of columns. The ceiling of the nave is of wood, but the aisles are vaulted. Unlike the Classical capitals of the Roman basilicas, here they are ornamented with spinous acanthus leaves, and between the capital and the springer of the arch is a trapezoidal block called an impost capital, which in Byzantine art takes the place of the frieze. The mosaics above the columns in the nave are perhaps the finest production of this new art which had come from the Orient. From the center of the nave the beholder cannot but admire the processions of saints on every hand. On one side, women and virgins come to adore the Madonna and Child; on the other, saints and martyrs headed by three angels and the Magi move toward the Savior. It is as though the scene in the cave at Bethlehem were mysteriously prolonged down through the centuries. The saints and virgins, dressed in the new style, are undoubtedly the work of Oriental masters. It is impossible to describe the charm of this church with its long lines of ecstatic figures, Oriental princesses and learned divines, who raise their great pensive eyes in devout self-forgetfulness.

The two Baptisteries of Ravenna are perhaps the most ancient of these

Byzantine buildings. They are octagonal in form and in the center of each is a handsome marble font. One was originally for the orthodox Christians, and the other for the Arians. Both preserve their old mosaic decoration on the walls and in the domes. Outside, they are constructed of large bricks which offer little indication of the gold and brilliant colors within. In the center of the dome we see represented the baptism in the Jordan; below, a row of Apostles bear books and rolls. In a still lower zone is a mosaic representation of curtains and niches containing objects connected with the ritual. These mural decorations of hanging curtains, furnishings, and even fountains, all done in brilliant polychrome, were a favorite Byzantine theme.

Portrait head of a Byzantine emperor, probably Heraclius. From a colossal statue in bronze.

The last great work of the Exarchs of Ravenna and originally the most richly decorated of all is the Church of San Vitale. This building has been preserved intact except for its mosaics, many of which were destroyed at the time of the Renaissance. The plan of this church is based on the Byzantine principle of grouping all the elements around a large central cupola which was supported by piers and columns. Here is the complex system of vaults which originated in the Orient. The base of the central cupola is an octagon which gradually merges into a hemispherical dome. The lateral thrust is resisted by seven semicircular recesses; on the eighth side is the cross-vault of the chancel which ends in an apse and contains the choir and altar.

The dome of San Vitale is constructed of rings composed of terra-cotta jars embedded in cement. This lightens it sufficiently to be supported by the thin walls beneath. The aisle surrounding the central cupola is covered with cross-vaults which intersect one another in a very irregular fashion. Both dome and aisle are covered with a roof of timbers and tiles, a feature never found in the churches of Byzantium where the dome itself is seen from the outside. There is a narthex, or vestibule, which is oddly set against one of the corners of the octagon.

The only mosaics which have not been destroyed are found in the choir and apse, and from these we gain some idea of the rich appearance of the rest of the interior in former times. Trees, flowers, plants, and animals, standing out from a gold background, still decorate the chancel-arch and vault. This design is interrupted by medallions containing the figures of prophets and apostles. On the side walls of the apse are mosaic compositions of historical personages of the Byzantine court. On one side we see Justinian bringing gifts to the new church, accompanied by Bishop Maximianus and a number of priests, courtiers, and soldiers. On the opposite side is the Empress Theodora. She is covered with jewels and bears a handsome bowl, as she leads a brilliant cortege of court ladies and eunuchs. Here, too, are the hanging curtains, fountain, and distant buildings which the mosaic artists loved to picture. The figures are the work of a contemporary artist. The austere face of the bishop is surely a portrait. Possibly a personal resemblance is intended in the faces of Justinian and Theodora.

Ivory plaque of an empress. National Museum, Florence.

Ivories, icons, and miniatures made in Constantinople reached the west of Europe in great quantities and fostered there the growth of the Romanesque styles. This fact alone ought to be sufficient excuse for turning our attention to Byzantine art. But in addition we are attracted by the inherent beauty of the Byzantine objects of art. They are a curious combination of Roman subjects interpreted by the mind of the Near East, with a fragrance of Persia

Archangel, on one leaf of an ivory diptych.
British Museum.

somehow about them. Let us look first at Byzantine sculpture. What is the meaning of this predilection for the low relief rather than the round? Was this a reminiscence of the Oriental fear of the excessive likeness? Was it a repugnance for material reality? Not one single Byzantine statue of a divine being has been rescued till now. We know there were several equestrian statues of the emperors in the main squares at Constantinople. The Venetians took one of them, with great difficulty, in the loot of 1202 and tried to ship it home. Portrait heads of Byzantine emperors and empresses in marble have been preserved and are in western museums. Therefore, we cannot say that the Byzantines disapproved of sculptures in the round, but we can surely say that they preferred the low relief.

The Byzantine marble workers excelled in the carving of slabs. Some of the decorations of their buildings were of unsurpassed beauty. They were considered as precious as gems by the Venetians. So many were carried away for the embellishment of St. Mark's that the great domed building is as much an archaeological museum as a church. We shall have occasion to speak of them later, when we describe St. Mark's Cathedral in the next chapter.

Many Byzantine marble slabs simply repeated earlier icons painted on wood and worshiped at altars of churches at Constantinople.

The icons of the great metropolis had a reputation all over the Empire and eventually reached the West. Some of them were repeating very old catacomb types. In Constantino-

Deësis, or perfect prayer. Mary and St. John the Baptist, praying to Jesus.
Byzantine relief. Venice.

ple, in the church near the Blachernae Palace, is the icon of the Praying
Madonna, called the "Blachernitissa." In this icon the Madonna does not
carry the Child, but raises her hands in prayer like an orans. Another icon
represents the Madonna as walking with the Child; she was named the
"Madonna Odegetria," because she stood at the Church of the Guild of the
Mail Carriers, or the Odegon Church. She carries the Child, symbolizing the
mail, and He carries a scroll symbolizing the Gospel he preached. Both the
"Blachernitissa" and the "Odegetria" were painted icons. Perhaps they
did those slabs for export to foreign lands, where plastic representation
was not so feared as it was by the people of Constantinople. For knowledge of Byzantine sculpture the smaller reliefs of ivory are more important than the carved marble slabs. Perhaps the most beautiful existing specimen of this type of work is the panel from a triptych representing
the Archangel Michael, now in the British Museum. It is most imposing:
the angelic hierarch descends a stairway from a columned portico like the
entrance to the sanctuary of a Greek church. In one hand he bears a spear,
and in the other a globe surmounted by a cross, as though in the act of trans-
mitting his dominion to the emperor, whose figure probably occupied one of
the missing panels of the triptych. The central panel probably represented
the coronation of an emperor and empress, a favorite subject with the artists
of Byzantium. Upon a small pedestal in the center would be the Savior
placing a crown on the head of each of the royal pair, thus indicating that

The Virgin of the Church of the Blachernae, as an orans. From Constantinople. Venice.

their imperial rank was divinely conferred.

The Byzantine ivory carvers also made beautiful diptychs for the consuls to distribute to their friends upon their installation in office, as was the custom in Rome. There was great competition among the officials in presenting gifts. Coins were thrown to the common people, corn was distributed to the poor, and carved ivory plaques were given to important personages. In time many of the delightful little carvings passed into the treasuries of the churches, where they have been used to carry the lists of names of benefactors for whom the priest had to pray. The subjects represented in the consular diptychs were very seldom religious in character. Some represented the games that the donor subsidized for the people's amusement, the donor himself appearing in the upper part of the relief, handkerchief in hand to direct the games; and below, the races, the fighting beasts, or the acts of the mimes, with the impression of the noisy scene well portrayed.

Many Byzantine ivories are portable altars and miniature icons reproducing the most venerated images of the great metropolis. We have already mentioned two of the Madonnas of the churches at Constantinople that found their way into the West, the "Blachernitissa," which did not prosper there, and the Madonna of the Mail Carriers. Another, the Nea Madonna, or the Madonna of the New Church, sat on a throne.

The figure of St. John often appears on ivories. He is never called the Baptist, but the *Prodromos,* or the one who walks before. Facing on the Mesé, the Broadway of Constantinople, was a great church dedicated to St. John, who was always represented as a patriarch of the church, with long robes and a cape, not at all like the eater of locusts or like the semi-nude figure of John accepted in the West.

Many of the ivory carvers of Constantinople either were monks or were

assisted by monks. For this reason
theological subjects are often found.
A favorite theme was the *Deesis,* or
the perfect prayer, which might have
been the prayer for mankind made
by Mary and the Prodromos, as both
were the first to acknowledge the
divine character of Jesus. Sometimes
the perfect prayer is the one by Mary
and the Beloved Disciple at the foot
of the cross. More mystical was the
subject called *Etimasia,* or the divine
throne. This was a chair decorated
with a lamb and a cross, about which
twelve lambs worshiped. It is difficult for us to understand how the
Byzantines saw there the representation of the Trinity. Only the Byzantine artists could have produced such
beautiful objects with such involved
theological themes.

The painted icons must have been
the supreme achievement of the Byzantine artists. Some were so revered
that they were covered with veils and
shown to the public only on certain
days. One was supposed to be shown
only when the veil miraculously
moved of its own accord—which
must have been rather seldom. Unfortunately, no original icon of the
Golden Age of Byzantine art has
been preserved. The themes that appeared on them are known only because they were copied in subsequent
works of art, such as coins or seals.
Some of the dignitaries of the church
had seals made depicting their favorite image from some icon.

We must go to the mosaics and
miniatures for an understanding of
the great art of the painters of Constantinople. We have already mentioned the important mosaics of
Ravenna and Santa Sophia. Those

Ivory copy of the "Madonna of the Church
of the Mail Carriers." Constantinople.
Metropolitan Museum of Art, New York.

Silver plate from Cyprus, representing David fighting with Golia h. Above, the dispute before the duel, with the figure of the *genius loci* of the Valley of Elah. Metropolitan Museum of Art, New York.

at Salonika are our best source of information. During the Golden Age of Byzantine art, Salonika was the second and most important city in the Eastern Empire. Although the mosaics there suffered badly from the fires of 1911 and 1917, enough remains to prove that they must have been among the chief jewels of the artistic treasury of mankind.

Miniatures in books reflect perhaps better than anything else the peculiar beliefs which surrounded the Byzantine artists. For them ideas were real; in fact they were almost as tangible as bodies are to us. We have, for example, a precious manuscript of the medical text of Dioscorides, that belonged to a Byzantine princess of the fifth century. We have no reason for believing her extraordinary; yet she is portrayed on the first page between figures representing Magnanimity and Reflection. On the next page is the portrait of the author Dioscorides, approached by the idealized figure of *Euresis,* or Discovery. The book contains still another portrait of this author shown with the idealized figure of Attention. So, not only theological ideas, but also intellectual concepts, were portrayed as everyday realities by Byzantine artists.

The biblical texts also contained a great number of personifications of ideas, places, and concepts. In some beautifully illustrated manuscripts of the Psalter done during the Golden Age of Byzantine art we find historical persons like Samuel,

Miniature from the Psalter of Paris. Representing Isaiah praying between Night and Dawn.

Saul, and David accompanied by allegorical figures of the Desert, the Dawn, Melody, and Echo. Inspiration is represented as a nymph in Classical dress.

David as a Shepherd between Melody and Echo. At the lower right, the figure of the *genius loci.*

Very likely the Byzantine miniatures of the aristocratic manuscripts of the Psalter originated in Antioch, the place where the tradition of Hellenistic refinement found its haven. But the Constantinople copyists enjoyed repeating these creations, and learned from them how to make the allegorical subjects real. This seems to prove that the Byzantine artists kept and made more popular the themes of the Hellenistic schools.

May we say that Byzantine art is a natural development of Greek art? In some respects, yes. Many students of Greek literature consider the Apostle Paul as the last of the Greek writers; some go farther and include the works of St. John Chrysostom, John of the Golden Tongue; while others go even farther and consider Greek the literature of the Byzantines up to the fall of Constantinople. If we accept these views of literature, then Byzantine art may be considered only another chapter of Greek art. We have the beginning of allegorical personifications in the pediments of the Parthenon, where the Sun rides a chariot and the horses of the Moon go down into the Sea. And yet there is so much of the new in the interpretation of the old subjects by the Byzantine artists, and the theological spirit injected into them is so strong, that it is perhaps a scholarly snobbishness not to acknowledge their creative inventiveness and originality in the works they produced at the highest point of the Golden Age.

Mosaic of a bishop. In the Basilica of St. Demetrios, Salonika.

"Apotheosis of Alexander." The conqueror ascends to heaven in a chariot drawn by griffins which he lures upward by means of two sticks baited with rabbits. Byzantine relief of the Iconoclastic period. Venice.

THE BYZANTINE RENAISSANCE

(*900-1200 A. D.*)

THE CENTURIES that followed the long reign of Justinian up until the Iconoclastic dispute, about 800, were truly the Golden Age of Constantinople; but the Empire still had ahead of it six long centuries of glory. The Byzantine Renaissance after the period of Iconoclasm has amazingly dropped out of our knowledge, and even educated people today do not seem to have much respect for it. The explanation of this lies in the reluctance of the art critics to go to the original texts. Historians, from Gibbons on, remembered that the Byzantine Empire produced great characters: statesmen, warriors, philosophers, and churchmen. Not only were these men among the greatest of the time, but the Empire itself had so extraordinary an organization that many of its governmental ideas are still found workable today.

The western European idea of Byzantium might well be summarized in Taine's epigram: "A nation of subtle theologians and vainglorious idiots." This erroneous conception was largely due to a belief that Byzantine civilization was from the very first circumscribed by formal rules and precedents, as inflexible as religious dogma, which kept its artists and thinkers from producing any spontaneous or creative work. The etiquette of the court, the administration of the government, and the rules of art and even of the sciences, were all founded on the religious dogmas established by

Church of St. Theodosia in Constantinople, with the high domes of the late Byzantine style. Restoration by Kenneth J. Conant.

the Fathers in the Church Councils. "It is for the Fathers to dispose and command, and for the painters to execute," was the dictum of the Council of Nicaea. Indeed, certain artistic types were established which in a general way were faithfully reproduced for many centuries. Nevertheless, this tyranny was more apparent than real. The Greek artists of the classical period also had their fixed types which were transmitted from generation to generation, but which never ceased to acquire new beauty. The Byzantine artists also succeeded in infusing their secular productions with that variety which is essential in artistic forms. To the superficial critic of fifty years ago the entire repertory of Byzantine art seemed most uniform; but today our perceptions are more acute, and we see the rigidly imposed subject clothed with new and ever varying forms and styles. We now distinguish at least four different styles in Byzantine art. The first prevailed from the foundation of the capital down to the Iconoclasts; the second covered the reigns of these emperors; the third endured from the time of Basil II until the sack of the city by the Crusaders; the fourth, from this date until the Turkish conquest.

Cathedral of Santa Sophia at Kiev. Restoration by Kenneth J. Conant.

These four styles correspond to the four great periods of Byzantine political history, for it is wrong to suppose that everything stood still for so many centuries. We of the West are still unwilling to recognize the importance of that epic struggle with Islam on the battlefields of Asia Minor, when Byzantium was Europe's only real defense in the East. During the Middle Ages the European idea of the city of Constantinople was very different from that which is now generally held. To them it was the one and only capital of the world. When the largest European cities were little more than petty towns, Constantinople alone, with its populous wards, great buildings, and mighty battlements, recalled the greatness of Rome. Its pomp and splendor were a lure to adventurers from everywhere. Within its walls they saw a booty beyond their wildest dreams, and it was a ceaseless struggle to keep them at a distance. These defensive wars developed the talents of many an illustrious leader whose qualities we are only now beginning to appreciate. To repel the Huns, Bulgars, Russians, and Normans, and to defend the city from the Crusaders, Constantinople had pressing need of warlike emperors and astute generals. More than once was the Byzantine court the scene of a conclave of able leaders assembled at a critical moment when the fate of a civilization hung in the balance.

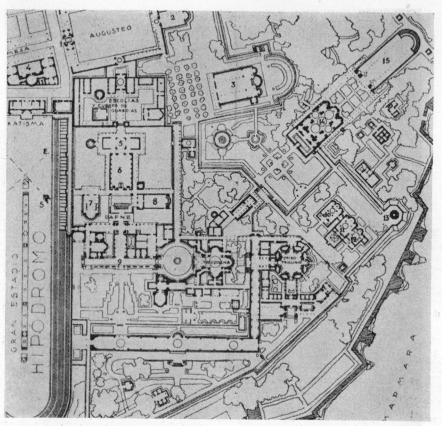

Plan of the Imperial Palace at Constantinople. (1) miliarium, (2) senate, (3) magnaura, (4) chalce, (5) tribunal, (6) consistorium, (7) triclinium, (8) Church of the Savior, (9) gallery, (10) Church of St. Demetrios, (11) Church of the Pharos, (12) St. Elijah, (13) Pharos, (14) the *Nea,* or New church, (15) polo grounds.

Partisan quarrels and revolutions at home also contributed to the growth of new ideas. It was natural that a period of disputes and revolts should be followed by one of artistic production in which the old subjects should take on new grace and vigor. At such times art rose again triumphant, and new churches sprang up in every part of the Empire. Brilliant mosaics and graceful porticos proclaimed the birth of a new Byzantine style.

Taking up the architecture of this nation where we left it in the last chapter, we note with interest that after the persecutions of the Iconoclast Emperors, the shape of the cupola was modified. The dome was raised upon a higher cylindrical drum in order to give the building a more imposing appearance when seen from a distance. These lofty domes could not assume the size of those of St. Sophia and St. Irene; but they increased in number,

Pier with Byzantine decoration, showing character of the work in the Imperial Palace of
Constantinople. Corner of St. Mark's, Venice.

and architects devised new and ingenious systems for combining a number
of them in a single building. The cupola continued to be the most prominent feature of Byzantine roof construction; but it no longer predominated

Byzantine railings. Brought from their original places for use in St. Mark's, Venice.

to the extent that it had in Justinian's time, when the plan of the entire building was subordinated to the dome and the massive piers supporting it. Many churches were built in this second style, and we see in all of them the same freedom of structural design. There was usually a portico or a cloister in front. This, too, is often covered with domes which rise from various levels but do not cut off the view of the church proper. The drums of these cupolas are octagonal, the windows are sometimes divided by small columns, and the exterior is often faced with alternating bands of brick and stone that are very pleasing. There are several churches of this style in Constantinople as well as at Salonika. Even in Athens and in far away Ukrania, at Kiev, there were churches built with numerous lofty domes.

During this Byzantine Renaissance a number of the more important buildings were constructed as additions to the imperial palace at Constantinople. This great group of buildings has disappeared completely today, and we have only contemporary descriptions to enable us to restore them. One of the most important sources of information is the BOOK OF THE CEREMONIES OF THE BYZANTINE COURT written by the Emperor Constantine Porphyrogenitus. The great palace must have been the most important example of secular architecture in the Byzantine Empire. Its original foundation dated from the time of Constantine, who traced out the site for its location on one side of the imperial forum, or Augustaion. It was rebuilt by Justinian and was from time to time enriched with new halls and porches by his successors. But it was not until the tenth and eleventh centuries that it became the stately assemblage of churches, pavilions, and gardens, which made it the ideal palace of the medieval romances of chivalry. The name of Sacred Palace was given to it.

Like the palaces of the Oriental monarchs of Syria and Persia, it consisted of an irregular arrangement of buildings and gardens. Owing to its proximity to western Asia, the Oriental character of the Sacred Palace became more and more accentuated. Indeed, the emperors who added to it

Byzantine capitals. Transplanted from their original settings for use in St. Mark's, Venice.

in the ninth and tenth centuries intentionally imitated the grouping of the palaces at Baghdad. With its gardens the Sacred Palace occupied almost a hundred acres, an area larger than that covered by the Louvre and the Tuileries. From a distance it must have been very imposing. The Kremlin at Moscow is the only building of modern Europe which can give us even a faint idea of what this great palace must have looked like. In addition to the buildings which formed parts of the palace itself, there were four large churches, namely, St. Stephen, the Church of Our Lord, St. Mary of the

Venetian Byzantine palace, with porch on the ground level and gallery on the upper floor. Venice.

Pharos, and the so-called *Nea* or New Church, as well as chapels, oratories, and a baptistery, comprising altogether twenty-three buildings devoted to religious rites.

The palace itself contained seven colonnaded vestibules, eight courts, and two porticoes which served as entrances. The accounts of historians seem to establish the fact that it was divided into three groups of buildings: those around the *Chalce,* or monumental entrance, which housed oratories and guardrooms; the *Daphne,* a building containing reception halls and administrative offices; and the Sacred Palace itself, in which were the *Magnaura* and *Chrysotriclinium,* the halls where ambassadors were received, and the private apartments of the emperor. In the palace there was also an *Xeno-dochium,* or school, where boys of good families were trained to be officials in one of the thirty types of service, into which the Byzantine government was divided. Half of them were required to become eunuchs in order that they might not make family ties or create a hereditary aristocracy, unknown in Byzantium.

The interiors of the palace buildings were extremely luxurious, with elaborate decorations which often produced a decidedly theatrical effect. Constantine Porphyrogenitus in his BOOK OF CEREMONIES gives us a vivid picture of the famous receptions, magnificent festivals, pageants, and processions which took place in the galleries and triclinia of the Sacred Palace. Each occasion had its own special ceremony. A visiting prince or ambassador from the Occident was conducted through long corridors gleaming with mosaics and carpeted with Oriental rugs and scattered rose-leaves, while lines of guardsmen stood at attention on either side. Passing through one apartment after another the visitor finally came to the Magnaura and Chrysotriclinium, the great ceremonial halls where he heard with bewilderment the peal of the organ and hymns in honor of the emperor entoned by the voices of hidden singers.

The Magnaura preserved its basilican arrangement of nave and two side-aisles, with a throne at the further end. Originally designed by Constantine himself, it underwent many changes of decoration, until for richness of effect it had no equal in the world. The Chrysotriclinium, on the other hand, was genuinely Byzantine in style. The form was octagonal; there were eight apses supporting the central dome, which was surrounded by a gallery for spectators. One of the apses served as the emperor's robing room and contained a small oratory as well; another served as the treasury in which were kept the crown jewels, famous pieces by noted goldsmiths, enameled crowns, and precious robes covered with designs commemorating the deeds of historical characters. In the apse opposite the entrance was the emperor's throne; two golden lions stood before it, and behind it a golden plane tree in whose

A Byzantine grating of marble. In San Vitale, Ravenna.

Façade of St. Mark's, Venice, showing the high cupolas characteristic of the late
Byzantine period.

branches were perched mechanical birds. At a certain point in the ceremony
a secret mechanism caused the lions to roar and the birds to flutter and sing,
while the throne itself rose high into the air, exalting the monarch who sat
upon it, veiled in clouds of incense. The reception of an ambassador is described by Constantine Porphyrogenitus as follows: "The ambassador, when
he enters the hall, prostrates himself upon the ground in reverence to the
emperor. He then arises and advances a certain distance while the organ
begins to sound. It must be noted that after the ambassador has been introduced, the most distinguished members of his suite also enter, and after
they have prostrated themselves, they separate and move, some to either
side of the hall. The master of ceremonies puts the usual questions, and
then the lions begin to roar and the birds (on the throne and surrounding
trees) break forth into melodious song. The animals at the foot of the
throne rise to their feet, and at the same time the pronotarius delivers the
gifts which the ambassador has brought in the name of his king or prince.
After the ambassador has retired, the senators and patricians begin to go
out, and after them, the other officers singing the "Polychronion." When
all have gone, the emperor descends from his throne, takes off his crown
and chlamys, and puts on his gold-bordered cloak. Whereupon he returns

Interior of St. Mark's, the most Byzantine of western buildings.

without any pomp to his palace, following the route by which he had come, attended by the grooms of the bedchamber and guarded by God."

All this occurred in the great hall of the Magnaura, but the same pomp and ostentation was often displayed in the palace as well. Our author also describes the imperial bedchamber constructed by the Emperor Basil. "Nothing can compare," he says, "with the beauty of this sleeping apartment. The pavement is of mosaic, and in the center is a peacock set within a circle of Carian marble. From this centerpiece extend bands of green marble like spokes to a second larger circle. The rest of the room is carpeted with eagles of mosaic so real that one might believe they were alive and flying. The lower portions of the walls are cased with tiles of colored glass which delight the eye with the variety of flowers represented upon them. A band of gold separates this decoration from the mosaics covering the upper wall space of the apartment. Here we see seated against a gold background the figures of Basil and his wife Eudocia. They are clad in purple and wear their crowns, while beyond them their children stand in line, with books in their hands as a sign of their piety. Amid the gold of the vault gleams the sign

The Palatine Chapel at Palermo. Built by Saracenic laborers and Byzantine decorators for the Norman kings.

of the cross in green marble; and here again we find the portraits of the Emperor and Empress with their children, who raise their arms to God and toward the visible symbol of the cross."

This description gives us an excellent idea of the character of the emperor's private apartments and the arrangement of the mosaics and rare stones in the upper walls and vaults, as well as the decorations covering the lower wall spaces. The former were sometimes ornamented with historical scenes and genre pictures. If they had survived, we would know more, perhaps, of the secular art of Byzantium, which was not so closely restricted by rules and precedents as the religious paintings in the naves and apses of the churches. Constantine Porphyrogenitus also tells us of the banquet-hall constructed by the Emperor Theophilas, in which were pictured the principal events of his reign. "The vault," he says, "is supported by sixteen columns. Eight are of green Thessalian marble and six of onychite; their shafts are covered with flowering vines and animals. The other two are also of onychite but are ornamented only with spiral fluting. In all of them the artist has sought by the variety of his designs to give the greatest pleasure to the beholder. The entire dome is covered with mosaics. In the center we see the Emperor Theophilas with the generals who shared the hardships of his campaigns, while others offer him small models of the cities which they have conquered with him. High on the vaulted ceiling are depicted the military exploits of the Emperor, his Herculean efforts to secure the happiness of his subjects, his courage on the field of battle, and the victories bestowed upon him by the Lord."

Though hardly a trace of the Imperial Palace remains in Turkish Constantinople today, we may judge of its magnificence to some extent from the fragments and columns which we find scattered among the mosques of Stamboul, in the Palace of the Seraglio, and even in Venice and other distant cities. Two famous pillars which were

Upper part of the Paschal candlesticks in the Palatine Chapel. Palermo.

Two Byzantine reliefs, with the peacocks that originated in the catacombs. The aristocratic style characteristic of the late Byzantine Renaissance. Venice and Torcello.

brought to Venice from St. Jean d'Acre give us some idea of the vine-covered capitals and columns described by Constantine Porphyrogenitus. In St. Mark's there are numerous marble railings decorated with reliefs, which the galleys of the Republic brought from the Orient. It is not unlikely that some of these are plunder from the Imperial Palace.

The Sacred Palace was almost completely abandoned in the twelfth century by the emperors who had constructed a new residence in Constantinople, called the Blachernae; and here the Byzantine court spent the last years of its existence. We know little of this palace. It is believed that we see its remains in the ruins of a handsome building which lie between the outer and inner walls of the city and bear the arms of the Palaeologus family. The façade at one end of a courtyard, with its gaping windows, displays a polychromatic design that is characteristic of later Byzantine architecture. It is decorated with bands of brick and stone, and a mosaic of marble marquetry like the neo-Byzantine churches which we have already described. Except for this ruin, which may not be a part of the Blachernae after all, nothing is left of the imperial palaces at Constantinople or of the handsome residences of the wealthy Byzantine families whose possessions rivaled those of the emperors.

The private houses at Constantinople must have been very similar to those of Syria and other parts of Western Asia, with their apartments lying behind the court. This was not the old Graeco-Roman type of house where the rooms were grouped around a square court. There was always a portico

The Christ of the narthex of Santa Sophia at Constantinople. Mosaic recently uncovered by the Byzantine Institute of America.

fronting upon the street; even when there was no room for a court, the portico was retained and a second story was constructed which contained the reception halls, as in the palaces of Venice. In the Madaba topographical map we see the cities of Palestine, with porticoes along their streets and two-storied houses like those of the miniatures in old manuscripts. We can judge of the external appearance of the private residences of Constantinople by the palaces of the tenth and eleventh centuries which still remain in Venice.

It is in Venice that we find the most perfectly preserved monument of Byzantine art that has come down to us, the famous metropolitan Church of St. Mark. The Republic long maintained close relations with Constan-

The Deësis. Mary and St. John praying at the foot of the Cross. In the Church of Daphne near Athens.

tinople. The Venetians had a quarter of their own in the capital, where great warehouses and stores of merchandise supplied their ships. In connection with their extensive commercial enterprises they had factories in many a city of Western Asia. Indeed, some of these places actually became possessions of the merchant-princes of Venice. Venetian ships brought the latest Byzantine fashions to Western Europe; and it was natural that this maritime state, so familiar with the splendor of the East, should copy the magnificent styles of Byzantium in its own buildings, rather than those of the rude nations of the West who could only imitate the old Roman structures falling to ruin about them.

Venice sent to the East for her first architects, when the original Church of St. Mark was begun in the ninth century. It was destroyed by fire during the insurrection of 916 and rebuilt during the next two years, although somewhat altered in both size and arrangement. There remains only a portion of the walls of this second church, which was constructed under the Doge Orseolo. It is believed to have been built of a variety of materials and ornamented with alternate bands of brick and stone, in the manner of the Byzantine buildings of the period following the persecutions of the Iconoclastic emperors. Like the rest of the church, these walls are now covered with marble of various colors; but a careful investigation of the floor and walls has furnished data from which it is possible to obtain some idea of the character of the older church. Its plan was like that of the usual basilica, with a nave and two aisles separated by two rows of twelve columns each.

In the time of the Doge Domenico Contarini, in 1063, both the plan and the appearance of St. Mark's were greatly altered. It lost its original appearance of a Roman basilica and became an Oriental church with five domes, probably with the same arrangement as that of the five-domed Church of the Holy Apostles at Constantinople.

Miniatures from the MENOLOGION of Basil II. Joseph's dream.

Thirty years were required before the church was ready to receive its decorations. Domenico Selvo, who was then doge, issued directions to all the consuls, ambassadors, merchants, vessel-owners, and wealthy citizens living in the East to collect zealously the precious materials needed for the decoration of the new church. The plan was well received, and all vied with one another in bringing treasures, shafts of columns from ancient temples, capitals from Byzantium, and slabs of handsome stone, and precious marble in great quantities.

St. Mark's and Santa Sophia are equally rich and splendid. Although they differ from one another in some respects, the spirit animating the two churches is the same. St. Mark's, perhaps, gives us the better idea of the pomp and ostentation of Byzantium in the old days. The Venetian church is still a place of worship where an imposing ritual is carried on, and its mosaics are intact; while Santa Sophia has been desecrated, and its decorations have been badly defaced.

Compared to Santa Sophia, St. Mark's is a small church; but its well-balanced proportions, skillful arangement, and certain ingenious perspective effects cause it to appear larger than it really is. For example, the three domes covering the transepts and chancel are smaller than the two over the nave, making them appear farther away and giving the entire building a more monumental effect. The interior of the church is sumptuous beyond description; in the far end the chancel gleams with its columns of rare stones; pulpits on either side of the altar are carved from the most precious marble; and antique lamps hang from the ceiling. In the most holy place is the High Altar radiant with gold and enamel, the sacred palladium of the great maritime republic. The interior is lighted entirely from above; the springers of the five domes are pierced with small windows through which the rays of the sun filter in, to be reflected from the magnificent mosaics inside.

We learn from an old chronicle that they sent to Constantinople for artists to execute the mosaics, but among the Greek inscriptions we see Latin distichs explaining the significance of each scene. The exterior of the church offers an aspect of richness and beauty not found in most Byzantine monuments. During the prolonged death struggle of the Byzantine Empire, the Venetians took advantage of the abandonment of certain provinces to carry away rich marbles and handsome carvings for the embellishment of their national church. Indeed, they even plundered some of the deserted buildings of Constantinople as well.

To complete our description of the exterior of St. Mark's, we should not neglect to mention the ornamentation of the cupolas. Upon the brick domes are set wooden frames surmounted by lighter metal cupolas which stand out from the mass of the building. The five domes with their gilded pinnacles and the delicate tracery of the spires round about them strike a joyous note as they cast their radiance across the lagoons.

About the time St. Mark's was being built, the Byzantine army again

Miniatures from the MENOLOGION of Basil II. The Nativity. Vatican Library.

Miniatures from the HOMILIES of St. Gregory owned by the Emperor Basil II. Christ is
represented with the facial likeness of the Emperor. National Library, Paris.

occupied southern Italy, which had been devastated by the Lombards and
later by the Saracens from Sicily. The fortunes of war resulted in a parti-
tion of the southern portion of the peninsula; Capitanata, Apulia, and the
territory about Otranto remained Byzantine, while Calabria and Sicily fell
to the Saracens. Bari, the residence of the *Kapitanos,* or imperial deputy,
with its port and fortress became what Ravenna had been in Justinian's time.
But this state of affairs was soon brought to an end by a new disturbing
element, which first overthrew the domination of the Saracens, and then,
two or three centuries later, forced the Byzantine garrisons to retire. This
third element consisted of a band of hardy Norman adventurers who had
come from the misty shores of northern France to found a kingdom among
the orange groves of Sicily and southern Italy. Although these northern
conquerors were only a small governing aristocracy and never exceeded one

St. George. Enamel from Yumati.

percent of the population, they were quick to appreciate the capabilities of the Saracen and Byzantine artisans and artists who still remained in the country. The Norman monuments of Sicily, though they were due to the initiative of princes and bishops newly arrived from northern Europe, were largely the work of Mohammedan artisans and Byzantine sculptors and mosaic workers. These placed their own stamp upon the interiors of the buildings, lining them with bright colors of the Orient.

The combination of Saracenic and Byzantine styles gives the buildings of the Norman kings of Sicily a variety that is most delightful. At times the Byzantine element predominates; again the Saracenic builders had their way, and we see structures that are decidedly Mohammedan in character. Not many examples of the civil architecture of this period have come down to us. One of the halls of the old royal palace at Palermo is still preserved, although it is now incorporated in a building of later date. Decorated with flowers and hunting scenes in mosaic, it might well be taken for the residence of an Oriental emir.

Arabian travelers, like Eldrisi, describe the palaces of King Roger built by the sea that the monarch might enjoy the fresh breezes from the Mediterranean. Much of the richness of these structures is due to the fact that the Byzantine artists in the service of the Norman kings still retained a knowledge of working the hardest stone, such as porphyry and red granite. The technique of this art was known to the sculptors of Classical times, but it was lost to western Europe during the Middle Ages and was only rediscovered at the time of the Renaissance.

St. John the Baptist. Byzantine enamel from Yumati in the Caucasus. Metropolitan Museum of Art, New York.

Byzantine book cover in gold and enamel, showing the use of medallions such as those reproduced on the opposite page. Evangelistary of the tenth century. Library of Siena.

In Russia, the last land to be conquered by Byzantine culture, we still find this type of art alive and vigorous. According to the old chronicles, the art and religion of Byzantium were introduced into Russia about the year 1000. After his conversion, the tsar Vladimir moved his capital to Kiev,

Two archangels, Michael and Gabriel. From the "Pala d'Oro," St. Mark's, Venice.

where he built the mother church of Russia, Santa Sophia. This church was covered with domes and decorated with mosaics in the purest Byzantine style. From Kiev, Byzantine art spread all over Russia; indeed, it was well suited to the innate love of the Slav people for pomp and display. The exteriors of the various buildings probably did not change so much. The climate almost required the continuation of the old wooden construction. Walls were ornamented with roses and interlaced patterns, which recall the Byzantine mosaics.

During the time, however, that Russia was under the tutelage of Byzantium, the art of the country was also influenced to some extent by countries lying still further to the east, such as Armenia and Persia, for the Russians came in contact with these nations as well. This accounts for the bulbous

domes with which they sur
mounted their cupolas and
which became so characteristic of
Russian architecture. Of the later churches in Russia, that of the
Russian navy at Kronstadt was
built in almost purely Byzantine style; but the rich Church
of the Resurrection at Petrograd,
erected on the spot where Alex
ander II was assassinated in 1881,
was made more typically Russian in character, with its towers
crowned with bulb-shaped
domes. The national art of Rus
sia expressed everywhere its love
for resplendent domes, and mosaic walls and floors borrowed
from Byzantium.

Monasteries played an important part in the political and
social life of the Empire. It is
interesting, therefore, to know
something of the character of
the communities out of which
surged the fanatical passions
which at times shook Byzantine
society to its foundations. In
Constantinople only the mutilated remains of the Studium
still remain. It was from this
monastery that candidates were
chosen for the position of Metropolitan Patriarch of the Church
of Santa Sophia and other high
posts of the Eastern Church.

St. Demetrios, the Strategos, or soldier-saint, of
the Byzantines. St. Mark's, Venice.

But to know what these reli-
gious communities really were, we must turn to the provincial convents
which did not suffer so severely from the effects of the Moslem invasion.
There are St. Luke of Stiris, Daphne near Athens, and most important of all,
the monastic colony on Mt. Athos. The sacred mountain of Athos forms a
promontory, extending out from the coast of Thrace; and on this green
peninsula is a series of Byzantine monasteries, beginning on the level of
the seacoast and extending step-like up the slopes on either side. The most
ancient of these is St. Laura, founded by St. Athanasius, and was distin-

The "Stroganoff Madonna." Probably reproducing the famous icon of the *Nea*, or New Church, built by Basil I within the Imperial Palace grounds. Cleveland Museum of Art.

guished by the patronage of that warlike emperor, Nice phorus Phocas, who enriched it with many gifts, as did his successor, the terrible John Zimisces. Later on, the monastery of Vatopedi was built on this wild mountainside and was richly endowed in its turn. Next, the Iviron was founded by monks from Georgia and was later occupied by Greek monks. Other monasteries afforded a refuge to their saintly founders who had retired from the turmoil of politics, and continually sent out artists and writers into the world. Crowded together on the habitable space afforded by the sacred mountain, they remind us of the numerous monastic establishments which filled the old capital. Each is generally arranged in a square composed of the various buildings which are grouped about a court, in the center of which stands the principal church by itself.

Christ crowning Romanus II and Eudocia. Ivory plaque. National Library, Paris.

The monks of Mount Athos developed an extensive commerce in icons and religious paintings, in which they reproduced the old Byzantine religious themes; and these were purchased for their weight in gold by pious Russian pilgrims who carried these survivals of the old art to the far-off steppes of their own country, as long as Orthodox believers preserved the rites of the Greek Church.

Even more than architecture, the national art of Byzantium was painting, and this also reappeared when the storm of the Iconoclastic quarrel was over. The themes remained the same; the painters represented the old subjects which the monks wrote down, with the position specified for each personage. The treatises of Byzantine painting specified the precise manner in which the biblical scenes from the Old Testament were to be represented. The same was true of the twelve principal church festivals, the ecclesiastical councils, and the lives of the saints. For this reason the succession of Byzantine artistic types is, perhaps, the most stable of any in the history of art.

Front view of the "Harbaville Triptych." In the center, Christ with his Mother and
John the Baptist; below, the Fathers of the Church; and on the sides, military saints
and confessors. Louvre.

Not only was this ecclesiastical supervision exercised over the composition
of every scene, but even its position among the other mosaic decorations of
the church was determined by precedent. In the apse the most important
figure was of the great Pantocrator, or All Powerful, giving his blessing and
bearing in his hand a book inscribed with the text from the Gospel of
St. John: "I am the light of the world." Sometimes, instead of this figure
we find the Virgin seated upon a throne, but with the Child in her arms
as a prophetic variant of the same theme. On either side of the church
are scenes from the Old and New Testaments set in their chronological
order, to simplify the teaching of their content to the faithful assembled in
the nave.

The end wall was considered the most suitable place for the "Last Judgment," and upon the side walls of the aisles were depicted lines of the saints
of the Greek Church, the face of each being represented in the prescribed
manner. It is especially interesting to note the ascetic and immobile coun-

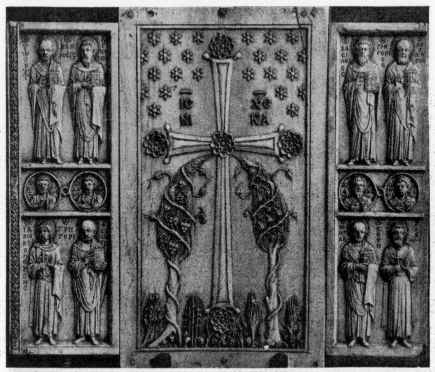

Back view of the "Harbaville Triptych." The cross is glorified by stars and worshiped by Nature represented by bowing cypress trees. On the sides are patriarchs and hermits. Louvre.

tenances of the knightly saints, George, Demetrios, Nestor, and Theodore; all are dressed in the uniform of the imperial militia. The Fathers of the Church and the confessors of the faith are clad in long mantles, like Byzantine priests; while the Apostles still wear the toga of the ancient philosophers. Among the latter, Peter, Paul, Andrew, and John are bearded, while Thomas, Philip, and others are always represented beardless. In the pendentives of the cupola we usually find great six-winged seraphim; and above, in the dome itself, a band composed of a series of prophets and the hand of the Creator issuing from a cloud.

During the artistic revival which followed the persecutions carried on by the Iconoclastic emperors, the spaces formerly destined for biblical scenes were filled with episodes from the lives of the saints and of the Virgin, whose life was most often treated. The touching episode of Joachim and Anna, the Presentation in the Temple, the Visitation, and the Annuncia-tion finally prevailed as the favorite themes of the Byzantine mosaic artists. To the scenes from the life of Mary taken from the New Testament, many from the Apocryphal gospels were added. Indeed, the latter furnished many

"Dormition," or Death of the Virgin, commemorated as one of the twelve great Byzantine feast days. Christ takes the little figure representing the soul of Mary, and the disciples weep as St. Peter touches the feet already cold. Metropolitan Museum of Art, New York.

Byzantine ivory casket, with medallions of saints. Metropolitan Museum of Art, New York.

a new theme to the painter, as the stories found therein lent themselves more readily than the canonical Gospels to be treated like novels. The Byzantines made of the doubts of Simeon and Joseph concerning the behavior of their wives, Anna and Mary, a real psychological novel. The trials to which they were put to prove their purity, and the divine guidance which brought them through successfully, filled many books and, more important still, covered walls in the form of frescoes and mosaics.

We now come to the iconography of the secular painters. The decorations of the apartments of the Imperial Palace with their historical scenes, portraits, and representations of flowering branches have already been described. In addition to these subjects, there were, no doubt, scenes from the Hippodrome, a love for which the Byzantines had inherited from the ancient Romans. There were probably hunting scenes as well, like those of the Persian palaces. None of these large wall paintings have come down to us, so we are obliged to fall back upon the literary descriptions. But the miniatures of the manuscripts also give us some idea of what they were. There are paintings of gardens in a manuscript copy of Nicander's treatise on poisonous plants, and there are examples of historical paintings, with scenes of battle and civil conflicts, in the illuminated history by Skylitzes, in the National Library at Madrid.

Byzantine religious books abound in miniatures, and we can readily understand that the emperors and patricians, who were so prone to theological controversy, should be fond of books illustrated with figures. The Gospels, the Octateuch, and the Psalter each had a fixed repertory consisting of the same subjects and executed

Ivory plaques with two portraits of St. John Chrysostom, one showing him as preacher and the other as patriarch. Walters Art Galleries, Baltimore.

"The Deësis." Mary and John at the foot of the Cross. The wood enters the body of Adam. Roman soldiers gamble over the garments. Eleventh century. Metropolitan Museum of Art, New York.

in the same style. The Gospels, for example, were always headed by a picture of the Evangelist seated at his desk and in the act of writing, as in the early Christian EVANGELISTARY of Rossano.

The most noteworthy religious manuscripts, second only in interest to these books of the Bible, are the calendars recording episodes from the lives of saints—their tribulations, their failures, their victories, their final glory in overcoming sin and temptation, and in gaining heaven with their martyrdom. Saints were represented as of all nations, though chiefly Orientals; they were men and women, old and young; they practiced all professions, even those of mimes, actors, and soldiers; some started as robbers; others who reached a great reputation for modesty started as prostitutes. These compilations of the lives of the saints of the Byzantine Church were called MENOLOGIES. They held the place taken today by adventure stories with a happy ending. They were often illustrated.

Among the many writings of the Fathers of the Eastern Church, certain favorites were also illustrated with miniatures. Among these we might make special mention of the HOMILIES of St. Gregory of Nyssa, and those of a certain monk, James, which were written in honor of the Virgin Mary. St. Gregory indulges in relating sentimental episodes in church history which he thought would appeal to the piety of his audience. He trims the stories with dialogues which he dramatized in preaching the sermons. So much real drama is introduced into these HOMILIES, or sermons, that it is supposed they were finally used as religious plays in the theater. We know that mystery plays were frequently given in Byzantine churches. Luitprand, a German ambassador to Constantinople, attended one of them in Santa Sophia and was struck by the realistic presentation of the "Ascension of Elijah"—the actor sitting in his chariot was carried to the top of the dome by means of mechanical contrivances. The magician's tricks—*deus ex machina*—were frequently used in the Byzantine theater. A Scandinavian saga speaks of mimes that spat fire, jumped to great heights, and did other

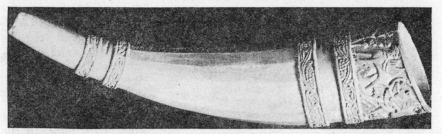

An oliphant, or ivory horn. National Museum, Zurich.

amazing things in the Byzantine circuses. King Sigurd, the Norwegian crusader, and his suite were amazed by the stunts of Byzantine actors, who had inherited most of their accomplishments from the Greek stage. The lives of saints, to be played well on the stage, required miracles; and these could be staged only with complicated machinery.

Another important branch of Byzantine art was the production of icons, or sacred pictures, painted upon boards or metal plates. Most of the icons that have come down to us date from the twelfth century or later. The method of execution was usually the same; the board was covered with a preparation of gypsum and then gilded. Upon this background the pictures were painted in bright colors. The folds of the garments were outlined with a burin which cut in far enough to show the gold background beneath, so the lines of the draperies are of gold.

Some of these Byzantine icons miraculously escaped destruction under the Iconoclastic emperors. In the Patriarch's residence itself, near Santa Sophia, were two hiding places for icons. We know that some images were whitewashed, since we have miniatures in manuscripts which show the iconoclasts with long brushes whitewashing icons and mosaics. Naturally they were restored to light after the storm was over.

Enamel work was really a branch of painting and bore the same relation to painting on boards that mosaic did to fresco painting. Here the figure was outlined by strips of flattened gold wire applied to a metal background. The spaces between were then filled in with enamel paste which was fused in place and polished to an even surface, so that it resembled a fine painting on glass. Enamel was also employed to ornament gold work, hanging crowns, altars, pulpits, reliquaries, crosses, and bookbindings. It was usually applied in a finished state to the objects to be decorated, and it consisted of medallions which were used for any of these pieces of goldsmith's work and was not restricted to particular ones.

We now come to Byzantine sculpture. We can readily understand that a certain prejudice against the reproduction of the human body, which has at all times existed in the Orient, also impeded the development of sculpture in the Byzantine Empire. With the exception of the carved capitals and friezes, this branch of art played but an insignificant part in the decoration of buildings. Our knowledge of Byzantine sculpture is largely derived

The "Wheel of the Elephant," one of the most frequently used patterns in Byzantine textiles. Museum of Berlin.

from the smaller figures carved in ivory, and from the Byzantine plaques, diptychs, and caskets which are now in the museums and cathedral treasuries of western Europe. The coronation of an emperor is a subject frequently found represented on these smaller objects. Jesus is the giver of the crown; he delegates his power to the autocrats here on earth, with no sovereignty reserved for the senate or the people.

The shops of jewellers and metalworkers in Constantinople opened under porticoes in the Mesé (main street). They received many orders from the Occident for bronze gates and doors, for western Europe had by this time lost the secret of casting bronze. The artisans of Byzantium were also skillful at *repoussé* work, and we have a very respectable series of *clypei*, or bronze shields, ornamented with raised figures. Some of these were discov-

ered in the most distant provinces of the Empire. Chalices,
plates, crosses, and covers of
Evangelistaries, which were
either made in Byzantium or
were copies of Byzantine work,
are found in various parts of
western Europe.

Another art in which the
Byzantines excelled was the
weaving of textiles, which were
most highly esteemed throughout Europe during the Middle
Ages. The designs, sometimes
copied from Sassanian fabrics,
are composed of rich combinations of lions, birds, and hunts-
men, interspersed with flowers
and branches. The figures are
usually enclosed within large
circles and the background is
of cloth of gold and silver. The
patterns in the circles were
called by the Latins *rotae* or
wheels; within them were animal forms, and each pattern
gave a name to a textile, such
as the ram, the white lion, the
eagle, the peacock, or the vine.

Byzantium first learned the
art of making handsome pat-
terned textiles from Egypt. The
earliest Byzantine fabrics were
ornamented with designs borrowed from the textiles of the
Copts. Soon, however, the artisans of Constantinople turned
to the Persians who had a

Three of the most popular designs in Byzantine
textiles: the elephant, the sigmurd and the griffin.
Museum at Cooper Union, New York.

monopoly of the trade in silk which they brought from Ceylon to the ports
of the Persian Gulf. From here it was transported by caravan to Syria and
Asia Minor. But this dependence upon Persia for materials soon became
irksome, and finally the emperors managed to procure the larvae of silk-
worms and introduced the manufacture of silk into their own territory.

Nevertheless, Byzantine fabrics always retained certain themes, such as hunting scenes and the strangling of lions and other wild animals, which remind us of the Persian designs. We also find designs of charioteers, chorus girls of the Hippodrome, hunting scenes, and representations of the Nativity and the Annunciation. The imperial manufacture for textiles was in the old Roman Baths building called the Zeuxippus, beside the Hippodrome. The exportation of the best textiles of the Byzantine looms, called *Koloumena,* was strictly forbidden. Luitprand, the German ambassador to Constantinople in the tenth century, tells us how the imperial customs officials confiscated some fabrics which he had packed in his baggage when he left. The textiles he was permitted to export were marked, and lead seals were affixed.

Miniature from the HOMILIES of the monk James, showing a scene from a mystery play in which the emperor and empress acted as Jesus and Mary. Vatican Library.

Façade of the Gate to the Palace of Theodoric the Great at Ravenna.

ART OF THE TEUTONIC PEOPLES
(600—800 A.D.)

OUR KNOWLEDGE of the barbarian peoples of Europe, until the last century, was derived solely from literary sources, such as references in the works of the Fathers of the Church, the medieval chronicles, and even the Roman histories. Tacitus in his monograph entitled *Germania* has given us a most valuable account of the character and psychology of these nomad peoples, whom the Roman legions were still able to keep from crossing the Rhine and from continuing their progress westward across the provinces of the Empire. With a sober eloquence seldom equaled by our modern anthropologists, this writer describes to us the religion, family relations, epic songs, arms, and costumes

The Tomb of Theodoric the Great at Ravenna.

of the barbarian tribes. The Classical representations of these people show them wearing jewelry in great profusion; and their own legends dwell on the handsome armor and necklaces of their ancient leaders. The heroes of the "Nibelungenlied" fight with one another for the possession of Odin's ring, and a father and his son recognize each other in a battle by their bracelets. Before the gates of Rome Totila incited his warriors with the offer of paniers of jewels that should be the reward of those who dis-

Detail of the cornice of the Tomb of Theodoric at Ravenna.

tinguished themselves in the assault upon the Eternal City. In the epic, *Waltharius,* the hero fights against several enemies to defend the jewels he stole, with the assistance of his betrothed, from the Huns. Indeed, Tacitus himself tells us that a barbarian chieftain was buried with his arms, jewels, and favorite horse, and that the site of the tomb was then marked by a simple mound of earth. Sooner or later some of these tombs were bound to be discovered in the country occupied by the barbarians, and their interesting relics brought to light.

The architectural monuments of the barbarians are few in number and of little importance. Tacitus is very positive on this point in his description of their dwellings in Germany. He remarks, "that there is in the German towns neither contiguity nor contact with one another of the houses which make up their settlements. Each lives apart wherever a spring, a meadow, or the forest attracts him; there he sets his dwelling, which is made of clay, either to avoid fire or because of his little knowledge of architecture. Instead of mortar and bricks, of which they are ignorant, they employ a rude material with no pretension to beauty, although some houses are coated with a sort of varnish which is so fine that it resembles paint." He goes on to explain that some of these people lived in caves hewn in the rock. These were doubtless the dwellings of the chiefs, supported by rock pillars and more spacious than the mean huts of clay and straw scattered in the forests.

The Teutonic peoples retained their fondness for separate dwellings even after they had settled permanently in western Europe. The old Roman cities were abandoned to their fate; they were not destroyed by the barbarians, but their existence was precarious because of the disturbance of trade. The barbarian chieftains settled with their families and retainers in fertile valleys or on hilltops easily defended. They surrounded their homes with palisades,

Interior of the Visigothic basilica built by King Receswinth at Baños. Palencia, Spain.

and on these fortified sites grew up the castles of the Middle Ages. There were royal palaces in Paris, Toledo, Metz, Monza, and Milan; and we have information about the arrangement of some of these buildings. The one at Metz, for example, had terraces on the River Moselle, from which the king could watch the fishermen catch the salmon for his table. The one at Paris had an upper-story balcony covered with vines, where important decisions were often made. The royal fortress, or *Arx,* at Toledo had a chapel, probably on the main floor, while the apartments were on the next level. At Ravenna may still be seen the façade of the Palace of Theodoric the Great. Nobody would dare to plan a reconstruction from that wall alone, but there is evidence from a mosaic representing the Ravenna palace that it was made up of separate halls rather than of a single building. The peculiar character of the Teutonic residences is due to the system of roofing each room independently. The present Palace of the Bishop of Iceland still consists of a series of adjacent rooms, each with its own roof.

The preferred residences of the Merovingian monarchs were not these city mansions, but royal farms in the country. At Quierzy near Tours, Chelles near Paris, Nogent in the North, and Gerticos in the heart of Castile were the favorite farms of the Frankish and Visigothic kings.

The *History of the Franks* by Gregory of Tours describes episodes that occurred in the royal villas, but it does not tell the plan of the buildings. However, we learn from the text that they were more like farms than suburban palaces, and were generally located in places where there was good hunting. In the center there must have been a monumental reception hall, like the one described in *Beowulf.* The miniatures in the books of Charlemagne's time give us some idea of the appearance of these villas. For example, in illustrations of the Psalms we see the palace of King David pictured just like the palace of a Teutonic king, with scattered buildings,

Merovingian Baptistery of St. John at Poitiers. Sixth century.

some having two stories and many porticoes leading from one to another.

The barbarian monarchs also built churches in some of the cities of the royal domain. While some of the towns remained semi-independent and preserved their municipal rights, others were governed by dukes sent by the king and were vassals of the crown; and in the latter the kings built monasteries and churches. We have a vague notion of how the first churches of King Clovis in Paris looked: in plan they were basilicas, their walls were decorated with mosaics, and their ceilings were gilt. Even larger than these churches was the one built over the Sepulcher of St. Martin of Tours, the holiest place in France. It was also a basilica in plan, with columns, and with a great porticoed atrium in front, which the Frankish kings could enter on horseback. We have descriptions also of a church at Toulouse, called *La Daurade,* or "The Gilded One," probably because of its mosaics of bright colored glass against a gold background.

We know that the Frankish churches on the Rhine were built of wood, which material, having the advantage of lightness, permitted the erection of three high towers, one at either side of the entrance and one over the crossing. This style was admired by the Franks of the more Romanized south, who were impressed with the carvings of these wooden churches. It was, indeed, the last step in the evolution of the wooden buildings of the Germans described by Tacitus. We find two conflicting elements in the

Reliefs by Longobardian artists. On railings in the Church of Santa Maria in Transtevere.

architecture of the Frankish kings—a conflict that is seen most clearly in the literature of the time, where the old Roman traditions and the Teutonic folkways clashed. It was a conflict that the barbarians never solved. We sense it in the works of Venantius Fortunatus, and other Frankish writers, Romanized in form but Teutonic at heart. We recall that Ataulp, one of the earliest Visigothic kings, tried to Romanize his people with no success; and a century later the great Theodoric at Ravenna tried the same thing with the same result.

There are two reasons why the few barbarian buildings that are still standing look somewhat Romanized: first, they are built in stone; and second, they are churches, and the ecclesiastics were more Romanized than the people as a whole. It is probable that some of the barbarian nations remained Arians only to avoid the supervision of the clergy. They wanted to keep their pagan superstitions, and at the same time to go to church. The Franks, a rougher people than the Visigoths and the Longobards, had not reached an advanced state even of Teutonic culture before they accepted Christianity. Probably the aristocratic cult of Odin was not an impediment for them, as it was for the Goths and the Longobards. Therefore the

Wellhead of the Longobardian period in Italy. Correr Museum, Venice.

Franks were Catholics from the very beginning after their conversion.

It is very significant also that the Teutonic warriors kept Germanic names even when they were established in the lands of the Roman Empire and were nominally Christians. Some of their names may have been traditional in their families, but others like Ataulp and Theodulf are related to the wolf of Odin.

The most important monument preserved from these Teutonic races in western Europe is the Tomb of Theodoric the Great at Ravenna. It is a decagonal building on the first floor, and becomes round on the second. The roof is a monolithic stone, a gigantic block of marble cut in the form of a dome, which weighs three hundred tons. On this block are carved ten hooks, which probably served to raise the stone into place. It has been said that this dome structure is an imitation of the mausoleums of the emperors in Rome—a vivid and tangible proof of the incapacity of the barbarian races to adjust themselves to the Roman culture.

Top of a ciborium in Longobardian style. Dated 816 A.D.

Theodoric visited Rome and admired its great buildings. In one of his edicts he provided for the preservation of the ancient buildings of the city. He used to say that he wanted the Teutons to live like the Romans, without losing their youthful energy; but the fact is that, in spite of all these efforts to Romanize himself and his followers, he and they remained pagan. His ministers, Boethius and Cassidorus, could not tame his indomitable nature. Theodoric was undoubtedly the greatest leader of the Teutonic races before Charlemagne, and an understanding of his character serves to explain the peculiar style of his mausoleum. The structure may have been intended to be Roman, but the result was an entirely Nordic building. In its present state it is denuded of ornaments; even the reliefs that originally decorated the façade are gone; and there remains only the frieze around the top, which is an entirely Teutonic decoration. The design is exactly the same as that found on some of the Teutonic fibulae, which show human forms schematically treated. Quite probably the round motifs represent heads of warriors, and the tongs are the limbs of those warriors who follow Odin in his cavalcade. It is touching to see that Theodoric wanted to perpetuate in his mausoleum the memory of the warriors who followed him in his great campaigns. The only allusion to Christianity is found in the small crosses, which are quite compatible with the Odin cult.

We have made mention of other buildings raised by Theodoric in Verona and Pavia, but there is no trace of them today. In fact, the Tomb of Theodoric at Ravenna is the only civic building of the barbarian races that remains in Italy, France, or Spain. At Toledo there stand parts of the walls from the time of the Goths, but these have no artistic interest.

All over Europe, nevertheless, are scattered fragments of barbaric decorations, mostly sculptures in low relief. They are quite uniform in style throughout France, Spain, Italy, and northern Africa, where the Vandals founded a long-lived kingdom. The patterns are always geometric, though some show remote connections with natural forms, so denaturalized, however, as to have become abstract. One wonders whether the Teutons attempted to reproduce floral forms without success, or if they deliberately reduced them to symbols. It becomes difficult in many cases to ascertain whether the forms have any meaning, or whether they are simply used to fill space. We are charmed by them because we see a naïve approach to representation made not by a single individual but by a whole race. It is surprising that Rome should be the place where barbaric reliefs exist in the largest number. We might apply the saying of Theodoric here, "that when the Roman became vile, he tried to imitate the Teuton."

Teutonic and Celtic arts are held by modern critics to be at the very roots of artistic expression in Europe. But the reader should be careful to differentiate between the Teutonic and Celtic styles. The Teutons and Celts are, racially and spiritually, different peoples, and their arts express their differences. For one thing, the Teutonic reliefs are not so strictly geometrical as the Celtic. Both have in common the non-representative q u a l i t y; but quite often the Celtic art is purely linear, without even a remote allusion to ornament or plant forms, while the Teutonic art retains some vestiges of natural objects.

Originally the languages of the two peoples were quite different, and they developed distinct and separate religions. The Celts originated in southern Germany in the region of the Black Forest, and from there expanded spasmodically into Galatia in Asia Minor, Galitzia on the Danube, Gallaecia in

Pulpit in the Church of San Giovanni, Val d'Arno, Tuscany.

Frieze of the Virgins at Cividale, capital of the Longobardian duchy of Friuli.
Eighth century.

Spain, Gallia in France and Italy, Wales, Ireland, and Scotland. The
Celtic migrations took place somewhere between 9000 and 500 B.C., several
hundred years before the Teutons started to move.

The Teutons originated in the Baltic lands. The location of the Pan-
Teutonic sanctuary at modern Upsala in Sweden, far from the Celtic tribes,
gives evidence of the separation of the Teutonic and Celtic cultures. But
both Teutons and Celts spread and wandered before they finally settled
in western Europe outside the pale of the Roman Empire. Love of adventure,
as well as necessity, pushed them from one place to another for centuries.
When, however, the vanguard of Mongolian hordes, the Alans, Avars, and
Huns, arrived in central Europe, Teutons and Celts were compelled to take
refuge within the borders of the Roman Empire. It is a great mistake to
think that they overran the borders in the fourth century A.D. When the
Teutons entered the lands of the Empire, in most cases they sought the
protection of the Romans and were granted concessions of lands in exchange
for military service. They were the crack militia and in times of peace
remained as *federati,* or confederates, of the Empire. If they overran a
province or destroyed towns it was because the corrupted Roman officials
failed to keep the promises made to them.

Alamannic helmet of the Migrations
period. Museum, Stuttgart.

But let us return to art. Both
Celtic and Teutonic cultures suffered
the influx of Classic civilization, and
through common experience their
arts resemble each other. They remained quite different in spite of
this. In no place did Celtic and
Teutonic culture mix. An Irishman
remains quite different from an
Englishman to this day. In the next
chapter we shall take up the subject of the Celtic art of the Middle
Ages, but let us finish here with
a short survey of the evolution of
the Teutonic art through the period

Fibula of Wittislingen. Alamannic jewel of
the seventh century. Museum, Munich.

of the Migrations. At the very beginning of the Christian Era the Teutonic
peoples around the Baltic showed a marked preference for what we call the
"animalistic style." In this style animals are the basic motif, but it is difficult
to discover the form upon which the fantastic design is based. These animal
motifs never entirely disappear from Teutonic decoration, because when
the Teutons became superficially Christianized, such animals served as representations of beasts associated with the cult of Odin. The Teuton nobles

Panel from an Anglo-Saxon casket. Episodes from the "Siegfried Saga", with Runic inscriptions. Left, Odin asks Grani (Siegfried's steed) about the crime; center, the steed is neighing over Siegfried's tomb; right, Hagen and Gunnar swear before Brunhild. Museum, Florence.

wanted to keep up their religious fraternities, and had to keep secret and involved the symbols of their superstitions. For this purpose they employed a great many brooches and buckles in which we can discern geometric lines, and the nebulous forms of the horse, the wolf, or the raven. The horse was important because Odin rode an eight-legged horse called Sleipner. The wolf was the shape that Odin's warriors took when they fled to Valhalla; and the ravens flew before and behind Odin. The one flying ahead of the god brought him information about the future, and the one flying behind

Nordic gravestone, with idealized horses and ravens of Odin. Museum, Stockholm.

recorded the past, symbolizing Premonition and Memory, since Odin, the god of knowledge, knew everything. Salvation for the Teutons was not by faith and redemption, but by knowledge and mighty work.

Odin was the last of the pan-Teutonic gods. At the beginning he was adopted as a son by Frey, and as the brother of Thor, he remained at Uppsala. But he gradually supplanted Frey as the ruler of Valhalla, and the Teutons of different nations agreed in their worship of him. The cult of Odin was secret and was reserved for the grandees, so his worship could be carried on without offending the clergy or the common folk. The fraternities of warriors addicted to Odin met only four times a year for

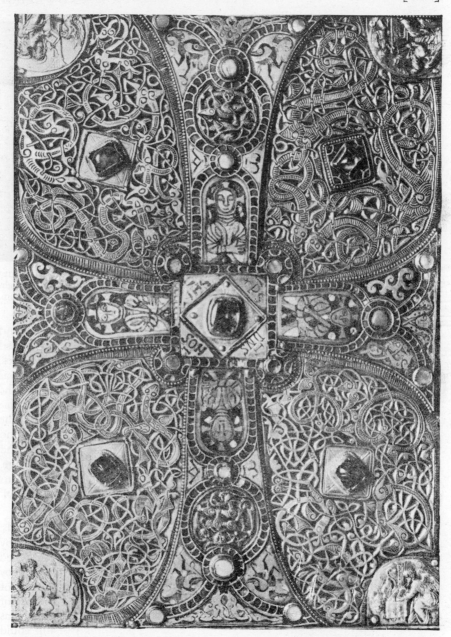

Back cover from the LINDAU EVANGELISTARY. Viking art of the eighth century. The four corner-reliefs showing the Evangelists are modern. Morgan Library, New York.

Visigothic ravens in gold and precious stones, representing Premonition and Memory, the birds that accompanied Odin. From a sixth-century necropolis in Spain.

The Plague. With Odin and Sleipnir. Metropolitan Museum of Art, New York.

a week's feast of horse meat. In Scandinavia, the worship of Odin continued until the tenth century, and in Saxony and Switzerland until the time of Charlemagne. It has been suspected that the last Visigothic kings of Spain were hailed or demoted by those who resented conversion from the Arian faith, because previously they had been able to enjoy the aristocratic cult of Odin. Probably the betrayal of the country, that is, opening it to the Saracens, was the foolish move of discontented Teutons.

The traditional zoomorphic style

Golden crowns placed as offerings in front of altars by Visigothic kings and lords of Toledo. Found at Guarrazar, Spain. Cluny Museum, Paris.

of the Teutonic decoration was disturbed by two influences; one was that of Roman art which the Teutons admired very much at the military posts on the border of the Empire. We believe, however, that this Roman influence has been overemphasized by scholars. Today Nordic students go so far as to deny any originality to their Teutonic ancestors. They see only in their

buildings and ornaments a degeneration of Roman forms. A Scandinavian
royal hall, like the one described in *Beowulf* is, for the German scholars, only
a Roman basilica; the involved patterns of the fibulae of the first Teutons
are simply degenerate Roman meanders and frets. There is no room here to
discuss this obsession of the professors. The objects speak for themselves.

The second and more permanent influence, however, is the one of Oriental art. The Germanic people received jewels through the fluvial routes
from central Asia and Persia. These were more fascinating for them than
the plain and logical Roman forms. The jewels were made with stones of
bright colors set in gold, and garnets cut in very thin flakes and set in paste.
These little mosaics of red stone and yellow gold were liked so well by the
barbarians that they adopted the style as a national technique, discarding
the old patterns of chiseled zoomorphic forms in solid metals, gilded bronze,
or gold.

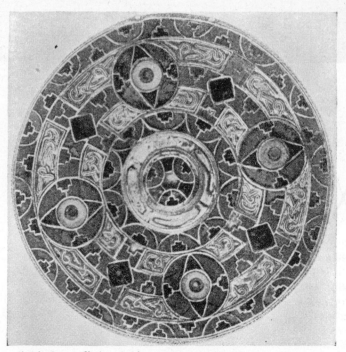

Anglo-Saxon fibula. Gold, set with garnets. Museum, Liverpool.

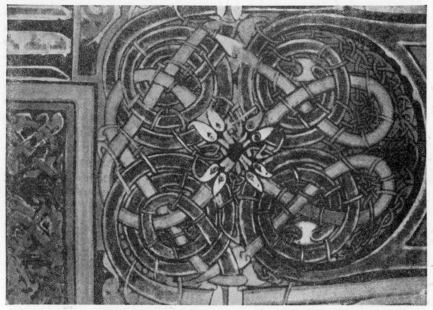

Detail of a miniature from the BOOK OF KELLS.
Trinity College Library, Dublin.

CHRISTIAN CELTIC ART

(600—1000 A.D.)

WE SAID in the previous chapter that the Celts spread from southern Germany north to Ireland, south to the borders of Etruria, east to Asia Minor, and west to the Atlantic Ocean. In all those regions in prehistoric times the Celtic race showed a taste for geometric patterns. These Celtic decorations are not regular combinations of straight lines, but are made up entirely of curves, circles, and spirals in trumpet form. The intersecting and interlocking curves cover a flat background with an amazing number of variations of this shape. The prehistoric Celtic style is called *La Tene,* because the first and also the largest number of Celtic objects decorated in this way were found at the modern village of La Tène on Lake Neuchatel.

Early in the fifth century A.D. we find Celtic Ireland still a mysterious realm inhabited by descendants of the prehistoric tribes and clans. Some of their warriors, like Fingal, we are told, visited the frigid volcanic islands in the Far North or crossed the channel to carry aid to the Celtic tribes of Scotland who were holding the Angles in check.

The small and geographically isolated Irish nation was destined to play

A Celtic Cross.

an important part in the history of European culture. She not only preserved the ancient traditions of an art native to Europe, the Neolithic art of La Tène, but she also later became a refuge for the culture of the early Latin Church, which was scorned by the first Germanic invaders. In the sixth and seventh centuries her monks visited France and Rome and brought back valuable manuscripts to the only spot in Europe where they could be studied undisturbed.

The conversion of Ireland to Christianity by St. Patrick is a beautiful legend. Knowing the strength of the people's faith in the old Druidic religion, this saint dressed in white like the Druids, and rode in a carriage drawn by white stags. A bell which the Pope had sent him was used to announce the meetings for prayer; and its sound, to which the people were unaccustomed, exerted an almost hypnotic influence on the susceptible people. In vain did the Druids vie with the saint in performing miracles; finally the Irish king and the people gave up the old religion and accepted Christianity. The development of the monastic life in Ireland was extraordinary from this time on. In the fertile valleys of the island are still to be found the ruins of the many monasteries that grew up at that time. They are surrounded by stone crosses, bell towers, and the remains of the cells of the monks.

In the solitude of their northwestern island the monks cultivated Greek and Latin scholarship and expounded the books of the Fathers and of Classical writers. During those years when few besides themselves were interested in such matters, at a time when it was rare to find at the courts of the Franks anyone who could read or write, The Venerable Bede, an Anglo-Saxon, was compiling the knowledge of the ancient world, in grammar,

The "Cross of Cong."　Ard Mhúsaeum nah-Éirian, Dublin.

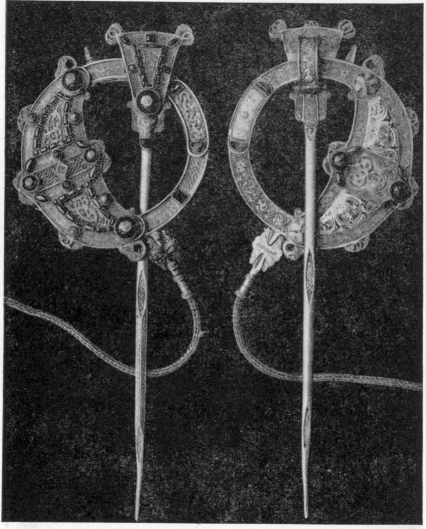

The "Tara Fibula," in gold and enamel. Front and back. National Museum, Dublin.

music, and rhetoric. It is not to be wondered that these learned Irish monks were summoned to the courts of the Franks to aid in the cultural development of western Europe, where for two centuries invasions of Germanic tribes and domestic warfare had been taking place. These monks took with them their books, the products of their romantic tastes and original artistic style, and their knowledge of letters and philosophy, as a contribution to European culture. Celtic genius never lost a certain freshness and spon-

The Reliquary of St. Patrick's Bell. National Museum, Dublin.

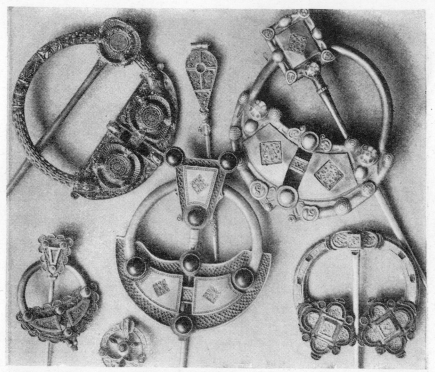

A group of Irish Celtic fibulae. National Museum, Dublin.

taneity, which was completely opposite to the sober classical spirit of Rome.

The study of the Irish art is important because of the influence it exerted on the Carolingian Renaissance, which in its turn may be said to be the starting point for that great French civilization so powerful in Europe during medieval times. Irish art, as we have said, is a continuation and development of that prehistoric Neolithic culture native to Europe and known as that of La Tène. Caesar describes the customs of the Celts, with the mysterious rites of the Druids conducted in sacred groves of oak trees by the light of the moon. He also describes their monuments, which consisted of great stones set up on end and of stones arranged in circles.

This culture lasted in Ireland until the conversion of her people to Christianity. With all the candor and faith of their ingenuous nature they accepted the new doctrines, but still they could not entirely give up their old, deeply rooted ideas. As they had placed their dolmens (or tombs) in the center of cromlechs (or stone circles) in prehistoric times, now they set their monasteries within a circular enclosure constructed of great stones. In front of the door they erected a cylindrical tower which the old chronicles call *cloicethec,* or house of the bells. More than a hundred of these cylindri-

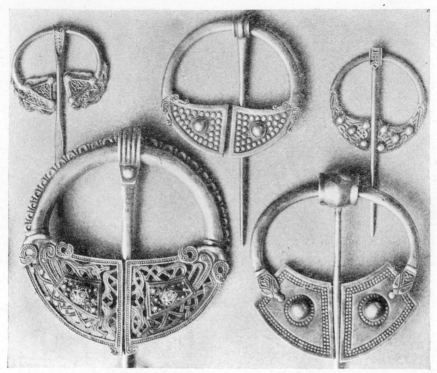

Irish Celtic fibulae. National Museum, Dublin.

cal towers are still standing. They are slightly conical in form, with small windows which suggest that they were used not only as belfries, but as places of retreat for the monks as well. They may also have served as refuges for fugitives who sought the protection of the monastery. Nearby we usually find upright crosses of stone, set upon large bases ornamented with interlaced designs and other types of carving. These Irish crosses are evidently very ancient. We are told in the history of the mission of St. Patrick that the saint was accustomed to visit a large number of them each day. They appear to have been set both within and without the circular enclosures of the monasteries, and each one to have been dedicated to a different saint. Their great number suggests that they were a continuation in Christian form of the old stone-worship, which seems to have been slow to disappear.

Most important to the history of art is the fact that they are almost completely covered with reliefs which show a further development of the interlaced designs of La Tène. Some of these reliefs represent biblical scenes, but for the most part they consist of geometrical patterns. The form of the cross is usually of great beauty, with its tall slender support and small central cross enclosed within a circle.

The Chalice of Ardagh. Ard Mhúsaeum nah-Éirean, Dublin.

Due to a quarrel for the possession of a book, St. Columba with a number of other Irish monks withdrew from the main group and went to establish colonies in Great Britain. Thus were founded the first monasteries on the islands of Iona and Lindisfarne. Monks from Lindisfarne went to the mainland, to Melrose, to York, and to Yarrow. In this way the Celtic church, which had formerly been only Irish, put its foot on the soil of Great Britain and also sent out other groups to found colonies on the continent. Luxeuil in France, St. Gall in Switzerland, Fulda on the Rhine, and Bobbio in Italy became centers of Irish culture which were excessively proud of their origin and somewhat antagonistic to the Roman Catholic faith. It looked for a while as if the Celtic monks would form an independent organization, for they refused to bow to Roman authority and asserted that Christ was on their side. A miniature on a Celtic manuscript made at Bobbio represents Jesus as freckled and beardless like an Irishman of fair complexion.

Since little architecture remains in Ireland with the exception of towers and crosses, the work of goldsmiths and miniatures must furnish our chief sources for the study of Celtic art. Some of the Irish fibulae, or brooches, appear to be very ancient. Their very shape, a circular ring crossed by a pin, is characteristic of La Tène work. Their scroll work decorations are also typical of that period of art. The earliest of these fibulae are usually of bronze, ornamented with enamels and incrustations of coral. The circular ring later was widened on one side, forming a surface on which were inscribed extremely complicated decorative patterns.

The most beautiful of the fibulae in existence is the so-called Tara Brooch discovered in 1850 and now in the Museum of the Royal Irish Academy at Dublin. It is of bronze and embellished with gold plates which are ornamented with interlaced designs, enamels, and pieces of coral. The style of its decoration corresponds to that of miniatures in manuscripts of the seventh century.

The art of the goldsmiths of Ireland, however, was not confined to personal jewels. Ritual objects seem to have been in great demand. The richness of the Tara Brooch is rivaled by the famous chalice discovered in Ardagh in 1868 and now in the Dublin Museum. The form of the vessel, the letters of its inscription, and the two handles, so characteristic of early church plate, place it in the ninth century. The variety of its interlacing knotwork designs is marvelous, and the grace and elegance displayed in the outlines of bands and medallions make it one of the most exquisite pieces of metalwork in existence.

Next in importance to these two pieces is the silver-gilt case which now serves as a reliquary for the famous St. Patrick's bell. Upon its face are four panels ornamented with interlaced designs and combined with medallions, while the back is decorated with Greek crosses. Around it runs an inscription requesting prayers for King Donnal, who ordered it made; for the bishop who succeeded St. Patrick in the diocese of Armagh; for the keeper of the bell; and for Gudulig, his son, who executed the work. The most interesting feature of this piece is the handle. Here among the interlaced designs typical of La Tène art we find dragon heads in Scandinavian style.

Another specimen of Celtic work is the cross from the Abbey of Cong in the Dublin

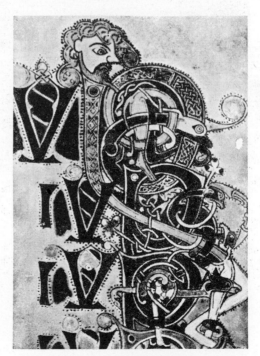

Detail of a miniature from the BOOK OF KELLS. Trinity College Library, Dublin.

Christ between two Romans. Notice the Irish face of Christ. Miniature from the BOOK OF KELLS. Trinity College Library, Dublin.

St. Matthew. Detail of full-page miniature from the BOOK OF KELLS. Trinity College Library, Dublin.

Museum. It was used as a reliquary for a fragment of the True Cross sent by the Pope to the abbey about the year 1123.

Representations of human figures are comparatively rare in Celtic art, and when they occur they show less skill than the decorative patterns. This fact leads us to conclude that the artisans of Ireland felt a certain disdain for natural forms. When they used them they deliberately simplified and conventionalized them, as calligraphic ornaments.

The portable ritual objects of metal were the principal vehicles for the spread of Celtic art forms on the continent; but the manuscripts also played an important part in making known the interlaced design of Celtic art.

The monks of Ireland must have begun very early to develop the art of calligraphy. The oldest Celtic codex with miniatures in existence is believed to be the BOOK OF DURROW at Trinity College; it dates from the seventh century and came from the Monastery of St. Columba. It is strongly reminiscent of the style of La Tène, in the interlaced designs which adorn the capitals and the margins of the pages.

The BOOK OF LINDISFARNE is another famous example of Irish religious art. This manuscript is known to have been copied by Eadfrith, Archbishop of Lindisfarne, between the years 698 and 721 in that famous Irish monastery in England. The BOOK OF KELLS, perhaps the best known of all Celtic manuscripts, is, however, the best executed of the manuscripts of its period. The capital letters are richly illuminated with typical Celtic designs and its miniatures often fill entire pages.

The first Celtic illuminations display curled and twisted shapes which archaeologists call "the trumpet spiral ornament," and which are characteristic of the art of La Tène. This type of ornament became more regular later, taking the form of symmetrical interlaced design. It was the contact with the Romanized European world which gave Celtic art this feeling for symmetry. When the Irish monks went to Italy they found there the Byzantine culture, which had acquired from Roman art a predilection for geometrical forms in mosaics and sculpture. These Byzantine patterns were more comprehensible to them than were those of Classical Roman art. Under their influence the Celtic art now began to lose its characteristic curved and twisted forms and adopted patterns resembling the interwoven splints of a basket.

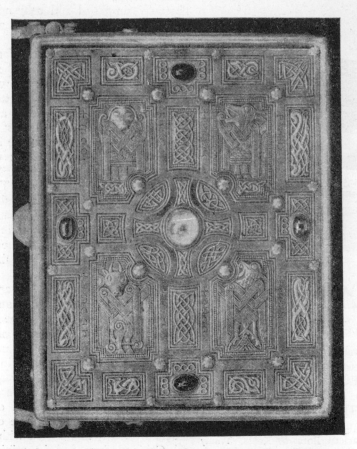

From the Shrine of St. Molaise at Ardagh. National Museum, Dublin.

Entrance to the Carolingian Abbey of Reichenau, Germany.

CAROLINGIAN ART

(800-1000 A.D.)

ALL THAT WESTERN EUROPE retained of its Classical tradition, all that remained of the art elements which the Teutonic peoples brought from their homes on the steppes, and all the artistic principles of the Celts which the Irish Church had preserved were united at the Court of Charlemagne, the great promoter of the culture of the Middle Ages. His reign we may consider as the turning point of European civilization, which began to develop anew. It is interesting to note the various forces which contributed to this development.

The Emperor and most of his powerful feudal lords were of Germanic origin. They were barbarians, it is true; but, like Theodoric before him, Charlemagne, the King of the Franks, strove to rid himself of Germanic traits and to assimilate the Classical culture which he recognized as superior. Nevertheless, he always remained a Teuton at heart.

Political conditions of the time, and his enlistment in the cause of the Pope to defend the Church against barbarian peoples, gave this young

Charlemagne's Palace-Church of Aix-la-Chapelle, consecrated by Pope Leo III in 804.
Restoration by the author in *Summa Artis,* volume eight.

Frankish monarch the chance to become the most prominent figure in western Europe. The best representatives of the Church of Rome were attracted to his court. They came because Italy was exhausted. Rome was but the phantom of its former greatness; and the other provinces of the West were powerless to bear the torch which was to illuminate the world. Northern Africa and Spain had fallen into the hands of the Saracens, and only the few Spanish bishops of the Visigothic Church remained, who, like Theodulf, had fled to Charlemagne for protection. Since little was to be expected from Germany, the Emperor summoned to his court the missionaries from Ireland, who alone had preserved a love for science and retained a sufficient knowledge of sacred literature, to be the schoolmasters of the second Roman Empire. The most famous of Charlemagne's ministers and the man who really inspired the educational reformation and much of the artistic initiative of this period was a monk named Alcuin of York. His correspondence with the Emperor still bears testimony to the great efforts made by these two men to restore civilization in the West.

Theodulf was a Visigoth, Alcuin a Celt, and Einhard and Angilbert, two other councilors of the Emperor, were Germans. We see the court of Charlemagne, like that of the Roman Empire, transformed into an international organization. The art of the period possessed the same mixed character. It was the combined product of a number of very different schools.

The most important architectural achievement of Charlemagne, a building that still remains almost intact, is the Chapel of the Imperial Palace at Aix-la-Chapelle, a small town near Cologne, which he chose for his capital. The rest of the buildings of Charlemagne's time at Aix-la-Chapelle are gone, but the Banqueting Hall, *Aula Regia,* is described in a poem by Theodulf. It was approached through four antechambers and had a *solarium,* or open portico, at each end. It was of great size, large enough to hold all the members of the court; the light came in through great windows, *fenestrae lucidissimae.* Theodulf describes a meal there: the Emperor seats himself at the supper table, and his daughters enter bringing flowers, fruits, and wine. As the girls are talking, singing, and dancing, the Emperor's sister enters. She wants to consult him about a question of theology, which Charlemagne elucidates "as God makes him to understand." After he has returned to York, Alcuin recalls in a letter to Charlemagne how they used to discuss theological questions, while bathing in the hot springs of Aix, in *fervente naturalis atque balneo.*

The biographers of Charlemagne in speaking of the buildings of the time never fail to mention Einhard as the mastermind that guided their construction. He succeeded Alcuin as head teacher of the School of the Palace and included among his many accomplishments architecture and jewelry making. There is no doubt that he tried to learn the Roman methods of architecture from the *Treatise on Architecture* by Vitruvius. He quotes from this text in his letters, adding that in order to popularize the teachings of Vitruvius he ordered little models of columns to be made of ivory and sent to the supervisors of the imperial works.

These efforts produced some results. There was a great advance in art and in all culture during Charlemagne's time. The Teutonic reliefs, as well as the Celtic frets, became more sober and were reduced to mere trellises of parallel l i n e s. This repudiation of the Celtic and Teutonic styles was accompanied by an outspoken taste for Classical forms. Was it affectation? Or was it sincere, but lacking in real understanding? This l a t t e r hypothesis seems the more likely. Charlemagne and his friends were romantics and

The Royal Grange of Charlemagne at Ingelheim.
Restoration by Rauch.

The Abbey of Centula at St. Riquier. Built by Angilbert, son-in-law of Charlemagne. As drawn by Mabillon.

took as their model the Augustan Age, because of its remoteness in the past. Because the Renaissance of Roman life and culture, which Charlemagne and his friends brought about at Aix-la-Chapelle, was artificially superimposed and contrary to the trend of the time, it was short-lived. Charlemagne called himself Augustus, Alcuin was renamed Horatius, Theodulf was called Pindar, and even the cook was given the name of Menalcas, from an *Eclogue* by the Latin poet Vergil. . . . But the names did not change their bearers into Romans.

The revival of Classical culture in the time of Charlemagne is called the Carolingian Renaissance. Better than in architecture its results can be appreciated in ivories and in manuscripts, of which we shall speak later on. In architecture the little model columns of ivory which Einhard employed to propagate the Classical orders were not very successful. The only building that is a frank imitation of Roman or Byzantine construction is the Church of the Palace at Aix-la-Chapelle. And yet the plan and general form of this building were evidently copied from San Vitale at Ravenna; and the latter, we know, was a faint echo of the Gilded Church built by Constantine at Antioch.

The church is octagonal with a central cupola; but, unlike that of San Vitale which was made lighter by its pottery construction, it was entirely of stone and therefore could not be so high. The octagonal ambulatory, which surrounds the space beneath the dome, resists the lateral pressure of the central mass, and for this purpose is constructed of massive vaults. At the corners of the octagon stand great stone piers. Between these are arches, those of the upper stories being divided into smaller ones which rest upon columns. The dome was covered with frescoes representing the Lord seated on a throne, with the Twenty-four Elders as described in the Book of Revelation. This is a new theme, and one certainly not imported from the East since the Apocalypse was a forbidden book for the Eastern Church. We emphasize this especially since the subject of the Lord surrounded by the twenty-four Elders was to become so popular in the West all through Romanesque times. During the long periods which the Emperor spent at Aix he worshiped daily in this church. Here he passed the declining years

St. Matthew. Miniature from a manuscrip. of the School of the Palace at Aix-la-Chapelle.
Trèves Library.

of his life, and here he was buried. The church was connected with the other rooms of the palace by porticoes, in which were displayed the artistic spoils of the conquered provinces. Among them was a bronze eagle with outstretched wings and wearing a crown, and an equestrian statue of Theodoric which he had brought from Ravenna.

Several churches, such as those of Werden, Fulda, and Goldbach, repeat on a small scale and with less beauty the plan of the church at Aix-la-Chapelle. But that palace-church and its poor copies had no consequences

St. Matthew. School of Reichenau. Würzburg Library.

Full-page illustration from the first chapter of Genesis in a manuscript of the School of Tours. British Museum.

for the future. On the other hand, we know that the old wooden churches on the Rhine that aroused admiration in the southern Merovingians were repeated in stone without any changes of plan. To erect towers of stone as high as the wood construction permitted, was an ambitious program to try without changing their plan. But it was done! Angilbert, a son-in-law of Charlemagne, one of the members of the Renaissance club of Aix-la-Cha-

Miniatures from a Psalter of the School of Reims. Utrecht Library.

pelle, retired to an abbey in France, where he built a gigantic church. The building itself is gone; but from the views of it that have been preserved, we see that it was a structure designed for wood but made of stone. It retained the two high towers flanking the entrance, making a sort of portico between the nave, the two aisles, and the monumental tower over the crossing. The buildings of the time showed the Merovingian forms of the North translated into materials of the South. Wooden posts were replaced by pillars of quarried stone blocks, beamed ceilings by vaults, and painted wooden panels by frescoed stucco or mosaic.

The poor results of the efforts of Charlemagne in Romanizing architecture are clearly seen in a church built by Theodulf, Bishop of Orleans, at Germigny-des-Pres. Theodulf was probably the best educated of the palace group; his library contained a great many volumes of the early Christian writings, as well as works by classic poets, such as Vergil, Ovid, and Trogus, which he declared he read *frequenter,* day and night. That he liked objects of ancient art is revealed in one of his poems when he says that he had to resist the temptation of being bribed with a vase on which were painted the Labors of Hercules. Nevertheless, when Theodulf built his church at Germigny-des-Pres, he copied an old Visigothic building, not a Roman one Another proof of his unchanged Visigothic preference occurred when he

Judgment of Solomon. Charles the Bald, the Carolingian emperor, is represented as the Jewish king. BIBLE OF ST. PAUL, Rome.

Panel from the altar of Sant' Ambrogio at Milan. A work by Volsinus,
probably a disciple of Einhard.

ordered two Bibles to be copied for his own use. The old Visigothic Spanish text was employed instead of the Vulgate corrected by Alcuin, which
was one of the great humanistic works of the great Palace School at Aix-la-
Chapelle. The Church of Theodulf at Germigny still retains in the apse a
mosaic with a very unusual subject, the Ark of the Tabernacle protected by
the wings of seraphim. This was a new theme. Nothing of the sort was
found in the art of Constantinople, but it was probably suggested to Theodulf by some decoration in mosaic that he had seen in Visigothic Spain in
his youth. The theme of the Ark of the Tabernacle was never repeated in
later times, and it was not destined to have as long life as the subject of
Christ sitting on the throne with the Twenty-four Elders, which was found
at Aix-la-Chapelle.

That the painters of Charlemagne were capable of invention, we know
from the subjects of the frescoes at the Aula Regia of the Palace at Ingelheim. They reveal an ambitious imperial program. On the left side were
painted the legends of the kings of old—Ninus, Cyrus, Phalaris, Remus,
Hannibal, and Alexander the Great. On the right the frescoes were conse-

crated to the mighty deeds of Theodoric, of Charles Martel, of Pipin; and finally, to the capital episodes of Charlemagne's history, his crowning at Rome and his campaigns against the Saxons.

To study painting of the Carolingian period, we have to turn to the miniatures of the manuscripts. These are the most successful works of art of Charlemagne's time. We still possess a considerable number of manuscripts, many of them dated and decorated with the portraits of the persons who first ordered them. We have been able to divide them into schools and to attribute them to certain cities. It is quite clear that the School of the Palace included, in addition to rooms for teaching, a scriptorium, or special place set apart for the making of books. The collection of manuscripts was dispersed long ago; and it is strange that in the testament of Charlemagne, which was copied by Einhard at the end of the Emperor's life, he ordered his books to be sold and the proceeds to be used for good works. Nevertheless, one Evangelistary which seems to have belonged to him has been preserved. According to tradition, Emperor Otto, when he opened the tomb of Charlemagne, found that manuscript in the sepulcher. Thereafter it was used in administering the oath of office to the German emperors, and it is now in the Treasure Room at Vienna. This manuscript has served as a model to identify others. Manuscripts of the School of the Palace at Aix-la-Chapelle accept most frankly the Classical style. They are decorated only with portraits of the four Evangelists wrapped in tunics and mantles like Roman philosophers. Those at least justify the name of Classical Renaissance that had been given to the Carolingian period.

Detail from the front cover of the LINDAU EVANGELISTARY. Probably by the same hand as the altar of Sant' Ambrogio. Morgan Library, New York.

Carolingian ivory with scenes from the Gospels. British Museum.

For curiosity we shall mention here how the other schools of this period have been identified. There is another BOOK OF THE GOSPELS at the Library of Trèves that belonged to Ada, a sister of Charlemagne. An inscription on the volume calls her "Mother Ada, the Handmaiden of God." As we know that Ada lived in the neighborhood of Trèves between 800 and 805, we have a clue to identify other manuscripts of the same school. The Gospel writers in this Codex and other related manuscripts are shown writing in pavilions upheld by columns. The type is Byzantine, but with a strong Western accent. Another school of illumination seems to have centered at Reims. Ebo, a friend of Charlemagne, went there as bishop, and a precious manuscript that belonged to him is still preserved. It is quite probable that Ebo established a scriptorium at his cathedral, and the style of the miniatures of this shop for bookmaking is characterized by an extremely "nervous" line. Finally, it is quite certain that a school for illuminating and bookmaking was established by Alcuin at Tours, where he was the abbot of the great Monastery of St. Martin, the patron of the Gauls.

The reader can easily imagine that scholars have played a great deal with attributions of manuscripts, tossing them from one school to another. We have disturbed the reader in these scholastic details in order to show how conclusions are sometimes reached in this field of the history of art. The illuminations of Carolingian manuscripts, besides being the supreme product of the art of the time, contain real beauty. They are interesting not alone from the purely archaeological point of view. Some of the figures represented are worthy of standing beside the greatest masterpieces of all times.

Degeneration finally ensued. The scriptoria after the death of Charlemagne lingered on, but their works can hardly be considered as belonging to that Classical Renaissance

The Church represented as a matron holding the cross (faith) and the spindle (works).
Metropolitan Museum of Art, New York.

which the Emperor encouraged. There was a reversion to the barbarian Teutonic spirit, and only the robes of the figures indicated the Roman style. The grouping of the figures into complicated scenes, and an infantile perspective in treating buildings and furnishings, reveal a lack of the organization and clarity so characteristic of the best of the Carolingian Renaissance. The painters fall back on the primitive methods of showing an important personage, such as the emperor, larger in size than the rest of the figures and of telling a story by putting many scenes on the same page.

We do not have a single large piece of sculpture from the time of Charlemagne. A very small bronze at the Musée Carnivalet at Paris seems to be a copy of a large equestrian statue of Charlemagne at Aix-la-Chapelle. The horse was probably brought from Ravenna from a group statue of Theodoric. So we have to judge the sculpture of the Carolingian Renaissance by the ivory plaques that have been preserved. Some are quite beautiful; a few contain non-religious subjects; and a few repeat the subjects found in the miniatures. Indeed, the two arts of illuminating books and ivory carving were very closely related because most of the plaques which survive were used for bookbindings.

The last of the arts that calls for our attention is by no means the least in the Carolingian era—the silversmith's art. The few jewels preserved from that period are even more beautiful and classic than the miniatures. In the records of the friends of Charlemagne, Einhard is always mentioned as an artist of the group. He was nicknamed Bezaleel, after the one who worked for Moses: "I have filled him with the spirit of God in wisdom and in all manner of workmanship, to devise cunning works, to work in gold, and in silver, and in brass, and in cutting of stones, to set them."

Ivory, representing a Carolingian church with a separate bell tower. Depicted on the porch of the church is Christ in the manger. Victoria and Albert Museum, London.

Gallery at St. Miguel de Lino. Chapel of the Royal Grange, near Oviedo.

EARLY ROMANESQUE STYLES

(1000—1100 A.D.)

THE TERM *Romanesque* is applied to western European art of the period between the eleventh and thirteenth centuries. The barbarian peoples had fused with the Latinized population of the old Roman colonies; and their descendants by this time had acquired a sufficient knowledge of the technique of Classical architecture and decorative art to unify the mixed culture, which may be said to have become during this period a reflection of that of the ancient world. The term, Romanesque art, is an allusion to the elements that it took from the art of ancient Rome. Just as the Latin dialects which grew up among the peoples of southern and western Europe came to be called Romance languages, so the artistic forms of this period in which we find preserved more or less of Roman culture came to be called Romanesque. It is interesting to note that just as the neo-Latin languages were not corrupted forms of literary Latin, but were derived from the Latin of the later Roman Empire; so Romanesque art was not based on the styles and methods of the imperial art of Rome,

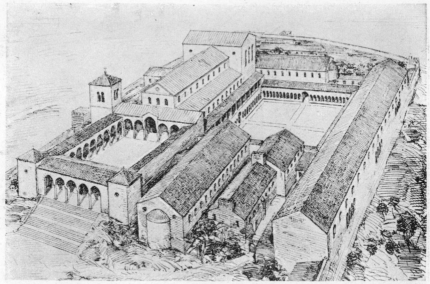

The Abbey of Monte Cassino, parent monastery of the Benedictine order. Between Rome and Naples. Restoration by Kenneth J. Conant.

but grew out of structural styles developed in the provinces that were often very different from those of the capital.

The geographical area covered by Romanesque art corresponded with that of the Western Empire. First in importance came Italy, although still somewhat subject to Byzantine influence during this period; then Gaul, especially Provence, which had been Romanized to the extent of becoming almost another Latium. Next in order came Spain, and the Rhineland, and finally Britain, whose strong Celtic spirit prevented full participation in the general movement.

We might fix upon the year 1000 A. D. as the starting point of the Romanesque period and mark the end with the thirteenth century, when the ogival arch of France was generally adopted by the countries of western Europe. Before 1000, Germanic ideas were still largely predominant throughout the Occident, and the term Romanesque, therefore, can hardly be applied. This date is merely an arbitrary one and of use only for classification. In some places Romanesque art developed earlier, and in others later. A monk, Raoul Glaber, is often quoted as saying that after the year 1000 Christendom was clad in so many new buildings that the world seemed to wear a new garment of radiant white.

The origin of the Romanesque style, in architecture at least, has been attributed to the increased building activities that followed the dissipation of the fear that the world would end on the first day of the year 1000. This theory, however, touches only part of the truth. It is also a fact that the

Interior of the Church of the Abbey of Monte Cassino. Built by Abbot Desiderius in 1050.
Restoration by Kenneth J. Conant.

large amount of rebuilding in connection with monasteries at this time was
a consequence of the reformation of the religious orders, which had already
taken place.

The work on so many new buildings, and the rivalry it occasioned,
caused the monks to become familiar with many already known structural
methods and to essay many bold innovations. The Romanesque period is
mainly characterized by the increased importance of the vault as an architectural feature, which involved a technique not to be acquired without
much practice.

Charlemagne had tried strenuously to change the character of the monastic orders, making them more strictly religious. In Merovingian times
the discipline and morals of the Benedictine houses on the continent were
extremely loose, and only the Celtic monks made a beginning of reform.
Charlemagne enforced further reform of this order; Count Witiza, the

Atrium of the Lombard Church of Sant' Ambrogio at Milan.

founder of the Monastery of Aniane in Provence, had previously made certain efforts in this direction. All these attempts were finally successful; and by the year 1000 the Benedictine houses, although not yet very strict, were much improved in morals and discipline. The monks were now compelled to remain in the monasteries and could no longer wander in the worldly manner to which they had been accustomed during the previous centuries.

At the beginning of the eleventh century all the monks of the west were still Benedictines, for the reformations of the Carolingian Age had been directed entirely to enforcing stricter observance of the monastic rules, rather than to creating new orders. Monte Cassino, the monastery in which the sepulcher of St. Benedictus, the founder of the order, was located, became a great center of pilgrimages as a result of this discipline. Situated between Rome and Naples, where it was exposed to raids by the Moors, the monastery had been abandoned a century before. But in the middle of the eleventh century, when that danger had passed, it was rebuilt under the leadership of the great Abbot Desiderius. The chroniclers tell us that he sent for architects, sculptors, and painters to come from Constantinople. We should expect, therefore, a structure of pure Byzantine style. No doubt the decorations were in this style; but judging from what remains of the building and from

Interior of the Lombard Church of Sant' Ambrogio at Milan.

the descriptions that have come down to us, its general appearance must have been more Romanesque than Byzantine. This is quite important to note, because to Monte Cassino has been credited most of the Byzantine influence that permeated to the Romanesque buildings of the West. According to the chronicler, after the works for Desiderius had been completed, the artists he imported spread throughout Italy and worked in their own styles *per castella and eremos,* on castles and farms.

The Romanesque period has often been called the time of monastic buildings, while the Gothic period is best represented by the cathedrals. After passing the much-feared year, 1000 A.D., Christianity felt optimistic and built enthusiastically. The Monte Cassino evidence seems to prove a survival in the West of the tradition of old Roman techniques and craftsmanship. The Goths at Ravenna used a method of building that was called *manu Gothica* in opposition to the predominant Roman style of the rest of Italy. We do not know exactly what was meant by *manu Gothica;* but it was evidently something different from the Roman methods of the western provinces of the Empire, where, especially in Spain and southern France, we see quite clearly the persistence of the Roman building techniques.

The best known of the building guilds of this period is that of northern

St. Guilhem-le-Desert at Aniane, Provence. Built in Lombard style. Side and apse of the church, with the simple decoration of blind arches.

Italy whose members were called *Magistri Comacini,* masters of the Como region. Tradition says that when Rome was sacked by Alaric in 410, the guild of master-masons fled from the Eternal City and took refuge on an island in Lake Como, and there, in northern Italy, the exiles preserved the secrets of their trade when the art of architecture had fallen very low. We do not know whether this story of flight from Rome is true or not; but it is a fact, however, that the Magistri Comacini were summoned to different parts of the country, even beyond the Alps. They were called Lombards or Lambards, since they came from Lombardy, and were respected as masters of their trade. Still extant contracts which they signed for work abroad state how many Lombards and how many local workmen were to be employed on a job. We cannot give here a more detailed history of the Magistri Comacini, but considerable data about them can be found in the documents and on the monuments of the period. Even today, wandering Italian masons are quite often found in the valleys of Switzerland and in the south of France, while in America the Italians almost monopolize a large number of the building trades, especially that of cement work. We must not suppose, however, that the Lombards were the only ones who preserved the tradition of the old Roman guilds.

Since they are so well documented, let us examine some of the monuments that were built by the Lombards in Italy and elsewhere. They are chiefly stone buildings, with very little or no sculptured decoration. The ornamentation is entirely subordinated to the architectural requirements. It consists mainly of moldings that accent the arches blind arcades, pilasters, and friezes of protruding stone that decorate the exterior and interior walls.

Aula Regia, or Royal Hall, of the kings of Oviedo, built in 830 A.D.

The most important element in a Lombard building is the vault, which was to have much influence on later building. The old barrel vault was pierced at right angles with a series of other vaults, to admit more light into the building, and the resulting vaults were called groins. They were divided from each other by ribbed arches and reinforced by diagonal ribbings where the surfaces came together.

These vaults would have looked poor and bare if they had not been decorated with frescoes, and except for this embellishment they would have looked more like the work of engineers than of architects. They are always impressive, however, because of their simplicity and sincerity, and some of them are doubly so because of their great size. Especially in Italy, the cradle of the style, very noble buildings were built. The great Church of Sant' Ambrogio in Milan, still standing in all its magnificence, may perhaps be called the masterpiece of the Magistri Comacini. Other cities of Lombardy boast of similar buildings of smaller size, however. The Milan basilica still preserves its great atrium before the austere façade of the church.

The Lombards penetrated into the Rhine, but there they had to conform with the Carolingian tradition. Churches were built with two towers on the front façade and one over the crossing. The decorations, however, of some of the churches in Cologne and its vicinity still exhibit in their decoration blind arcades, pilasters, projecting stones, and other details of the Lombard style; while the plan still remains Teutonic. In Provence, where the Lom-

Capital in Mozarabic Romanesque style. From Palencia. Walters Art Galleries, Baltimore.

bards also worked, they were under the control of local architects whose tradition was too strongly rooted to permit much influence by these Lombard masons; although the latter were able to contribute a few building ideas. The styles adopted at first by Provence are almost Classical. The columns of the façades have excellent proportions and the capitals are strictly Classical. In the friezes we see processions of figures evidently copied from Roman sarcophagi. From Provence the marble carvers exported sarcophagi to distant lands, and Classical sculpture never died. The early Romanesque churches of Provence took advantage of these traditions; Arles and St. Gilles still manifest a revival of the southern art of sculpture. It is interesting to consider that later some of the Provençal sculptors were forced to migrate to Italy, when the northern French crusaded against the Albigenses. In this way, the lessons of architecture that were learned in Provence from the Lombard masters were repaid to Lombardy by Provençal marble carvers.

In Spain, the influence of the Lombards was limited to the northeastern corner, which is now called Catalonia. There they were less unfettered than in any other place, and there they erected large churches entirely in Lombard style. These churches seem to be even more Lombard than the monuments of the same kind in Lombardy itself. The rest of Christian Spain, however, continued in the Visigothic traditions of the land before it was overrun by Islam. A renaissance of Teutonic forms took place in the northern kingdom of Oviedo, where the Visigoths had taken refuge, while in the lands of the Moors further south, the Visigoths remained faithful to the old styles in spite of their contact with the art of the Caliphate. The Cordoba monks employed in their buildings a style called *Mozarabic,* an architecture and decoration strictly Visigothic.

This should not surprise us; for during the centuries when the Visigoths had been in power in Spain, they had accepted the advice and help of the Romans who were subject to them. When they re-established their kingdom after the Arab conquest, their own national spirit began to predominate again. The civil laws of Christian Spain in the tenth and eleventh centuries were more Teutonic in character than in the time of the Visigothic kingdom of Toledo. The same thing occurred in art; Mozarabic monuments were more Nordic than those built by the Visigoths in the fifth and sixth centuries when they were the undisputed masters of the land of Spain.

Perhaps the earliest Romanesque monument in England was the first Westminster Abbey, constructed by two French architects prior to the Norman Conquest. We have indications of its appearance in the tapestry of Bayeux, called the "Tapestry of the Countess Mathilda." It depicts in needlework the abbey built by Edward the Confessor, and it is represented as a church of the Rhineland type, with many towers, a nave, two side aisles, and a transept. How much faith we can put in it for archaeological research is uncertain. The Romanesque buildings in England, parts of the Tower of London, and a few parts of Canterbury, as well as some of the smaller churches, seem to show a progress in the style, which finally blooms in the Cathedral of Durham, the most conspicuous Romanesque monument of Great Britain.

The story of almost all Romanesque monuments is obscure. Documents in archives often speak of buildings erected at the beginning of the eleventh century, but it is difficult to identify the buildings mentioned with the ones actually on the spot. The documents usually describe acts of consecration in involved phrases very punctiliously naming the relics brought to the sanctuary and mentioning each patron in flattering words; but they are very meager in the description of the monument itself. As a consequence, the dates furnished by literary sources are constantly questioned by the modern historian, who closely examines the buildings themselves, who compares one with another, and who very often decides against the evidence furnished by the documents. Other historians prefer to remain faithful to the texts unless they are proved forgeries. As a result, we have two schools of investigation in the field of medieval art, which are rather antagonistic to one another and rarely agree on anything. They are the so-called Archivists, who hold to the written word, and the Stylists, who, as their name indicates, depend entirely upon the style of the monuments, that is to say, upon the stones themselves. The latter are acute observers, and a minute detail which would pass unnoticed by the ordinary person becomes for them a definite criterion and a dependable source of information.

As a matter of fact, the method of either school is faulty when

Romanesque capital of the eleventh century. From Palencia. Walters Art Galleries, Baltimore.

Cain hears the voice of Abel speaking from the ground. Portal of Santa Maria, Ripoll, Gerona.

used alone. To put blind faith in a literary text written in a period so devoid of any historical sense as the Middle Ages, will lead to countless errors, of course. It has been proved beyond question that many of the dates of the medieval chronicles were either falsified or honest mistakes. But, generally speaking, to disdain the old documents as useful sources of information is to reject an arsenal of facts which history has preserved. Frequently they have been altered or enlarged upon, it is true; but in many cases the written accounts are honest and accurate.

It has often occurred that after the Stylist believed he had corrected some date from a literary source, a closer examination of the monument compelled him to admit that he had made a mistake. In trying to rectify the date furnished by the document by means of a superficial study of the buildings in question, he has fallen still further from the actual truth. The fact is that both the old document and the modern critic are liable to error, but the probabilities are usually in favor of the former. Until the contrary has been proved by conclusive evidence, it is safer to hold to the literary tradition.

What has been said on the previous pages leads us to expect little of sculpture in the early Romanesque period. Painting, on the other hand, is exceedingly important, not only in its rôle as decoration but also as an essentially useful element. The simple structures built by the Lombards and other post-Carolingian masons required a coat of cement as a covering on the interior walls, and these areas needed to have their bareness relieved.

Head of an Apostle. Eleventh century. Archaeological Museum, Madrid

Mozarabic ivory crucifix. The figure of Christ is at Léon and the cross is in the Louvre.

Thus, frescoes decorated almost every building of the early Romanesque period. Unfortunately, the majority of these paintings were destroyed even as early as Gothic times because of their crudeness. A survey of the Romanesque churches in France, however, has disclosed more than a hundred churches with small fragments of fresco decoration still remaining, and only a few whole compositions which belong to the late Romanesque period.

In Germany, on the contrary, Romanesque frescoes are quite plentiful, and if their popularity has not been great, it is because they are either too

The Angel of the Revelation passing the Book to Saint John. Miniature from a manuscript
of Beatus. Cathedral of Gerona.

faded, or their original color, where it is unchanged is too pale to attract the
eye. In England, there are Romanesque frescoes in the crypt chapels at Canterbury Cathedral. In Italy an interest in Romanesque frescoes started only
thirty years ago, and since that time a large number has been found in Lombardy and in the neighborhood of Rome. In northern Spain, too, in recent
years more than fifty paintings in churches of the Romanesque period have

Miniature from a manuscript of the Apocalypse by Beatus. National Library, Madrid.

been recovered. We use the word "recover" because these fresco decorations had previously been either covered with whitewash or hidden by high altars. It was thrilling to discover them one after another.

Many Romanesque frescoes have a stylistic resemblance that makes us suspect them to have been the work of traveling masters, like the masons of

The Prophet Isaiah, one of the four seers, who at different times had the same vision of the Almighty within the mandorla with the tetramorphic beasts. The other seers were Ezekiel, Daniel, and John the Divine. Fresco from Esterri. Museum of Barcelona.

An Apostle and Mary with the Holy Grail. Mozarabic frescoes from Tahull.
Museum, Barcelona.

the Como guilds. As exceptions we shall count those in the Rhineland, which, as we have said, are pale in color. Although many colors were used in these, the tones were kept soft. Like them in their exquisite refinement are the late French Romanesque frescoes, which are forerunners of Gothic decoration. In Italy and Spain and in the chapels at Canterbury the forms are sharply outlined, and the colors are vivid. Were they done, perhaps, by painters associated with the wandering Lombard builders?

Other exceptions are found in Castile, where the Lombard style did not penetrate. Here the fresco decorations are entirely different. There is no trace of that international style of painting which we have associated with the Lombard style of architecture. The Castilian paintings seem, rather, related to the Mozarabic builders. The background is divided into horizontal bands in strong color. These strips, it has been said, represent abbreviated landscapes. This, however, seems unlikely because the blue band is not invariably at the top, nor is the green always at the bottom. The figures stand out against the background with great intensity of movement and expression. The Mozarabic artist has a more forceful manner of depicting his subject than has any other artist of his time. In piercing penetration no European painting of the eleventh century approaches the works of the fresco painters in Spain. These Spanish artists are often crude and violent;

apparently they deliberately refuse to make any concessions to conventional beauty. Yet how beautiful their frescoes seem to us who are seeking the same results in modern art. The Mozarabic school of fresco painters dislodged the early international style in Catalonia. The work of the late eleventh century is much more Spanish in character than the earlier.

In the Rhineland there continued very much alive the miniature style of the Carolingian schools. The Ottonian miniatures of the Rhine display an inventiveness and vitality of line and color that make the early works done during the reign of Charlemagne appear academic and pretentious. The manuscripts remain large in size, and the full pages of illumination show a great deal of fantasy in the grouping of figures and in the poses, which are often very striking. Sometimes they appear even too alive; the figures gesticulate as if possessed; and the eyes stare as if having magic power. In Spain the Romanesque miniature paintings exhibit a process of change similar to the one we have noted in fresco paintings. For a certain time, at least in Catalonia, the miniature style remains Carolingian; but the force of the Mozarabic schools could not long be held in check, and all the Christian lands of the peninsula eventually fell under its influence.

Famous works by Mozarabic painters were the illuminations of a commentary to the Apocalypse, written by a monk called Beatus. The text is an insignificant, unorganized compilation of commentaries from the Visigothic age, two of them even of African origin. The mediocre quality of the literary work hardly deserves the tremendous popularity that it enjoyed for two centuries—as many as twenty-four manuscripts have come down to us, for the Beatus text was widely copied. All of these texts except two, however, are richly illuminated, and these illuminations justify the fame of the work. Its source was Castilian, and the original artists did for the illuminations what Beatus did for the text; they took ideas from miniatures of earlier manuscripts. In spite of the diverse

Virgin carved in wood. From Santa Maria de Tahull, Catalonia. Now in the Fogg Museum, Cambridge, Massachusetts.

influences which went into its formation the style finally became set in that cruel, passionate, rebellious, forceful, Spanish manner which makes the miniatures of the BEATUS CODEX a source of exotic delight to the sophisticated critic of today who is looking for Surrealistic delirium. There is nothing comparable to them in the whole of the Romanesque miniature art. Perhaps nothing like them has ever been produced. So strenuous, so ferocious, they surpass even the fantasy of the apocalyptic text itself. The illuminators picture flying stars, scorpions devouring men, the great harlot who was the Anti-Christ, the Four Horsemen, and all the tricks of the devil, with such vivid reality and so much inventiveness, that beside them the centaurs, sirens, and satyrs of the Greeks appear like harmless and infantile amusements.

The few extant statues and reliefs of this period are equally as interesting as the miniatures. In Italy, the old Classical tradition continued without any complete break, and we have already spoken of the Classical influence of the marble carvers in Provence. In Spain, the Mozarabic sculptors break the bounds set by Classical tradition and imbue their work with all the fervor of a passionate faith. The sculptured figures are wrapped in mantles falling in stiff vertical folds, but their ecstatic souls shine through their wide-open eyes—they envision a "kingdom that is not of this world." The Spanish sculptors have achieved the almost unattainable; they have carved out of stone a spiritual world.

The Pantocrator, or Almighty. Museum of Barcelona.

Restoration of the apse of Cluny. The tower at the left is the only part still standing from this Romanesque building. Drawing by Kenneth J. Conant.

LATE ROMANESQUE STYLES

(1100-1200 A.D.)

UNTIL THE TWELFTH CENTURY there had been no other bond between the Benedictine monasteries than the Rule laid down by their founder, which was common to them all. Monte Cassino, it is true, was a kind of mother house, but St. Benedict had made no provision in his Rule for an official head of the Order, such as the Dominican and Franciscan monks had later on. Lacking thus a central authority, the monks of each community were accustomed to elect their own abbot, and each Benedictine house was equal in importance to every other. Without any central control, the monasteries in the course of time again fell into the habits of indolence and profligacy that Charlemagne had striven to correct. In the eleventh century, therefore, the need for re-ëstablishing the old spirit of devotion came to be felt anew.

The monastery of Cluny, a Benedictine abbey in Burgundy, took upon itself the task of curtailing the undesirable independence of its sister communities. It may be likened to Monte Cassino in that here the Benedictine order was reborn. In a remote spot where no traditions of culture existed,

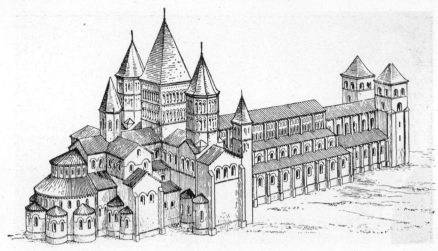

A restoration of the Church of Cluny.

Duke William of Aquitaine had established a company of monks and given them a perpetual grant of land, free from all feudal and civil obligations. Thus had Cluny been founded. For the early years of its existence the abbey was fortunate to have a number of able abbots at its head. Odo, the second of these, undertook the work of forming a federation of the Benedictine abbeys, in order that they might be better governed. At first only four abbeys were included in this union: St. Augustine at Pavia, Aurillac in Auvergne, Romanmourtier in Switzerland, and his own abbey, Cluny, which was the head of them all. Finally twelve houses altogether came under his jurisdiction. New monasteries were also founded by Cluny, and they in turn became centers of influence over the other older Benedictine abbeys. The power of the Cluniacs grew; kings and great feudal lords gave over great lands and smaller abbeys to their rule, and the influence of this mighty organization spread with extraordinary rapidity in France and abroad.

In the eleventh century most of the monasteries in the region around Barcelona came to be associated with the Benedictine houses of Provence, and often they were even ruled by Provençal abbots. Alfonso VI of Castile married a French

Façade of the Romanesque Church of Cluny, restored from data brought to light by the Harvard University excavations. Drawing by Kenneth J. Conant.

Two capitals from the apse of the Church of Cluny. King David with his harp, on the left side; and the Virtues, on the right.

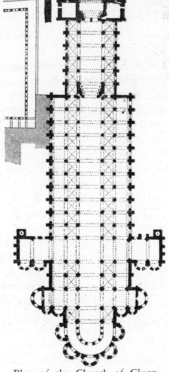

Plan of the Church of Cluny.

princess who brought with her many relatives, and a group of French Cluniac monks to occupy the most important ecclesiastical posts in the kingdom. Cluniac monks were taken also into Germany by the Swabian kings. The abbots of the more powerful abbeys now chose the priors for the subordinate houses, and often the abbot's choice fell on one of his own monks. Often the community to which the new prior went was in rebellion to the reform and it became his difficult duty to instill in the monks a respect for the Cluniac ideals. Many Cluniac monks became bishops.

It was not strange that with the tremendous resources at its disposal, Cluny should desire to rebuild its church. In 1089 the small original church founded by Duke William was replaced by a great church, larger than any of the basilicas of the Apostles at Rome and destined to become the greatest church of Western Christendom. A legend says that the Apostle Paul himself appeared and gave the plan to the monk Gauzo, who was to direct the work. This plan was believed to be so re-

Porch of the Cluniac Abbey Church of Vézelay in Burgundy.

markable that it was not possible to have been conceived without divine aid. A very long vestibule, or narthex, with a nave and two aisles, which was itself as large as a moderately sized church, led through a doorway into the basilica proper. The main part of the church had a barrel-vaulted nave with four aisles, two transepts, and a great choir, with aisled ambulatory and semicircular chapels. At one side of the great edifice was the cloister onto which opened the refectory, kitchen, storehouses, and libraries. On three walls of the refectory, we are told, were painted scenes from the Old and New Testaments and portraits of previous abbots and benefactors of the house, while a "Last Judgment" adorned the fourth wall.

The exterior of the church must have been very impressive, with its many towers and small projecting chapels. Over the crossing of the larger transept rose a great lantern, or tower with many windows, flanked on either side by a smaller tower, while the center of the smaller transept was marked by a fine octagonal tower. Two large square belfry towers with pointed roofs stood one on either side of the entrance, one serving as the archives of the abbey and the other as the prison. The sculptures which embellished the portal have been sketchily described in writings that have come down to us. In the center of the tympanum over the doorway there was a portrayal of the Lord seated in Majesty, with the symbols of the four Evangelists around Him; on the archivolt of the portal were represented the Twenty-four Elders of the Apocalypse; and above them, the four who had the vision

Interior of the Church of the Abbey of Vézelay, enshrining relics said to be those of Mary Magdalene.

of the Lord—St. John, Ezekiel, Daniel, and Isaiah. The group of buildings that composed the abbey, with their orchards and gardens, was enclosed within a great massive wall. Still another, larger fortification encompassed this enclosure and the little town of Cluny on the slope of a nearby hill. Of this great abbey, which survived almost unchanged to the time of the French

French churches of the twelfth century, showing the adoption of the central tower and apsidal chapels of the Church of Cluny.

Revolution, little now remains—only a portion of one transept surmounted by a tower marks the spot where the magnificent buildings once stood. A few capitals remain to convey an idea of the beauty of its decorations.

Fortunately, the subordinate Abbey of Vézelay, also in Burgundy, still exists almost intact and helps us to picture the plan and the decorations of the mother abbey. This also was a rich abbey; and because it preserved the bones of St. Madeleine, pilgrims from every land visited it and made donations to it. The church has a long vestibule and an ambulatory. In plan, perhaps, it was a smaller copy of the Church of Cluny, except that the nave has only two aisles while that of the Cluny had four.

The decorations are typical of all surviving Cluniac buildings and enable us to reconstruct in imagination the lost ones of Cluny. The portals have many archivolts, on which play numberless fanciful little animals: birds pursuing one another, lions, centaurs, and stags with antlers ending in spiral plant forms. The "Pentecost" represented on the tympanum is one of the

Two rural churches with the Cluniac type of apse. St. Saturnin at Puy de Dôme and St. Robert at Corrèze.

most extraordinary existing works of late Romanesque sculpture. In the interior, on the capitals and corbels, are found the same fanciful decorations and plant forms that are seen on the portal.

The style of Cluny so well represented in Vézelay spread beyond Burgundy and was adopted even in buildings that were neither Cluniac nor Benedictine. The central tower over the transept and the elaborate apse of Cluny in particular were copied at that time in many churches in France. The tower was treated in various ways; but it usually had two stories with arched windows, like the Cluny tower. The columnar ambulatory around the choir and the small radiating chapels of the apse were also imitated. The churches in this style found all over France show the beginning of a co-operation between the monks and laymen in carrying out a building program; for from this time on, many of the churches were built for the bourgeois of the towns and their building was overseen only by monks.

The decorative motif, as well as the architectural style, spread until the little sculptures depicting men, animals, and birds in the midst of curls and spirals of grapevines, were applied to buildings entirely outside the Order and became a sort of international style. Nor was the Cluniac style limited to buildings alone; it was used also in smaller articles, such as goldsmith work, and for furniture as well.

It is not surprising that before long there was a reaction against the luxurious ways into which the wealth of the Benedictines was leading them. The original reforms to safeguard morality and to centralize the authority over the abbeys had been outgrown, and another reformation became necessary. The next "purge" emanated from the Monastery of Cistercium (Citeaux), also in Burgundy, and was due to the initiative of St. Bernard who, like Peter the Hermit, was a preacher of the Crusades. The community at Cistercium was not a new establishment, like that of Cluny had been. In the early eleventh century three monks, after failing to reform their community at Molesme, had gone to Lyons and with four others had petitioned the bishop for a place to practice strictly the precepts of St. Benedict. They were granted some land in a swampy forest, where they were joined by others. Twenty-one monks finally established themselves at Cistercium and lived by the work of their own hands. To avoid the vices which accompany wealth, they refused to accept any donations.

When St. Bernard and his companions came to join these monks, the community, which before had been unimportant, received a new spiritual incentive and fought to hold what Cluny had won a century before. From the swampy forest where the monks of Molesme had first built their cabins with their hands, more than sixty thousand monks were to go forth over Europe and establish new communities. In Italy, Spain, and central Europe, more than two thousand Cistercian monasteries and nunneries were built. Thus the principles of Burgundian architecture, along with the new Benedictine spirit, were introduced throughout the West.

In a general way, the plans of the Cistercian buildings did not differ greatly from those of the Cluniac; the proportions and arrangement were practically the same. There was the large-walled enclosure which contained the monastery with

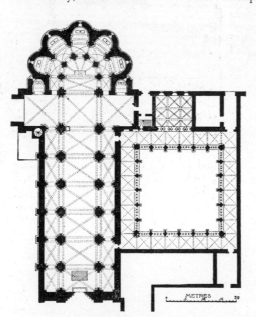

Plan of the Church of Veruela, Aragon. Notice the similarity between this plan and that of the Church of the Monastery of Poblet on the following page.

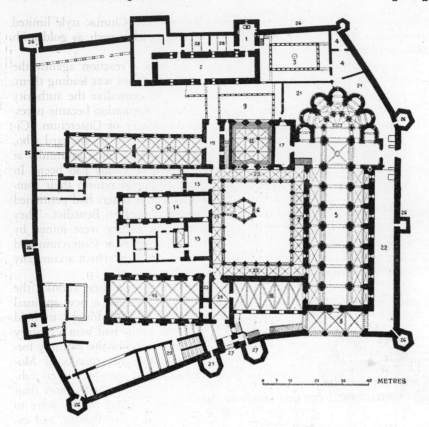

Plan of a typical Cistercian monastery. Poblet, Catalonia.

TWELFTH CENTURY. (1) Chapel of St. Stephen. (2) Large hall. This may originally
have been the dormitory. (3) Cloister of St. Stephen. (4) Ruined dependencies, unclassi-
fied. (5) Main church, begun at the end of the twelfth century and continued in the
thirteenth. (6) Small hexagonal building containing the piscina. (7) South wing of the
main cloister.

THIRTEENTH CENTURY. (8) Narthex. (9) Cloisters of the locutory. (10) New library.
(11) Old library. (12) Chapter-house. (13) Calefactory and barbershop. (14) Refectory. (15) Kitchen. (16) Originally the lay brothers' refectory, later the wine cellar.
(17) The old sacristy. (18) Wine presses, possibly the lay brothers' old dormitory. (19)
Ante-chamber of the libraries and locutory. (20) Stairway leading to the archives and
treasury on the main floor. (21) Monastery cemetery. (22) Lay brothers' cemetery.
(23) Stairway. (24) Vestibule. (25) Galleries north, east, and west of cloister.

FOURTEENTH CENTURY. (26) Battlemented walls and high towers. (27) Gateways. (28)
Apartments. (29) Granaries and bakery.

Portal of the Abbey Church of St. Peter at Moissac in Provence.

all its various buildings; on one side of the church was the cloister, with the chapter house, the refectory, the kitchen, and library opening onto it. Slightly removed from this group of buildings were the others which were necessary for carrying on the life of the monastery—flour mills, oil presses, the hospice for sheltering strangers, and living quarters for the lay servants attached to the monastery.

Though similar in plan, the Cistercian buildings appeared austere in comparison to the Cluniac, since their founder preached the frivolity of ornament. "Of what use," he asked, "is this foliage with its thousands of monsters, figures of centaurs and satyrs, moldings with wild animals, and other ornaments which distract the mind of the monk from his piety and turn him from the evangelical poverty enjoined by St. Benedict?" An assembly of the Order headed by St. Bernard in 1119 established the Constitution of the Cistercian Order, which laid down the rules for the building of their monuments. "Our abbeys shall not be constructed close to cities, villas, or castles, but in places remote from where men pass. . . . . In the monasteries there shall be neither sculptures nor painting; only simple wooden crosses. The doors of the churches shall be painted white. . . . . The legends on the wall shall be painted in but one color and the letters without ornamentation. . . . . There shall not be towers of stone for the belfries nor shall those of wood be too high." Without the great belfries,

Detail of the tympanum of the Abbey Church portal at Moissac. The Almighty with the
Four Beasts (lion, bull, eagle, and the beast with the face of a man), archangels with
rolls of prayers, and the Twenty-four Elders.

with no sculptured decorations on the capitals, and with no reliefs on the
portals, which all added so much to the charm of Cluniac buildings, we
find the Cistercian buildings simple indeed. With their efforts thus confined to structural problems, the monks developed churches of great size.
The plans of the buildings were monotonous, since each Cistercian monastery depended upon another by which it had been either founded or adopted.
For the same reason the practices in them all came to be nearly uniform,
as each new community carried out the forms of the mother house. The
Constitution gave specifications for the founding of the new monasteries:
"The monasteries shall be established, so far as possible, where there will
be water for the mill and gardens, that it may not be necessary for the
monks to wander about outside. . . . . Twelve monks, together with the
abbot, shall go out of the old abbey to found a new one, taking with them
only the necessary books, the missal, rules, book of usages, psalter, hymnal,
lesson book of the matins, antiphonal, and gradual. In the new house

Ezekiel, one of the four seers who saw the   "The Visitation." Relief on the east side
Almighty with the four beasts. Relief at   of the porch of the Abbey Church at
Moissac.   Moissac.

they shall install an oratory, refectory, dormitory, hospice, and porter's gate."

It is natural that we should find the houses similar on the interior. A comparison of any two Cistercian houses shows the churches of both to be identical in plan and architectural elements. Cross-sections of columns, moldings, and other features are alike. The chapter houses of the monasteries are rectangular and divided into nine sections, covered by vaults supported by four columns in the center of the hall. The refectory is always a rectangular hall with a tribune for the reader, and a fountain.

The Cistercians had spread very early to England, where they settled in 1185 at Waverley Abbey in Surrey. During the century that followed this establishment, no fewer than a hundred houses were founded, seventy-five for men and twenty-five for women. Subsequently the Cistercian ardor declined. Only one new foundation is recorded from the middle of the thirteenth century to the time of the Reformation in the sixteenth century.

The suppression of artistic beauty by the strict prohibitions of the Constitution did not entirely crush the imagination of the monks. With their artistic efforts restricted, the monks concentrated on structural problems and succeeded in constructing vaults that to this day are considered great en-

The Western Pantocrater, Creator and Ruler of Heaven and Earth. From the
Church of Tour d'Auvergne. Pitcairn Collection. Bryn Athyn, Pennsylvania.

Moses and an Apostle. Detail from the left side of the tympanum of the portal. Church of Charité-sur-Loire.

gineering feats. By means of these they erected tremendous buildings, many of them far out of proportion to the needs of their communities. These Cistercian vaults, which were higher and more elaborate than any that had been built before, marked a great progress over the simple ribbed barrel vaults made by the Lombard builders. The vaults were groined and ribbed at the intersections; their construction was facilitated by using the ribs as the framework upon which the vault is built, whereas, in earlier times great

Elijah and two Apostles. Detail from the right side of the tympanum of the portal.
Church of Charité-sur-Loire.

temporary wooden scaffoldings had been necessary. We must not imagine,
however, that the Cistercians achieved the perfection of the vault. Their
buildings always remained static, non-organic structures, in contrast to the
dynamic Gothic buildings, with their acting and counteracting forces which
seem to be struggling for equilibrium. In the Cistercian edifices the vaults
were held by the massive weight of the walls.

Two sculptured Elders. From Parthenay. The lower parts of the figures have been incorrectly restored; they are in Glory, where there are no monsters of sin, and for this reason should not be trampling the creatures under foot. Two other figures from the same portal, now at the Louvre, are correctly shown standing on flowers and diminutive churches.
Gardner Museum, Boston.

The Cistercian houses became the greatest centers of learning in Europe at the end of the twelfth century. In this lay the real source of their power. Out of the teachings of their great scholars, Bernard, Anselm, Abelard, and others, grew the doctrine and mode of thinking known as Scholasticism.

By the end of the twelfth century in western Europe, Cistercian techniques for building were being combined with the elaborate Cluniac decorative style. The sculptures created under the influence of Cluny grew to be so fantastic in proportion and shape as to deserve comparison with the Baroque of the Renaissance. This "Baroque of the Romanesque" represents the final development of Cluniac sculpture. Angels, men, and beasts became so exaggerated with their striking, distorted movements that the realm of probability is left behind. A style so intricate and animated we shall not meet again until we reach the school of statuary fostered by the Jesuits seven centuries later. This Romanesque Baroque is exemplified by the great reliefs of Vézelay, Moissac, and Autun, which delight the modern Surrealists, who declare these sculptures to be, like their own work, the products of natural disorder, normal insanity, perfect dream, exact unreality!

Cluniac sculpture, born in Burgundy, came to the full bloom of this extreme style in Provence. It is not strange that the mad figures of this school, contorted and expressive, were adopted there. Although the Classical sculptural tradition had long existed in Provence, by the end of the twelfth century romantic ideas, far removed from anything Rome had bequeathed them, had come to flourish there. Social relations, morals, and religion reached a high point of sophistication in this land which was the cradle of the troubadours. The Albigensian heresy with its absurd and immoral ideas, the poetry and music of the troubadours, and the late Romanesque reliefs reveal how far Provence had grown away from Classical ideas.

A group from the Twenty-Four Elders on the portal of Sainte-Croix, Gironde.

Head of an Elder. From Parthenay. Pitcairn Collection, Bryn Athyn, Pennsylvania.

Capitals from Vézelay and Toulouse, showing the styles of Burgundy and Provence.

Two Apostles. From St. Etienne (1145).
Museum of Toulouse.

The involved stanzas and complicated melodies of the troubadours offer the greatest contrast to the plain chants used elsewhere at this time, and still used by the Church today. The troubadour songs, full of unexpected variations of tune and meter, are the antithesis of the Gregorian chant with its simple succession of notes.

The subjects preferred by the Romanesque sculptors facilitated the growth of a new style. We have already mentioned the sculptured works on the portal of Cluny. The same composition was repeated thousands of times by the late Romanesque schools of sculpture. It became the fad of a whole century. Artists never tired of representing the Lord with the four symbolic beasts and the Twenty-four Elders, sometimes adding to this company two archangels carrying rolls of prayers for the living and the dead.

Since in representing this involved subject sculptors had to deal only with beings of another world, they were led to picture them as different as possible from those on earth. The Lord, the archangels, and the kings were elongated and twisted without limit; while the four beasts offered the artist a chance to use his most fantastic imagination, and the Twenty-four Elders gave them a welcome opportunity to represent lords with heavenly manners. The urbanity and courtly affectation of these aristocrats were far above anything to be found in the castles of the living Provençal barons. Since the Apocalyptic Elders

The Journey to Emmaus. Capital from Moûtier-St.-Jean. Fogg Museum,
Cambridge, Massachusetts.

lived in celestial mansions, they were entitled to bodies and limbs quite
extraordinary in proportions.

Early Romanesque portals have statues attached to columns and serving
as supports. We have seen nothing like this before, except in the caryatids
of Greeks and Romans. At the end of the Romanesque period these statues
become almost entirely independent of the column, merely resting against
it, slender and elongated, like fluted shafts.

On the base of many Romanesque portals are high reliefs representing
the fights of animals, which symbolize the conflict of good and evil, as
described by Prudentius in the book, *Psycomachia* (Fights of the Soul).
Saints are depicted as trampling on horrible creatures with human faces
but with hairy bodies and claws, personifying sins. The devil, or Satan,
was the most difficult problem for the artists of the Middle Ages: how to
concentrate in a single image all the perversions possible to creatures and
all that is detestable to the creator. Indeed, the Romanesque artist did not

Sculptures of the portal of St.-Loup-le Naud. Auvergne. Photograph by Kingsley Porter.

succeed as well in making images of the devil as in making
images of God. To make a
devil, he simply put the wings
of a bat, horns, and a tail on
the figure of an uncouth man.
Thus he represented the Evil
One tempting Eve and harass-
ing Job. Certainly the Romanesque artist did all that he
could in his sculptures to make
evil repulsive.

On the capitals of cloisters
we have more profane subjects.
They constitute the first attempt toward a plastic encyclo-
pedia of the age. Rude and
primitive, these reliefs take advantage of all the previous
synthesis of knowledge. Use is
made of *De Universo,* the contemporary work of Rabanus
Maurus Magnentius, of the *De
Imagine Mundi* of Honorius
d'Autun, and also of Pliny's
Natural History, especially the
parts describing fantastic animals and monsters of remote
lands. All the unusual beings
of a different world, described

Statues on a pillar in the cloister of St. Bertrand
de Comminges, Haute-Garonne.

fully in the *Bestiarium,* a book of zoology of the time, were carved on the
capitals. Sometimes the animals were depicted in pairs with necks inter-
twined as if they had been tamed by the Christian artists.

In addition to carving reliefs and capitals, the Romanesque sculptors
were called on to make images of the Madonna and of the saints. These
statues must have been some of the best works of the twelfth century. Unfortunately they were movable and breakable, and most of them were
destroyed by revolutionary mobs. We can see their types reproduced in
more modest figures. For example, the "Virgin of Chartres," the most
famous in that age in central France, is repeated in innumerable statues
of the seated Madonna with the Child in her lap. Very seldom does the
Romanesque Madonna stand.

Other subjects very popular for capitals of the Romanesque period were
those relating to the various trades. The life of the craftsman of the twelfth
century was illustrated in full detail. We are given an intimate acquaintance

Cloisters of St. Trophime at Arles, France, and of St. Mary at Ripoll, Spain.

with the daily occupations of the burghers of this time. The depictions are sometimes as picaresque and abusive as those in the engravings of the street vendors of Paris in the eighteenth century or of the "Cries of London."

The Romanesque repertory of scenes and the style of the Cluniac sculp ture were introduced into southern Europe along the pilgrimage routes. It has become clear that during those last years the pilgrimages were stimulated by Cluny in order to keep the layman interested in Cluny. A string of Cluniac houses was built along the road and offered the pilgrims hospitality with food, lodging, and hospital care. The route, starting in the north, led through Cluny, Vézelay, Toulouse, Comminges, and other places in the south of France where relics were preserved. Besides the bones of saints, there were to be visited the tombs of heroes of Charlemagne's time, such as Oliver, Gari, Otgier, and others. The tomb of Roland was at the Abbey of Blaye; his horn, at the Abbey of St. Seurin at Bordeaux; and his sword, Durendal, at Brioude. After visiting these places where they could refresh their memories of the chansons and epics so popular in France, the pilgrims entered Spain over the Ronccsvalles Pass. This took them first to Pamplona, from where they followed a road that is still called *Camino Francés,* or French road. Visiting Cluniac houses as they went, they finally came to *Finis Terrae,* the world's end, where the body of St. James was supposed to have come ashore miraculously.

Other routes through the passes in the Alps took the pilgrims to Milan and Venice. The *Strada Francigena,* or French road, led from sanctuary to sanctuary, until it finally reached Brindisium, where the pilgrims set sail for Cairo and Jaffa. Camping, hiking, leaving cares behind, and looking toward a mystic goal, the pilgrims enjoyed every kind of sport and devotion of the time. Yet the travelers risked their lives and their purses as well, not only with the heathen Saracens in Spain and Palestine, but even more with the highway robbers who infested the routes.

Example of late Provençal Romanesque style as it had developed in Languedoc by the time of the Albigensian Crusade. St. Trophime, Arles.

Pilgrimage sculpture in Spain. Reliefs in the Cloister of Santo Domingo de Silos, Castile.

Many pilgrims, dying on the way, bequested their estates to Cluny. It is no wonder that the Cluniac style in architecture and sculpture spread to the ends of the route at Brindisium and Compostela. Cluny itself became rich and powerful, and three popes in succession came from her abbeys.

Marking the progress of the pilgrims, we find all over Italy records of Roland and other heroes of the Carolingian cycle, mingled with stories of the prophets and saints; and in the reliefs and mosaics, even as far away as Brindisium, are the echoes of the *chansons de geste,* or French epics.

In Spain, hundreds of popular songs, still repeated by simple folk, mention the deeds of Roland (whom they call Roldan) and Oliver (Oliveros), Turpin, and the sluggish Charles who was "great only when not drunk." The Pilgrimage sculpture in Spain repeats French models, but it nationalizes them as it has nationalized the literary subjects. So greatly transformed are many of them that they seem not to have been imported but rather to have been created in Spain. In fact, there is the radical theory that Pilgrimage sculpture was a creation of the Spanish people, and that it was

King David, and the "Creation of Man." Reliefs on the Puerta de las Platerias, Santiago de Compostela.

Detail from the "Porch of the Glory" of the Cathedral of Santiago de Compostela. The latest development of Pilgrimage sculpture in Spain.

Two columns decorated in the Pilgrimage style: one from the Santiago "Porch of the
Glory"; the other from St. Denis and now in the Louvre.

imported into France from Spain. But this theory is untenable: the facts
are confused by partisans; passion and pride are still disturbing the scholars.
The pro-Spanish detest the pro-French, and *vice versa*. A cloud of dust
and hatred conceals the facts more than do arguments.

It is preposterous to believe that in Mozarabic Spain there was germinated
the Pilgrimage sculpture that bloomed in Provence one hundred years later.
An excuse for the pro-Spanish theory may be found in the fact that the
latest and most beautiful work of that school is in Spain—the portal of

Statues on the west portal of the
Cathedral of Chartres.

St. James Cathedral at Compostela. In
that Finis Terrae of the West a master
called Matheus carved a portal which
is the synthesis of perfection of sculptural art in the two preceding centuries. The tympanum represents the
familiar subject of the Almighty surrounded by the four symbolic beasts
and the Twenty-four Elders. The statues are attached to the columns, and
angels in rows complete the noble
screen of stone on the portal of the
church. Magnificent work! All that
we know of the master Matheus is his
signature on the portal. He was probably a Spaniard trained in the school
of Pilgrimage sculpture, which in his
time was essentially Provençal. The
Battle of Muret, which put an end to
Provençal culture, was fought in 1200,
eight years before Matheus finished
his great work. This portal of St.
James at Compostela carved by this
unknown master is a terrible indict-
ment against the northern French who
with excessive Catholic zeal destroyed
the Provençal civilization. Great for
its beauty and craftsmanship, the
portal of St. James seems a prelude to
the Florentine Renaissance.

Romanesque sculpture served as
preliminary studies for the statues and
reliefs created two centuries later for
the great Gothic cathedrals. The bene-
ficiaries of the Romanesque attain-
ments in sculpture were the artists
who decorated the first cathedrals of
northern France at St. Denis and
Chartres. There we see, growing from
the tree of Pilgrimage sculptures, a
branch that eventually grew larger
than the parent itself. The portals of
Chartres and St. Denis are the binding
links between the Romanesque and
the Gothic. Their slender figures at-

Statues on the west portal of the Cathedral of Chartres. End of the twelfth century.

Detail of a statue on the west portal of the Cathedral of Chartres.

Two statues of saints and statue of a queen. School of
Chartres. Museum of Bourges and the Metropolitan
Museum of Art, New York.

Upper part of a bishop's folding chair. Decorated in the late Romanesque style.
Cathedral of Roda in Aragon.

tached to the columns, or serving as columns, have that peculiar flavor of an art caught halfway between the old and the new. When looking at the long figures of Chartres and St. Denis, we are uncertain whether we enjoy them more for their archaism or for their novelty.

In paintings of the late Romanesque period we are much poorer than in sculptures. Only a few altars have been preserved, and these are in rural places where the later styles did not dislodge them. A group of altars from the Pyrenees, rather rustic in treatment, preserves all that remains from the paintings on wood in the south of France and Spain.

Miniatures of this time are likewise less interesting than of the previous century. There is nothing at this time to compare with the Mozarabic illustrations of the BEATUS in Spain or the Ottonian Bibles in Germany. Many of the twelfth-century illustrated books which have come down to us are insipid, vulgar, and uninspired.

All the art of color in the late Romanesque style seems to have been concentrated in the making of enamels. This ancient technique had a tremendous revival in the twelfth century in the region of Limoges, in central France. We have in our museums so many plaques, medallions, caskets, and platters of this period, that it is a question whether we should call this craft at Limoges an art or an industry. The answer is, both! Much of the Limoges enamel ware is valued only for its superior workmanship, the colors being opaque and comparable rather to those of a porcelain coat stuck over the metal than to a transparent vitreous paste fused onto the metal object. Some of the works of the Limoges enamel masters, however, are splendid objects. Reliquaries of gilded bronze in the form of a miniature chapel are enriched with enameled plaques portraying saints.

The technique of the opaque enamels was not limited to the Limoges shops. Enamels similar to the French Romanesque were made also in Spain. The pastes of the Spanish enamels are coarser and more opaque; but the colors are more intense, and the designs are more personal and livelier.

In the region of the Rhine, another great school produced enamel works superior to those originated at Limoges. The objects were larger; in fact, they were so large as to deserve the qualification of monumental. Still pre-

Limoges enamel plaques, with the popular Romanesque subject of the Almighty and the four symbolical beasts. Metropolitan Museum of Art, New York.

served in the churches of Cologne and neighboring lands are certain reliquaries, lined with enamel plaques, which have no rivals in France.

Enamel work quite often is a combination of sculpture and painting. The most important parts are independently-worked flat reliefs, applied on top of the enameled plaque. The chisel helps to accentuate details with engraved lines, and some places are emphasized with inserted gems.

The handsomest of the enameled objects is probably the chasse, or reliquary, at the Cathedral of Cologne, supposed to enshrine the bones of the Three Magi. It has the shape of a roofed church made of gilded bronze, with friezes and panels richly enameled. The contemplation of this masterpiece of metalwork makes the beholder proud of belonging to the human race. How many days of toil to bring to completion that marvelous object! What a fund of perseverance and faith was required for perfecting every detail. But also what skill and taste! And back of the great master, who, in the shop near furnaces and ovens, planned and finished the Cologne chasse, are centuries of experience and generations of artists—searching, searching for beauty.

Relief showing evidence of the penetration of Pilgrimage sculpture into southern Italy. Museum, Bari.

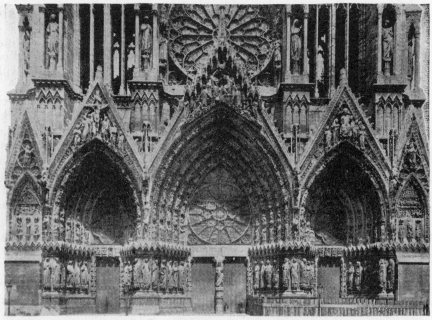

Front portal of the Cathedral of Reims.

EARLY GOTHIC ART IN FRANCE

(*1200—1350 A.D.*)

THE TERM *Gothic* originated in an unfortunate confusion in the minds of the writers of the Renaissance. The wide-spread use of this adjective, which is quite unrelated to either the origin or the character of the style, is due to Giorgio Vasari, a Florentine writer on art. He began his book, which contained the biographies of the Italian painters, with a number of short chapters on the arts of painting, sculpture, and architecture. In discussing the styles of the Middle Ages, he tells us that the monuments were built in a style which originated in Germany as the invention of the Goths, and he consequently calls it Gothic. He goes on to state that it was extremely bad art compared with the ancient Classical, the Gothic being nothing more than a confused conglomeration of pinnacles, spires, pilasters, and leaves, without any orderly arrangement and entirely lacking in any sense of proportion such as constituted the perfection of the Greek Classical styles. Vasari's statement was much quoted; and, strangely enough, the dictum of the Florentine writer continued to be generally accepted until nearly the middle of the last century. Romanticists such as Chateaubriand and Victor Hugo first recognized the Gothic cathedrals as among the most glorious achievements of man and turned the tide of opinion in favor of Gothic art.

Interior of the Abbey of St. Denis, near Paris.

Yet, it is surprising that many famous people of the nineteenth century lacked an appreciation of the Gothic style. Goethe, so open-minded, so capable of understanding remote and exotic styles, died without having realized the profound beauty expressed in the German cathedrals. When he was a student at Strasbourg, he climbed the tower of the cathedral there, but it was a stunt of youth. He never crossed into France to admire the Gothic buildings there. Byron, in spite of the many Gothic subjects mentioned in his poems, remained a worshiper of Classical beauty.

The resistance of officialdom to the idea that the Gothic style was worthy of being used as a background for ceremonies of the court is exposed by the fact that when the last of the Bourbon kings of France, Charles X, was anointed at Reims and crowned in the cathedral there, the beautiful church was masked with plaster columns, so that it appeared as a faked and cheap Greek temple, but it was esteemed by the chamberlains and prelates of the France of the nineteenth century as more beautiful than the magnificent Gothic structure of the time of Jeanne d'Arc and Dunois.

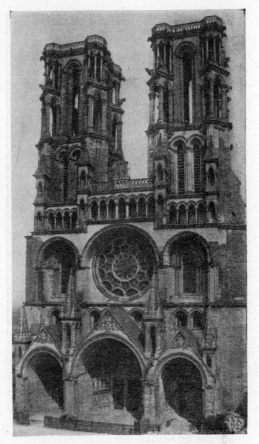

Façade of the Cathedral of Laôn. Example of Early Gothic.

But this foolish lack of appreciation did not continue. Soon protests were made against the term Gothic, and an attempt was made to substitute for it the word *ogival*. *Pointed* is also employed in connection with the architecture of this period. Discussions, too, arose concerning the origin of the admirable forms of the Gothic portals and vaults and magnificent structural systems, with their skilful combination of thrust and counterthrust. According to some misinformed scholars, the pointed style had been imported from the Orient, where it had grown out of an imitation of the rows of palm trees of the desert groves. Others to whom Gothic architecture seemed barbarous, believed that it had originated in Germany, whence it passed over to France and then spread over the whole of Europe. The ogival or pointed arch, it was asserted, had the form of the Egg of Isis. Some sought Christian symbols in the various Gothic forms: the vault stood for the ship of St. Peter; the columns, for the twelve Apostles; the cruciform plan alluded to Christ crucified; and devout writers discovered by means of texts and comparisons many other subtle and finely drawn symbols.

Finally, a number of careful investigators acquired proper perspective and worked out the origin of the Gothic forms, establishing a criterion for

Façade of the Cathedral of Amiens.

judging the value of these admirable monuments of medieval France. It is now generally recognized that the Gothic style was a natural development from the forms of the Romanesque schools, particularly those perfected in Burgundy and disseminated by the Cluniac and Cistercian monks. It was not in Burgundy, however, that the early French Gothic reached its highest development, but rather in Normandy, and the Ile-de-France, which was most completely under royal control. From these two centers, it spread rapidly over the various provinces of France. By the middle of the thirteenth century it was generally adopted in Germany and was in the process of being introduced into Spain. It may be said that it reached its definitive form by the end of the twelfth century. The collateral development of the style in England is interesting.

The main characteristics of the Gothic style are the pointed, or ogival arch, the ribbed vault, and a new taste in moldings and other ornamentations. Since the groined vault had been widely used in the Romanesque period and was traditional in the ancient Classical structures, it might be well to examine more closely the difference between the Roman groined vault and the Gothic ribbed vault. To cover a rectangular area, the later Romanesque builders sometimes adopted a system of throwing diagonal round arches from corner to corner, and filling in the intermediate spaces with masses of concrete which solidified in the form of a vault. In the Gothic style the diagonal arches are really independent and have an elasticity of their own. Upon them rest the stone blocks of which the vault itself is composed. These diagonal arches, therefore, play the same part as the wooden frame upon which an arch is constructed. The vault has an elasticity of its own and the weight and lateral thrust come at the corners. These corners, therefore, are the only points which require strong supports, for upon them rests the entire weight of the vault. They are, therefore, buttressed with segments of arches, or flying buttresses, which appear to be propping up the wall. There is nothing so dynamic in Romanesque architecture. As we have already said, the vault was usually cylindrical, and the thrust, being uniformly exerted along the top of the wall, was resisted by the weight of the wall itself. When the main vault was strengthened by re inforcing arches, these were indicated on the exterior of the building by solid strip buttresses. Briefly, the mechanics of Classical and Romanesque architecture was static, force was opposed by weight; while Gothic mechanics was dynamic, one force resisted another. For this reason a Gothic church is so complicated and so perfect that one part of the structure cannot be touched without affecting every other part. The moment a flying buttress breaks, the arch which it sup-

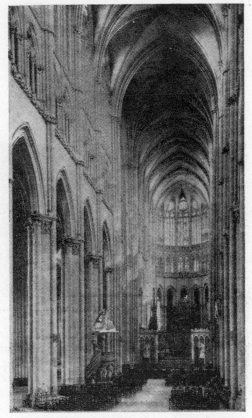

Interior of the Cathedral of Amiens.

ports will spread, as will the diagonal arches which are supported at the same point. Consequently, if but one element is lacking the entire building will fall.

However, it is not by this structural technique alone that the Gothic style is characterized. We also find a new taste in moldings and ornamentations. Romanesque moldings were round, many of them corresponding to those of the Classical styles; while in the Gothic buildings they assume an infinite variety of convex forms. These often project from a concave surface and produce remarkable effects of light and shadow in the interiors of the buildings. The degree of elaborateness of these moldings serves to determine the date of a monument. The more sharply edged and elaborate moldings belong to a more advanced style, and hence to a later building. It is interesting to note the variety of arrangements of moldings in a Gothic building. They begin in the diagonal vault ribbings, rest on the capital of the supporting pier, and are often prolonged as thin, engaged shafts to the

Façade of the Cathedral of Notre Dame of Paris.

floor. The columns thus become a core for a bundle of moldings. The vaulting of the nave is usually much higher than that of the aisles, and its lateral thrust is resisted by the buttresses on the exterior of the church. We no longer find the high galleries of the barrel-vaulted Romanesque churches. Instead, the walls of the nave rise high above the aisles and form a clerestory with immense windows, since in the more northern regions of France, where the style originated, light is sought after and not shunned as in the brighter regions of the south.

This arrangement of buttresses and high nave gives the churches their characteristic appearance. The nave rises like the inverted hull of a ship, supported on either side by the extended arches of the great flying buttresses. It is hardly necessary to add that the arches, windows, and flying buttresses are all ogival. It is only rarely that we find the round arch employed in a Gothic edifice. The large windows are divided by a border of slender columns and curved stone ornaments, (mullions), which often form a very complicated tracery. The thin columns and tracery of the windows are purely decorative. As the whole strength of the building is concentrated at the spring of the reinforcing arches, the light walls have no function in upholding the main structure, and the space they occupy could have been left entirely open, so far as the strength of the building is concerned. In the nave of a cathedral it was customary to have above the aisles a sort of gallery, called a triforium, which is also indicated on the main façade of the exterior.

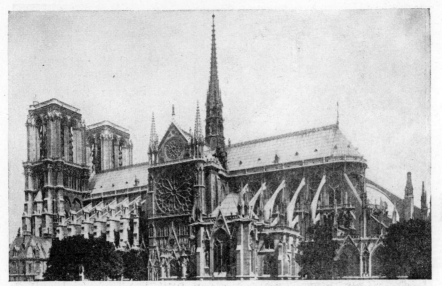

Apse of the Cathedral of Notre Dame of Paris.

The pinnacles on the buttresses, the towers, and spires are usually ornamented with finials of plant forms carved in stone, as, for instance, an
opening bud. The moldings of the arches are often accentuated by means
of vines with leaves and flowers, and we also find the capitals and the
bosses of the vaults at the intersection of the ribs decorated in the same
manner.

The forms used are taken from the commoner flowers and more modest
field plants; and they are applied to the moldings with a love for nature
not displayed since Greek art. Twisted ivy, tender shoots of grapevine, and
branches of oak climb the arches and moldings of the Gothic structures.
With their very twists and curves of decorative forms they adapt themselves
so completely to the character of the building that it seems as though Nature
herself were taking part in the creation of these new cathedrals. In Classical
art only a few plants, such as the acanthus, ivy, and laurel, had been accepted
as suitable for decorative motifs. The Gothic artists did not limit themselves to the vegetable kingdom, but represented birds as well, and even
fanciful monsters sitting erect on high parapets, like guardians. Sometimes
these figures in the form of gargoyles serve to carry off the water from
the roofs.

The Cluniac houses visited by pilgrims had elaborate façades; but the
Cistercian houses, which did not harbor relics or cater to pilgrims, were
entered by the monks through a passageway from the monastery and were
without decorative entrances. In the Gothic cathedrals, the Cluniac taste for
elegant façades reappears. The guilds of artisans and burghers vied in dis-

Interior of the Cathedral of Notre Dame of Paris.

playing their devout spirit and artistic taste, and the cathedral fronts were richly clothed with sculptural decoration. There were usually three portals, corresponding to the nave and aisles of the interior. This division was also marked by two buttresses between the portals, thus emphasizing on the main façade the plan of the building. The archivolts of the portals were loaded with niches which sheltered the statues of apostles and prophets, and the central doorway was frequently broken at the center with a column bearing a statue of Christ, the Blessed Virgin, or the patron saint of the church.

Above the portals there was usually a frieze of kings, which might represent the previous kings of France, put here by the burghers who were grateful for the liberties granted to them; or it might represent the kings of Judah, the forefathers of Christ, bearing branches from the tree of Jesse instead of scepters. However, these kings were probably a later edition of the Twenty-four Elders of the Apocalyptic visions so popular throughout Romanesque art. Royal figures adorn the façade of Amiens, Reims, Chartres, and Paris.

Over this frieze the three spaces were filled with rose windows, or, as was more often the case, there was a rose window in the center with an arched and mullioned window on either side, elaborately decorated with delicate stonework. Through these windows the afternoon light penetrated into the interior, for the façade was still usually turned toward the west as were the early Christian churches. The fact that the aisles are much lower than the nave is sometimes emphasized on the exterior, by a central gable, which is placed above lower ones on either side. The usual arrangement was the use of two towers at either side of the front. These towers were all originally intended to terminate in tall spires, as they do at Chartres; but most of the churches were never finished, and today we have only the tower on which the spire was to be placed.

Each city rivaled its neighbor in the magnificence of its cathedral, and they all vied in raising their buildings with towers and spires to such great heights that they could be seen from a great distance. On the plains of "sweet France," as the minstrel in the "Song of Roland" calls his native land, where no mountains or high hills break the line of the horizon, the low houses of the old cities are dominated by the enormous masses of their cathedrals, with their towers and spires piercing the sky. As the traveler draws nearer and nearer, he can distinguish the pinnacles of the innumerable buttresses, the great traceried windows, and the details of the façade. If, after entering the cathedral and exploring its chapels and crypts, he will climb to the top of the tower, he will see stretched before him the fair land of France, with its vineyards, groves, and peaceful rivers winding off into the distance. These will be seen over countless crocketed pinnacles and flying buttresses beneath him, which tell of another France of long ago, the France that in an outburst of religious zeal, at the time of the Crusaders and St. Louis, gave the unsurpassed beauty of Gothic cathedral art to the world.

Gothic image. XIIIth century. Pitcairn Collection.

Within a few decades after the first expression of Gothic art, there spread over the land a remarkable series of Gothic monuments, which even to the present day constitute the most precious heritage of France. Nothing has been done since that can compare with these Gothic monuments. Some of them suffered from the French Revolution: for example, St. Denis, which was almost destroyed, and Notre Dame at Paris, which was not so badly damaged. But none of them suffered materially from ill-advised restoration. The structural system of a Gothic building is such that it cannot be much altered without requiring a change from the beginning. The forces are so balanced that any remodeling of large dimensions would throw the whole structure out of equilibrium; the elaborate vaulting would fall apart if modified in the slightest degree. During the reigns of Louis XIV and Louis XV those who wished to introduce elements in the current mode, had to content themselves by displaying their Baroque taste in a new chapel or a doorway. When an artistic type achieves perfection, it possesses a vitality and coherence never found in a monument of a transition period. This is true of Greek temples as well. The Parthenon has served as a Christian church, but a building so perfect in the relationship of its parts could not be remodeled to fit the new needs.

Interior of the Chapel of Sainte Epine (Sainte-Chapelle), Paris.

The Palace of the Popes at Avignon.

The building of some of the great Gothic cathedrals was completed within a few years; for example, the old Cathedral of Chartres was burned in 1193, and only five years later, in 1198, the choir of the new one was consecrated. Most of the cathedrals, however, rose slowly; and a century or two was taken to decorate their façades. The Cathedral of Noyon, one of the earliest, was built in ten years, between 1140 and 1150. Notre Dame at Paris was built in twenty years, between 1163 and 1183; but the main façade was not finished until 1245. The Cathedral of Amiens, which is the most perfect in France in the intricacy and beauty of its exquisite decoration required for its completion the sixty years between 1220 and 1280, with three masters following one after the other in directing two generations of workers. The names of a few architects of this time have come down to us, and we happen to know that the three architects of Amiens were Robert de Luzarches, Thomas de Cormont, and his son, Renaud. Reims Cathedral was begun in 1211 and the work on its magnificent structure and rich decorations continued until the year 1400, but many of its parts have never been entirely finished.

During the Gothic period modern nations began to take shape, and it is not easy for this reason to classify the monuments by local schools. On the one hand, the kings, exercising greater power, were able to impose a national uniformity which had not before existed. On the other hand, in this great heroic time, this golden age of learning and universities, international ideas were spreading; and in their universality they were as antagonistic to the formation of local schools as were the limitations set by royalty. We may speak of the great architects who planned the cathedrals and built the most famous monuments as having started personal schools only in the sense that their work was copied to a great extent by other architects. Sens, Senlis, and Notre Dame at Châlons can be grouped together in this way as having been influenced probably by St. Denis near Paris, which was built by Suger in the middle of the twelfth century. He

House of the merchant Jacques Coeur at Bourges.

records in his chronicle to what pains he went to establish a school for training sculptors, bronze casters, stained-glass workers, and jewelers.

Although the French cathedrals were all built at approximately the same time and are very similar in plan and elevation, each has a character, or personality, of its own, depending upon the circumstances of its foundation

Patron saints of two important groups in the thirteenth century, the knights and the pilgrims. On the left, St. Theodore the knight, and on the right, St. James the pilgrim. Cathedral of Chartres and Sainte-Chapelle, Paris.

and the particular conditions it was built to satisfy. Chartres Cathedral still retains the old crypt and some of the parts of its original Carolingian structure. Notre Dame has a certain incomparable grace that cannot be found

Two French Gothic Madonnas. At the Metropolitan   French Gothic Madonna.
Museum of Art, New York.   Notre Dame of Paris.

elsewhere; Reims is rich and splendid as befits a cathedral destined for the crowning of kings.

Their architects were specialists, without vanity, sincere, and loyal. We have a glimpse into the character of one of them in the *Album* of Villard de Honnecourt, which is preserved in the Bibliothèque Nationale at Paris. It is a portfolio of drawings with notes, having no literary pretensions. "Villard de Honnecourt," it begins in its Picard dialect, "salutes you and begs all of you who engage in the works treated in this volume that you pray for his soul and be mindful of him." We cannot identify positively any of the buildings by Villard de Honnecourt; but the notes in this album reveal much of his life and education in matters of art. This French master-builder of the thirteenth century seems to have studied and worked with the Cistercian monks and to have been familiar with their churches.

He was a great traveler and eagerly sketched all that he saw. Actual architectural plans, as well as his own solutions of the problems presented,

Three French Gothic statues: Christ, John the Baptist with the Lamb, and the Apostle
John at the foot of the Cross. Toledo (Ohio) Museum of Art and Metropolitan Museum
of Art, New York.

are carefully set down in his book. Interested in everything and possessing
a keen sense of humor, he once sketched a lion and wrote beside it, "Know
that this lion was drawn from life." He noted the same of his birds and
flowers. In another place he writes, "Once I was in Hungary and there
I saw a church pavement made in this manner," and a sketch of the floor
accompanies this statement. He appears to have been associated for a time
with one Pierre de Corbie, who was also a layman and a pupil of the Cistercians. There is one drawing of the apse of a cathedral, which he says was
made in contest with this fellow architect *"inter se disputando."* It was
customary for the master-builders of the Middle Ages, like the painters of
old in the Ceramicus at Athens, to engage in friendly disputes and compe-
titions in their art. Judging by what we learn from Villard de Honnecourt
and also from contemporary expense accounts which credit them with only
modest salaries, the great builders of the cathedrals must have been men who
lived very simply.

Melchizedek, Abraham, and his squire. Sculptures on the interior of the
Cathedral of Reims.

This unique architectural sketchbook of the period casts a little light
also on the lives and characters in general of the medieval architects, and it
is all the more valuable because no other writings or working rules of the
time have come down to us. Unfortunately, there is no treatise of this period
such as that on Ionic architecture by Hippodamus of Miletus, or that on
the architecture of Imperial Rome by Vitruvius. But the buildings themselves, if we examine them carefully, speak with so much sincerity that they
give us as much information as could be found in any book.

French Gothic architecture at the height of its development lasted all
through the fourteenth century; later the vault and the arches of doors and
windows began to deviate from the pure ogival line and to take on a more
flamelike character and a more elaborate decoration. This style development
is called Flamboyant Gothic and will be discussed in another chapter. During this first period, French architecture had held fast to the fundamental
principles which we have already noted: the ribbed vault, the ogival arch,
the flying buttress, and the varied moldings. The many Gothic monuments
which are still standing attest the unity of this style. The structures are not
all cathedrals, but include monasteries, civil and military buildings, palaces
and castles, bridges and gateways.

One of the monasteries most worthy of note is the great Abbey of Mont-

Saint-Michel, which rises on the rocks of a small island near the coast of Normandy. Foremost among the palaces was the Louvre, the royal residence at Paris. Only one or two of the towers of this early building now remain, for it was rebuilt in the sixteenth century by Francis I; but a miniature in the famous BOOK OF HOURS of the Duc de Berry shows us how it looked, with its circular towers crowned with conical roofs and its battlemented wall surmounted by turrets.

Some palaces were great massive structures, like the Palace of the Popes at Avignon; some present a lighter appearance, proudly displaying their countless towers and peaked roofs at varying heights, and their sculptured pinnacles of a fanciful character, in the manner of the house of an eccentric millionaire of our own time. An elaborate structure of such a kind, no doubt, was the castle of Jean, Duc de Berry, at Mehun, if we can judge by miniatures and literary descriptions. It was not unlike the palace erected at Bourges by the wealthy merchant, Jacques Coeur, the treasurer of Charles VII. The stairways were usually set in circular or octagonal towers placed at the corners of the court. The steep slopes of the roof were pierced by lucarnes, or dormer windows, which lighted the rooms directly under the rafters.

The "Annunciation" and the "Visitation." On the front portal of the Cathedral of Reims.

Charles V and his wife, Jeanne de Bourbon. From the Church of the Célestins
at Paris. Louvre.

Some of the great halls of the palaces or residences were vaulted with
stone, but more often they were roofed over with wooden beams carved with
reliefs and decorated with color. The tall chimneys rising above the walls
produced a monumental effect. Perhaps the finest existing example of this
combination of dormer windows and chimneys is the hall of the ducal palace

King Charles V and the Dauphin, later Charles VI. Metropolitan Museum of
Art, New York.

of Poitiers. Above a stepped façade rise three immense chimneys from the
fireplaces which heated the great hall.

The use of the same decorative features is found in all the public buildings
of the period, the town halls, hospitals, monasteries, and guildhalls. The
hospitals boasted a splendor which may not have been in accord with modern
hygienic principles, but at least everything possible was done to beautify the
lodgings of the sick. A number of Gothic hospitals still exist in France. The
finest of all is that of Beaune on the Côte d'Or, with its court decorated with
lucarnes, its large galleries for convalescents, and its well-ventilated hall with
high ceilings and wooden screens.

The Gothic walls of many French cities are still in existence, with their
typical square merlons and towers at the angles; but few of them remain

The "Coronation of the Virgin." Ivory group of the thirteenth century. The garments of
Christ and the Virgin are decorated with the fleur-de-lis, the coat of arms of the French
royal family. Louvre.

with the entire enclosure intact, as do the walls of Avignon. The beauty of
these walls, with their battlemented parapet and their corbel table decoration,
is unsurpassed in all France. The cities were laid out according to the nature
of the ground, and the streets seldom conformed to a regular plan. The
towns were divided into wards for various trades and occupations. As the
business of an entire district often had to be crowded into a very restricted
space, the streets were narrow and the houses projected above the first floor
to almost the middle of the street. The ordinances of Perpignan, for instance,
permitted the houses to jut out as far as was thought necessary, provided they
cleared the head of a man on horseback. Below the stories set forward on
beams was a covered passage containing shops and sheltering street vendors.
Bourges and some of the cities of Normandy still preserve many such Gothic
houses. The houses were often built of a combination of wood and plaster;
the reinforcing timbers visible from the outside were frequently decorated
with carvings. The houses were very small for the number of people they
had to accommodate. Each story usually consisted of only one or two rooms
which had to serve every domestic purpose.

The highways were far from being the broad paved roads which extended
across the civilized world in Roman times. The tradition of Roman bridge
construction still continued, but the pointed arches permitted the spanning
of a greater space than formerly, with less lateral thrust, so that instead of
a series of round arches only one arch was now necessary and fewer piers

Two French Gothic ivories of the thirteenth century, depicting the glorification of the Mother of God. Metropolitan Museum of Art, New York.

were needed. Sometimes a chapel was placed midway on the bridge for the benefit of the devout wayfarer.

Even more than in its magnificent architecture, the glory of medieval France was reflected by its sculpture, which had been slowly developing since the Romanesque period. The monks of Cluny had given this art its first impulse; it had been checked by the preaching of St. Bernard and the austere rule of the Cistercian order; but by the middle of the twelfth century it again resumed its progress and before long achieved a success which might be compared to that of sculpture in ancient Greece. The earlier Gothic sculpture of France, which we may call archaic in comparison with later works, includes some of the statues of the great churches of St. Denis and Chartres. The drapery falls in straight folds and clings closely to the body, as in the work of early Greek sculpture. At Amiens, Reims, and Paris, the finest early work modestly decorates the façades of the ancient buildings with a touching simplicity. Here in the open, protected from the weather by small canopies, are the masterpieces of the French cathedral sculptors. These devout artists did not seek the plaudits of the crowd, but worked only for God and for art. Many of their statues are hidden between buttresses or placed so high on the roof that they cannot be seen by the multitudes thronging the streets below. It is only in our time that many of them have been

Ivory with scenes from the life of Christ. Metropolitan Museum of Art, New York.

rediscovered. Some of the works which were more accessible are gone forever, while others have found their way into museums. It is a miracle that, in spite of the devastation of the Revolution and the World War, so many of them have remained in their places to this day. There are thousands of figures on the Cathedral of Chartres. But one is saddened by a photograph of Notre Dame showing the arcade of the kings empty as it was before the statues were restored. The beautiful white marble figure of the Virgin was also missing from the center of the façade, as were the figures of Adam and Eve.

The representations of Christ and the Virgin, the two most important types in medieval iconography, show a change during the Gothic period. The Savior is no longer portrayed as the Pantocrator, the Omnipotent of the Byzantines, nor as the Christ in Majesty of Romanesque times, but rather as the Son of Man on His mission to earth. He has a spark of French elegance; His beard is combed, and His hair is soft and undulating. The Virgin, always youthful, is either standing or seated, but she holds the Child in her left arm or on her left knee. The seated Mother in the early sculptures recalls the Romanesque type in the simple treatment of the mantle which she wears, and she never wears a crown like the Virgin of the Byzantines. But by the middle of the thirteenth century her head is covered with a fine veil, and her brow is encircled with a royal crown. The story of Mary is told tenderly, in scenes of the Annuncia-

Two French Gothic ivories of the fourteenth century. Above, a tournament; below,
scenes showing the taking of the Castle of Love.

tion, the Visitation, Calvary, and her triumphant ascent to Heaven where
the Son awaits to crown her and seat her at His right hand.

Like that of the Greek artists, the repertory of the Gothic sculptors is a
definite one; and few variations were permitted presenting any of the scenes.
There were, of course, certain favorite themes; the Annunciation appears
more often than the Visitation; the Adoration of the Kings seems to be
more popular than that of the Shepherds. The three kings are usually represented: the first, as old and bald, laying his crown at the feet of the Virgin
and Child; the second, as tall and slender, raising his cup filled with gifts
and pointing to the miraculous star; the third, as young and beardless,

Love in Gothic France: playing, flirting, courting. Ivory casket of the thirteenth century. Metropolitan Museum of Art, New York.

contemplating the Holy Child with curiosity and amazement. These synthesize the three ages of man and the three characters of mankind.

In monumental sculpture, ivories, miniatures, and stained glass the iconography and treatment are the same. We see, for example, the Coronation of the Virgin with two kneeling angels on the tympanum of the Cathedrals of Paris, Chartres, Sens, Senlis, and Amiens, and in the marvelous ivory group in the Louvre, which may have belonged to St. Louis or his mother, Blanche of Castile. When there is not sufficient space to include the angels, as in a little ivory triptych, Christ and the Virgin appear without them but retain the same poses as in the monumental sculptures: the Virgin folds her hands and bows humbly even at this her most glorious moment, when the King of Heaven places the crown upon her head. Other themes of medieval Christian interest were also simplified by the great French artists, who slowly created them and finally brought them to perfection. These artists who

Ivory mirror back. Metropolitan Museum of Art, New York.

Three bishops' crosiers. Carved and enameled at Limoges about 1250. Metropolitan
Museum of Art, New York.

were entirely lacking in personal vanity were willing to be governed by
tradition, but inevitably added a little of their own inventiveness.

The original creative power of the Gothic artists is particularly evident
in their representations of local patron saints. Scenes from the lives of Christ
and Mary had their precedents in Byzantine and Romanesque art; and since
the types for these two figures had been created, the Gothic artists did little
more than modify them. This was not true, however, of the lives of the
patron saints, who had a part in every phase of life. For these the artists had
only literary models. The stories of their lives had been collected by a
Ligurian bishop, Jacobus de Voragine, in the GOLDEN LEGEND, which became
the most popular book of the fourteenth and fifteenth centuries. Upon its
legends the painters and sculptors based the themes of their reliefs and
paintings. Each saint had his own attribute which always identified him,
thus rendering unnecessary the explanatory legends that existed in Byzantine
art, to distinguish the very similar knight saints, the Apostles, and the
Church Fathers, one from the other. St. George, for instance, has a dragon;
St. Anthony, a pig; St. Jerome, a lion; St. Peter, a key; St. Andrew, a cross;
and St. Paul, a sword. In the cases where the symbol is not used, a relief
representing his story is placed at the feet of the saint.

Thirteenth-century wrought-iron hinges. Doors of the Cathedral of Notre Dame of Paris.

In the cathedrals we find a few subjects taken from history, such as the Charlemagne legend or the Crusades. But the history of the world always centers in some sense in the life of Christ or His teachings. Some of the sculptures are doubtless portraits of royal personages, which only rarely were introduced into the cathedrals. Often we find on the tombs the portraits of princes and prelates.

Miniatures of a French manuscript of the thirteenth century. Nuremberg Library.

Mary Magdalene with the jar of perfumed oil; St. Anne with the books of prophecy; St. Lawrence with the grill on which he was roasted; St. Margaret riding the dragon; St. Catherine with the wheel of her martyrdom; and St. Francis with the Rule of his Order. Miniatures from a French BOOK OF HOURS. Fourteenth century. Nuremberg Library.

Few Gothic mural paintings remain in France, and these few consist merely of imitations of architectural elements, sometimes ornamented with fleurs-de-lis. The scarcity of frescoes may be due to the fact that painting with tempera colors on wood had been perfected; and it may be due to the fact also that stained glass was serving in the same decorative function that fresco served in the earlier churches, which had greater wall spaces for paintings. Of the few religious and secular paintings that remain from that period some are excellent.

It is in the miniatures, which are numerous, that we can best study Gothic painting, which reached its peak in France during the reign of St. Louis. The principal center for this work was Paris, to which Dante pays a tribute in his *Inferno,* when he makes the most famous Italian miniature painter of his time praise the style of Paris. So richly illustrated were the manuscripts of the thirteenth century, that the university at Paris branded them as too luxurious and restricted the artists' use of colors.

The manuscripts of this period included short texts, psalters, evangelistaries, and prayer books, called BOOKS OF THE HOURS, rather than voluminous Bibles and sacramentaries like those of the Carolingian period. The Bibles were very small and sparsely illustrated, or they consisted wholly of pictures with no text. These latter were precursors of the so-called "Bibles of the poor" of the Renaissance.

The psalters with full-page illustrations were the books most characteristic of the reigns of Philip Augustus and St. Louis. These manuscripts, which were less unwieldy than the heavy Carolingian ones, were customarily carried around by the kings and nobles. The miniatures contained in them are of two types: one, an imitation of stained-glass windows, with the different scenes in circles which divide the page; the other, a single scene against an architectural background.

In the fourteenth and

French silver fountain for a dining table. Fourteenth century. Cleveland Museum of Art.

A French ironsmith of the fourteenth century. Metropolitan Museum of Art, New York.

fifteenth centuries, the BOOKS OF THE HOURS became most popular. They were bound with covers of enameled silver. Some of them have on the front page a portrait of the owner surrounded by his favorite saints or perhaps his suite. Also included in these books were calendars with illustrations depicting the activities of each month. The text of daily prayers followed, and there was an occasional full-page miniature. There were usually scenes from the life of the Virgin and from the lives of the saints, and sometimes scenes from the Old Testament, such as Bathsheba at her bath being spied upon by King David.

Another important manifestation of French Gothic painting is the stained glass windows of the cathedrals, which were marvelously decorative. Kings and prelates vied with one another in donating windows to the new churches. The shield of the donor was usually placed in the center of the border that he might receive recognition for his gift. As we have already noted, the first school of stained glass craftsmen was at St. Denis under Abbot Suger. The artists of Chartres seem to have learned the craft from the monks of St. Denis, and their school became the most important in France during the last half of the twelfth and the first part of the thirteenth century. The stained-glass windows of many other French cathedrals were probably the work of artists from Chartres, for they show themes with the typical treatment of Chartres.

During the reign of St. Louis, Paris became the center of stained glass workers in France, just as it was for miniature painters. At this time were made the great windows of the Sainte-Chapelle, through whose marvelously colored transparency the interior of the building is flooded with heavenly light.

Zephaniah and St. Thaddaeus. Stained glass windows from the Cathedral of Sens. Walters Art Galleries. Baltimore.

In the Gothic period, every artisan, carpenter, and ironworker, was an artist. The most trifling details were worked out by these modest craftsmen with meticulous care. Smaller articles, such as chests and caskets, were decorated with an emphasis on the structural elements, such as hinges, locks, metal bands; and even the vestments were adorned with designs related to the seams of the robes.

The old Romanesque enamel work of Limoges was superseded by the technique of painting in translucent enamel. It was discovered that the transparent colors took on a new brilliancy when applied to the polished surfaces of gold and silver. Ritual objects were often entirely enameled, or smaller plaques were enameled and soldered onto a larger object, as a chalice or a reliquary. The reliquaries sometimes had an architectural form, that of a church, for instance; and sometimes they were shaped like the relic they contained, like an arm, a head, or a hand.

Pentecost. Miniature from a French manuscript of the thirteenth century. Nuremberg Library.

Cistercian Monastery Church of St. Galgano, Tuscany. From here Cistercian monks went to teach the Gothic style to the lay architects of central Italy.

THE SPREAD OF GOTHIC ART

SPAIN

IN THE THIRTEENTH CENTURY, when Gothic culture was beginning to spread, Spain had two alternatives: either to throw herself into the arms of France and adopt French culture wholeheartedly, or to remain forever contaminated with Islamic art and civilization. She chose the former and it was the more prudent course. Only in this way could she develop as a Christian country, since the Moors were still a serious menace on the Peninsula. Nowhere has Gothic art been clothed in so pure a form and so completely adapted to the world of the spirit as in Spain. From end to end, the Peninsula came to be covered with monuments comparable to the finest Gothic creations of France. The Cathedrals of León, Burgos, and Toledo rival those of Amiens, Paris, and Chartres. The new style lost nothing either in spirit or in expressiveness when it crossed the Pyrenees. In Castile, especially, it acquired a splendor and magnificence which served to enhance it.

Façade of the Cathedral at León.

- So thoroughly did the Spanish people assimilate the style that we find it used everywhere: in rural churches, private houses, palaces, and castles, until the middle of the sixteenth century, when it was replaced by Renaissance art. Moreover, the Gothic style never ceased developing in Spain; and there it never remained aloof from the great international movement in art. The boldest innovations of the Flemish and Rhenish schools were adopted and always transformed into something characteristically Spanish. Not only in the thirteenth and fourteenth centuries did Spain profit by these foreign influences. In the fifteenth century also she adapted to her use the newer and more complicated moldings and ornamental features of the Flamboyant Gothic art of Flanders and Germany.

The rapid introduction and thorough acceptation of the Gothic style in Spain was greatly helped by the receptivity of the nobility and higher clergy to all new ideas and forms, and by their cordial reception of foreign architects, gentlemen, nobles, and travelers, from whom they gladly learned. Before undertaking the construction of a cathedral, a bishop might spend years in travel to study buildings in other countries. The kings often contracted marriage alliances with foreign princesses, who brought with them retinues of nobles and prelates who infused a new spirit into the nation. Foreign architects and builders were summoned to Spain to construct buildings that would rival the finest in the countries from which their creators came. From each important structure the new style spread, until the master builders of Spain finally learned to avail themselves of the Gothic forms without the aid of foreigners.

The Gothic influence also came into Spain through the Cistercian monks. We have already spoken of the influence of Provence over the monasteries in Spain. Early in the thirteenth century, great abbeys had been built and

Relief from the tympanum of the north portal of the Cathedral of Burgos.

some of their abbots had come from Provence. We know, too, of the close relations of the Counts of Barcelona with Provence and Languedoc, and the intimacy of the Catalan bishops with those of Narbonne. It is interesting to note that a number of Spanish Gothic cathedrals are even older and larger than some of the most famous Gothic churches of France.

The Cathedrals of Ávila, Siguena, and Ciudad-Rodrigo in Castile belong to the transition period and may be called Cistercian monuments, as they were started before the Gothic scheme was perfected. Their plans and walls are of the Cistercian Romanesque type; and only the vaults are Gothic.

The Cathedral of León is the first typical example of the imported Gothic style. Its presence in the heart of Spain is easily explained by the fact that its construction started immediately after the marriage of Alfonso VIII to a Plantagenet princess of Normandy. The building is a magnificent copy of the Cathedral of Amiens, though somewhat smaller in size. Having been neither attacked by revolutionary mobs nor spoiled by Renaissance embellishments, the Cathedral of León is perhaps the most homogeneous Gothic cathedral in the world.

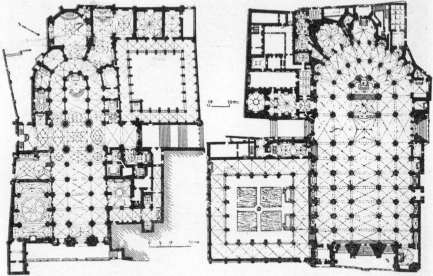

Plans of the Cathedrals of Burgos and Toledo.

The present Cathedral of Burgos was founded by its bishop, Don Mauricio. At the beginning of the thirteenth century he had been sent to Swabia to bring back Beatrice, the affianced wife of King Ferdinand III. On his long journey through France and Germany he no doubt saw many Gothic cathedrals in the process of construction. These inspired him with a desire to replace the old Cathedral of Burgos with a monument more worthy of being the leading church of Castile. In 1221 the cornerstone of the new building was laid; and when Bishop Mauricio died in 1238 the work on the apse was near enough to completion for him to be buried in the new cathedral. The plan is not unusual; it is composed of a nave, two aisles, a transept, and an apse with ambulatory and apsidal chapels.

The Cathedral of Toledo in its plan and arrangement has certain peculiarities which seem to show that its builder was of a more independent spirit than most of the architects who came from beyond the Pyrenees. It may be the work of a Spaniard; but our knowledge of him is limited to the fact that his name was Petrus Petri (Pedro Perez) and that he was of good antecedents and repute, if we may believe the inscription in the cathedral. There has been much speculation about this Petrus Petri who displayed so much daring and originality in the Cathedral at Toledo. French scholars believe him to be Pierre de Corbie who, *inter se disputando,* drew in the *Album* of Villard de Honnecourt the plan of an apse very similar to that of the cathedral in Spain. Spanish scholars on the other hand prefer to think of this master who planned the most highly esteemed monument of their land as a native architect. Unlike the churches of León and Burgos

Star-ribbed vault over the crossing. Burgos Cathedral.

which have slender piers and external buttresses, the piers of Toledo are
thick and massive, and the buttresses are hardly noticeable. It does not seem
that Petrus was familiar with the great French invention of the Gothic style
—the flying buttresses to counteract the thrust of the vaults. At any rate, if
he was familiar with it, he was not enthusiastic about it; and this leads us
to believe he was a Spaniard.

Seville has one of the most unusual cathedrals of Spain. It was begun in
1402, to take the place of an old Christianized mosque which was falling
into ruin. The resolution of the cathedral chapter was to build it so well
and in such a manner that there should never be another equal to it, even
though posterity might think them mad. It is very seldom today that directors ask their executives to be progressive to the point of madness. In its
details, the cathedral is French Gothic, but its arrangement is quite original.
It has a nave and four aisles flanked on each side by chapels, which amount
to a nave and six aisles.

In Aragon and Catalonia, the Gothic style takes on a somewhat different
character. Since the climate there is less severe than in central Spain, the

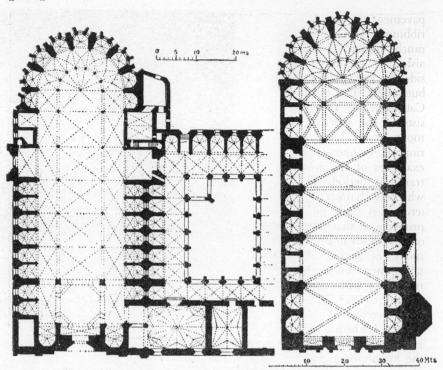

Plans of the Cathedrals of Barcelona and Gerona.

steep roofs habitual in those regions are not required. Flat roofs instead cover the churches, and the spaces between the vaults and the roof are filled with concrete and rubble. Buttresses are reduced to insignificance, and the thrust of the vaults is withstood by the heavy interior walls separating the chapels. In Aragon the transitional buildings were executed in accordance with the well established traditions of the Cistercian monks. The Cathedral of Lérida is a masterpiece of this phase of development. In it we find all the grace and delicacy of ornamentation prevalent during the last years of the Romanesque period. In plan it consists of a nave and two aisles with a dome above the crossing. The main entrance is approached through a cloister which forms a kind of spacious narthex. This great portico was open to afford a fine view from the hilltop on which the cathedral stood, down the steep slope and over the plain toward the city.

The Cathedral of Tarragona is another semi-Cistercian building which, however, was overtaken by the Gothic style. The apse is covered with a semi-dome without ribs, and it has no ambulatory. There is an octagonal tower over the crossing such as is characteristic of the great monastic churches of the Romanesque period. Heavy engaged shafts carry down to the pavement the line of the vault ribbings. The nave, which is much higher than the two aisles, is supported on both sides by very plain rectangular buttresses. The beauty of the Cathedral of Tarragona consists in the sobriety and harmony of the lines in its interior. It is one of the finest examples of the work of the transition period. The cloister, which is characteristically Cistercian, is built on the same principle as that of the Abbey of Fontfroide in Provence. The monks of Santas Creus, an establishment under Fontfroide, may have furnished the plans for the cloister and may have even directed the work.

Polychromed ceiling of a Catalan castle.

The Cathedral of Barcelona is the best Gothic building of the kingdom of Aragon. It is also the one in which the style has been most completely nationalized. It consists of a nave, two aisles, and a narrow ambulatory about the apse, which appears to have been inspired by that of the Cathedral of Narbonne. Other Gothic forms, however, are applied with great originality. The crossing is not marked by a dome or tower, and the transept is short and not emphasized, though there are two heavy towers, one over each arm. The aisles are almost as high as the nave, but the chapels which flank the aisles are low, and above them are galleries. A dim light filters into the nave through windows level with the galleries. This subdued lighting contrasts strongly with the illumination of the churches of Castile, where the brightness is almost excessive.

The Cathedral of Gerona has an ambulatory very similar to that of Barcelona, but on a somewhat smaller scale. It is evident that the canons of Gerona planned to make a smaller copy of this larger cathedral. When, however, the imitation became very apparent, the architect, Guillem Bofill, decided to abandon the two side aisles which had already been indicated in the ambulatory and to cover the nave with a single vault, the widest Gothic nave ever covered by a stone vaulting. Before adopting this proposition, the chapter called a consultation of the best-known architects of the country and some from as far away as Narbonne. Seven were in favor of going on

Detail of an altarpiece presented by Don Pedro Lopez de Ayala to a church of his domain. The Art Institute of Chicago.

with the original plan which seemed perfectly safe, but five voted to adopt Bofill's more daring plan. The bishop and chapter finally agreed to support Bofill in his adventure. Good for the executives!

In Palma de Mallorca the Cathedral presents all the features of Gothic architecture. The columns between the nave and aisles are tall and slender. There is no gallery above the low chapels, and the buttresses, instead of being on the inside as at Barcelona, appear on the exterior of the building. From the sea the cathedral looks like a giant boat capsized.

We have noted the stylistic differences between the cathedrals of central Spain and those of the territory subject to Aragon. The latter were the work of lay architects and of the people. A greater unity exists in monastic buildings, although they, too, were influenced to some extent by the artistic currents which manifested themselves in the great cathedrals.

In the middle of the thirteenth century new religious orders began to appear. The Franciscans and Dominicans, although they did not have the political power of the Benedictine Cistercians, built many convents on the Peninsula, in the cities rather than in remote spots. From this time on, the skylines of the large cities all over Europe began to be modified by the great silhouetted towers of the gigantic Franciscan and Dominican convents. There were at least two for each town, one for the men and one for the women of each order.

Turning to the civil and military architecture of the Gothic period, we note the same differences in the styles of central and eastern Spain. In the central region the civil structures often reflect Arabic influences. Castile is in truth a "land of castles." Every conquest the Christian kings made in neighboring Arabic lands had to be strengthened with a new line of castles along the boundary. Thus, several lines of fortresses of formidable character

Catalan altarpiece. By the Master of St. George. The Art Institute of Chicago.

The Doge's Palace, Venice.

were built. Many of them are deserted today, but even in their present ruined state they are imposing. It is evident that Moorish architects and Moorish workmen were employed in this work.

We have explained the enthusiastic reception of the Gothic in Spain in the middle of the thirteenth century, and the eagerness to adopt the most advanced European methods to maintain Christian integrity against the Arabs. By the middle of the fourteenth century the Christian kingdoms of Spain had very little to fear from the Moors. Aragon had conquered them as far as Almeria, and Castile as far as Algeciras or Gibraltar. Comparatively safe now, the Christians could afford to flirt with Moorish ideas, and they began to manifest a taste for Moorish customs and art. Peter the Cruel of Castile lived in Seville like a Moorish king in an alcazar. At this time there began to be developed the type of architecture called Moresque, or Morisco, which employed Moorish tiles, woodcarving, and metalwork, in buildings whose general plan was still purely Christian Gothic.

The Aragon Confederacy, with lands on the Mediterranean shores, in the fourteenth century strengthened its relations with Italy. The trade between Barcelona and Valencia and the Italian ports introduced into Italy the Hispano-Moresque ware, which was eventually imitated in Tuscany. From Italy there came to Aragon not only objects of art, but also manners of living. The Catalan cities built municipal palaces that rivaled the ones of

Palazzo Pisani. Thirteenth century. Venice.

Florence, Siena, and Pisa. Porticoes, or loggias, were built in Aragon for trading; and besides these open marts, the Catalan cities built Seamen's Exchanges. Here the charters and contracts were drawn up and the maritime laws (Consulat de Mar) were administered. Three of these exchanges are still in an excellent state of preservation: those of Valencia, Mallorca, and Perpignan. Of those in Barcelona and Saragossa only the main halls remain, and these are engulfed in modern Neoclassic structures. A seamen's exchange consisted of a large hall without seats, like a stock exchange, and of rooms that served for courts and offices.

The ceilings of many of the buildings of eastern Spain were formed by an ingenious and efficient system. They were made of flat parallel beams supported on arches thrown across from opposite walls. The arches and beams were decorated in bright colors and gave the room a very gay appear-

Spire over the crossing. Cathedral of Milan.

ance, contrasted with the greater somberness of the Gothic vault coverings in more northern lands.

What we have said of the influences on architecture holds true of sculpture as well. During the thirteenth century sculptors trained in the Gothic style came to Spain to decorate the portals of cathedrals; but not many were good, since it was hard to persuade masters to leave their native lands. The statues of the portals of León and Burgos are certainly works by the hands of French sculptors. In the fourteenth century, local sculptors entirely supplanted the foreigners and produced work much inferior. We notice in

Interior of the Upper Church of St. Francis at Assisi.

Aragon and Catalonia the same preference for Italian taste in sculpture that we found in architecture. Certain marble-carvers in Pisa appear to have gone to Barcelona at the beginning of the fourteenth century, and from this time on, the taste for French style in Catalonia is diverted to the Italian. As a whole, Spain did not produce anything in Gothic sculpture comparable to what she had produced in the Romanesque.

Painting in the thirteenth century is represented only by miniature work; there is no fresco painting. The most outstanding examples of the illumination of this time come from the royal scriptorium of King Alfonso the Wise, of Castile. He had a real love of learning and surrounded himself with great scholars—Moorish, Jewish, French, and Italian. The head of the scriptorium, *escribano mayor,* was a Spaniard, Martin Perez de Maqueda, whose assistant scribes were also natives, but their work reflects the French style. Alphonso was interested in the scholarship of all nations, but especially in

Façade of the Cathedral of Siena, in Tuscany.

that of the Moors and the Jews. In translating the Oriental works of science, he applied the interpretations of a Western mind. He was fond of Provençal music and poetry and copied their style. The miniatures of the many manuscripts from the royal scriptorium reflect that combination of Oriental and French traits, with a balance in favor of the French.

In the eastern kingdom of Aragon there was nothing so spectacular as the book illuminations made in Castile under Alfonso the Wise. On the other hand, we find here what is not available in Castile, a considerable number of paintings on wood that were preserved along with innumerable documents in the archives. So we are able to study the evolution of painting in Aragon in a way that has very seldom been possible in the study of other schools of Art of the Middle Ages. The principal center of painting in eastern Spain seems to have been Barcelona. Here, during the thirteenth century, France furnished the model for painting; and in the fourteenth century, Italy, especially Siena, influenced the style.

ITALY

For a long time the Italian people were thought to be less receptive to the Gothic style than any other people in Europe. Opinions have changed, however, in recent years, since Italian scholars have come to possess more exact information concerning the monuments of their country. First, there was found evidence of the influence exerted by the Cistercian monks of Fossanuova, Vercelli, and San Galgano on the medieval structures of northern and central Italy. Next, it was realized how large a part was taken by

Façade of the Cathedral of Orvieto in central Italy.

French architects in southern Italy under the Swabian emperors and the Neapolitan dynasty of Anjou. The final importation of Gothic forms into Italy was made in the fifteenth century, when the royal family of Aragon regained dominion over Naples and Sicily. Architects from Catalonia and Mallorca then went to these two southern kingdoms as they would have

The Church of the Holy Thorn at Pisa.

gone to the provinces of their own country; and in Palermo and Naples, painters and sculptors from Valencia executed many commissions for Spanish bishops and nobles residing there.

In our study of the various manifestations of Gothic art in Italy, we shall begin with Venice and continue south through Lombardy and Tuscany to southern Italy. The finest Venetian Gothic monument is the Palace of the Doges, beside St. Mark's Cathedral. It looks like a great marble cube gilded by the sun. The arcades on the street and second floor extend around three sides of the building and form its most prominent decoration. Above them the walls rise straight and plain, inlaid with small slabs of rose and white marble and pierced by large arched windows. Edging the roof is a parapet of Oriental crestings. The famous Porta della Carta, so called because on it were hung the placards announcing the decrees of the government, connected the palace with the cathedral. The courts and some of the additions to the façade are in the Renaissance style, which blends harmoniously with the general Gothic scheme of the building.

From the time of the ninth century, when the Doge Particiaco built the first palace, the residence of the chief magistrate of the Republic has stood on this same spot. It was twice burned and did not take its present form until its restoration by Venetian architects in the fourteenth century. The work took several generations and was directed by a number of different architects, some of whose names have come down to us.

There are several private palaces in Venice which are of the same period. The design of their façades, with balconies and arcaded windows, is that of the Byzantine palace, but the details are Gothic. Among these palaces of Gothic-Byzantine style, we might mention the Contarini, Giustiani, Pisani, Dandolo, and Foscari. There are also in Venice many churches which combine Gothic and Byzantine ideas.

In Lombardy the most important architectural achievement in the Gothic is the Cathedral of Milan, which is built for the most part of marble. It is a late work; and its Gothic style excited surprise at the time

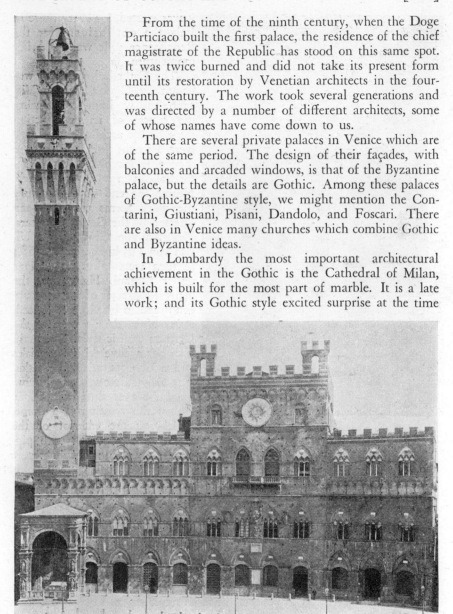

Palazzo Pubblico, or City Hall, Siena.

Palace of the Podestà, governor of the city of Florence, Tuscany.

it was erected, for everywhere in Italy the enthusiasm for the Renaissance style was gathering momentum.

The Cathedral of Milan was begun by Gian Galeazzo Visconti, and we know that during the course of its construction some of the architects in charge were French; for instance, the *ingegnere* (architect) of the cathedral in 1388 was French. Nearer the end of the century the work seems to have been directed by the German masters, Heinrich von Gmund and Ulrich von Fussingen. Their places in turn were taken by Italians under Organi. However, the general character of the structure continued to be Gothic; indeed, many of its details were of the German Gothic style. The main plan has a nave with four aisles and a transept with two aisles. The aisles, although of the same height, are of different widths. Above the crossing is a dome, which on the exterior of the cathedral is crowned with pinnacles and spires. The buttresses, too, are surmounted with pinnacles culminating in statues. The cathedral is a late manifestation of the Gothic spirit, carried out with little enthusiasm or faith. The colossal size of the structure and the great individuality of all its details make it so impressive that no cathedral in Europe can compare with it. Seen from a distance, or at night, when the monotony of its details is not noticeable, this white mountain of sculptured marble, with its myriad points rising toward heaven, produces in the beholder a deep feeling of awe.

Nothing like this great building exists elsewhere in Lombardy. It was an isolated phenomenon, a monument to the Visconti family, of the last of whom the *Chronicle* says, "while he lived he never stopped building." The Sforzas, on succeeding to the power in Milan, accepted the forms of the Renaissance. They completed, in a style decidedly Renaissance, the Carthusian Monastery of the Certosa di Pavia, begun by the Visconti in 1473.

Because of the deep-seated traditions of the Magistri Comacini, the Gothic forms hardly penetrated into the lake region of northern Lombardy. The same is true of Piedmont, where the country churches and numerous castles of this period, especially in the district of Montferrat, have few Gothic details. Strangely enough there is not a single Gothic monument in Turin.

In Tuscany only the walls of the church remain from the famous Cistercian Abbey of San Galgano. The vaulting which originally covered it has fallen, although the piers and the corbels on the walls enable us to trace something of its arrangement. Monks from this abbey directed the work on the Cathedral of Siena. This cathedral lacks the buttresses so characteristic of northern Gothic churches; and, instead of sculpture, bands of colored marble decorate the façade. Alternate light and dark bands also form a conspicuous feature of the decoration of the interior. An ingeniously constructed dome rises from the crossing, but the nave and aisles

Palazzo Sarracini. Fourteenth century. Siena.

are covered with Gothic ribbed vaults. In the construction, the general Gothic principles prevailed, while local secular artists of the country were responsible for the decoration. Among them were Andrea and Giovanni Pisano, and the latter's pupil, Arnolfo. At a later date the façade was further enriched by precious mosaics, which were done in the same marvelous colors that were used by the Italian painters of the first centuries of the Renaissance.

The Cathedral of Orvieto repeats many of the decorative features of the Siena cathedral. The general shape and appearance of the façades are very similar. Brightly colored mosaics distract the attention of the beholder from the structure as a whole. Sculptors who had learned from the Cistercians carried the Gothic vault through Italy. The arches of the cloister at the Campo Santo of Pisa are ornamented with Gothic openwork. The little Church of Santa Maria della Spina (Holy Thorn), also in Pisa, is another interesting example of the interpretation of Gothic art in Tuscany.

Cloth Merchants' Hall at Ypres. Destroyed in the World War in 1914.

A circumstance which furthered the spread of the Gothic style in Italy was the foundation and spread of the Franciscan and Dominican orders in the thirteenth century. As we have said, every town of any importance ought to have four convents, two for men and two for women. The principal house of the Franciscans was at Assisi, where the founder of the order was buried. The Church of San Francesco is one of the most curious Gothic monuments in Italy. It stands on the top of the hill, raised on a stout substructure over the burial place of the saint. There is a lower church, and an upper church which consists of a nave without aisles, a transept, and an apse. The thrusts of the vaults are counterbalanced by massive cylindrical piers, resembling towers, not unlike those of the Cathedral of Albi in Provence. The actual work seems to have been directed by two Italian masters; but since it was an international undertaking—the funds for its building were sent from every Christian land—various foreign influences crept in. It was built in a very few years, since it did not suffer the handicap of so many churches which had to stop work until sufficient funds were available to continue. The style necessarily had to be Gothic, the international style of the time.

The founder of the Dominican Order was buried in Bologna in a cathe dral of Gothic style dedicated to St. Petronio. This church was apparently intended to be much larger than it is, but it was never finished. Consequently we do not have any church of the Dominicans that is comparable to the church of the Franciscans at Assisi. The half-completed plan called for a nave, two aisles, and a transept with aisles. The work started at the façade and did not continue beyond the crossing of the nave.

In the free cities of Tuscany and Umbria we find great municipal palaces, which were usually built of blocks of rough stone. This gave them the air of fortresses, and they were crowned by high towers, from which the territory of the municipality could be surveyed. Such an edifice was called the palace of the Signoria; the largest is that of the Republic of Siena, which was built between the years 1289 and 1309. It occupies one entire side of the great semicircular piazza. Over its doors and windows is the double arch so characteristic of this city. On the lofty tower, more than three hundred feet high, is a superstructure bearing the arms of the Republic and containing the bells.

In Florence we find two buildings of this type. One is the palace of the Podesta, or captain of the Florentine army, and the other, that of the Signoria, or government, which stands at one end of a large square. Both are crowned by crenelated parapets and have high towers to house the bells that called the citizens to arms.

In the provinces of central Italy subject to the popes, the influence of Gothic art was felt less than elsewhere. At this time the popes were in Avignon, where they enjoyed both the art and the hospitality of France. During this time, the saddest in the history of Rome, a number of Gothic buildings were erected in the Eternal City, for example, the Church of Santa Maria della Minerva, which is entirely Gothic. We must not expect anything very original nor even very beautiful in most of these churches.

Besides the introduction of the French characteristic features

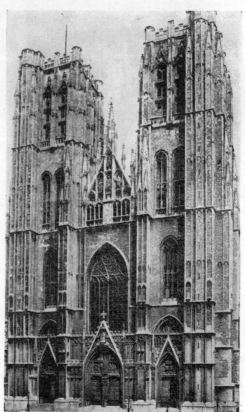

Church of St. Gudule, Brussels.

The Cathedral of Cologne.

of Gothic style by the monks of the reformed Cistercian order, there were other avenues for the Gothic influence, which were perhaps even more important. About the middle of the thirteenth century, southern Italy again acknowledged the suzerainty of the Holy Roman Empire. The heiress of the Norman kings of Sicily married a prince of Swabia, Frederick II, who by this marriage added to his domains the Norman kingdom of the two Sicilies. He made his home in southern Italy, spending most of his time in Apulia and Capitanata, his favorite provinces. In constant conflict with the Church, his northern neighbor, he hardly built or rebuilt a single church but devoted all his energies to fortresses and castles. He was responsible for the restoration of the Castle of Bari on the Adriatic, and for the rebuilding of the Castles of Syracuse and Augusta in Sicily, which originally had been constructed by the Byzantines.

In addition, Frederick II erected new castles on a plan which suggests French Gothic influence. Among these we might mention the Castle of Lucera, where the Emperor is said to have kept a harem and an Arab garrison which was greatly feared by the friends of the pope, we are told.

There was also the famous Castel del Monte, which is Gothic in construction. Its shape is hexagonal, and at each corner it has an octagonal tower for defense. The name of the architect who directed the work is unknown; but in the interior we see the structural techniques of Gothic architects. The vaults are perfect examples of the pointed style. The ribs carry the thrust of the vault to the corners and here they are re-enforced by pilaster strips. Over the doorway is an almost classical pediment. We shall see later how the first manifestations of a real interest in the old Greco-Roman art are to be found at the court of Frederick II. It seems undeniable that French architects were present in this strange court of a German emperor, whose tastes were like those of an Italian prince.

About the middle of the thirteenth century, southern Italy fell into the power of the House of Anjou, and from Naples a French court governed the country. There was a fierce struggle between Aragon, which claimed the kingdom of the two Sicilies through the marriage of Constance, the granddaughter of Frederick II, with Pedro of Aragon, and the French under Charles of Anjou, who had received Naples from the pope. But for two centuries Naples remained a French city. Charles took to Naples not only his court but also many French artists and architects, chief among whom was one Pierre d'Agincourt. Another French master, also named Pierre, worked on the Church of St. Maximino. The Gothic style continued to be employed in Naples during the fourteenth century, although it came later to lack both good method and good taste.

The two great castles of Naples, the Castel dell' Ovo and the Castel Nuovo, are fortresses originally constructed in the time of the Swabian

Interior of the Cathedral of Cologne.

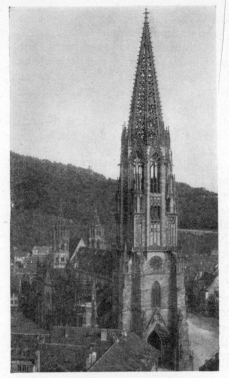

The Cathedral of Freiburg.

rulers, but portions of both date from the period of the Angevin kings. The Castel Nuovo, in particular, was almost entirely rebuilt by Charles of Anjou. It has the appearance of a *donjon,* or fortress, with high walls, barbicans, battlements, and circular towers which need only conical roofs to be taken for those of a French château like the old Louvre.

We now come to the last introduction of a foreign Gothic style into Italy by the kings of Aragon. Sicily was conquered by Pedro II, but it was separated from the kingdom of Aragon at the death of this monarch, who bequeathed it to his younger son. For a long time this branch of the royal family of Aragon maintained its independence, keeping weak political ties with the sovereigns of the House of Barcelona. But painters and architects continued to go to Sicily and constantly worked there in the Gothic manner that still predominated in their native land.

It is not strange, therefore, that we find Catalan and Valencian styles in Sicily, which maintained close relations with the two provinces during the fifteenth century. Many structures of Palermo and southern Italy which bear the marks of Catalan architecture are private palaces; and consequently, no data regarding them are to be found in the official records. However, the monuments speak for themselves. Not only the general lines, but even the details of the moldings and sculptural decorations are importations from Spain. The architects must have brought with them not only their own workmen, but also in many cases the carved materials, such as the typical Catalan Gothic capitals which we see in the Archiepiscopal Palace and the Palazzo Abbatelli at Palermo.

GERMANY

In Germany the Romanesque style resisted the invasion of the Gothic longer than in either Spain or Italy. Between 1261 and 1278 we find the first monument in the pointed style in process of building—the Abbey Church of Wimpfen im Thal. The master-builder was from Paris, according to the

Chronicle, and he built the church in the French style. Following this beginning, many churches were built in the French Gothic style, among them, St. Elisabeth of Marburg and the Liebfrauenkirche at Trèves. The general arrangement of the buildings as well as their structural and decorative features were adopted from the new style. The nave is usually flanked by two aisles; and there are a transept and an apse with ambulatory and chapels. Like the French Gothic churches, the G e r m a n have three portals; but a German variation is seen in the tower and spire which rise above the center of the main façade, as in the Cathedrals of Ulm and Freiburg. They may be reminiscent of the towers at the front of Carolingian churches.

The Cologne Cathedral is almost entirely French Gothic in style, although it is a truly national work of the German people, who continued to work on it almost down to our own time. It was completed only a little over a generation ago. An older church had stood on the same site, but a fire de-

The Carlsbrücke Tower in Prague.

stroyed it in 1248, and an entire new plan was drawn for its rebuilding in Gothic style. The work started with the apse, which was constructed by a certain Meister Gerard. The construction, however, progressed so slowly that he was succeeded about 1330 by one Arnold, whose son in turn directed the building operations. The fact that the choir was not consecrated until 1322 gives some idea of how slowly the work of building progressed. There was a long interruption from the sixteenth until the nineteenth century. Work was recommenced in 1817 and carried to completion in 1880. The cathedral, one of the largest in the world, is about four hundred and forty feet long, with transepts over two hundred and eighty feet in length.

Schöne Brunnen in Nuremberg.

Its plan is similar to that of Amiens, although at Cologne there are four aisles instead of two as in the French cathedral. The nave might appear too long and narrow if it were not for the splendid decorative effect of its clustered piers, its ribbed vaultings, and the great profusion of moldings which carry the eye upward and away from the limitations of space below. The exterior is elaborate with pinnacles and spires. The finest features of all, however, are the two towers which rise, one from either side of the façade. They serve as a landmark for many miles around the city, and their silhouettes are often shrouded in the mist which descends over the cities of the Rhine, giving to the cathedral a mysterious etherealness. The façade seems to be subordinated as a kind of base to its overshadowing towers, which are of different heights, one five hundred and twelve feet high and the other about four hundred and eighty feet. The portals, so important at Amiens and Chartres, are thus dwarfed into comparative unimportance in spite of their profuse decoration.

We also find evidences of French Gothic influence in some of the famous castles along the Rhine. They usually stand on a precipitous hill overlooking the river and are surrounded by heavily battlemented walls. The castle itself, with high square towers, frequently has a little church at one side. The fortress at Marienburg in Prussia, the residence of the Grand Master of the Teutonic Order, was begun in the thirteenth century in the pointed French style and was added to many times. The original nucleus of the building was a massive castle, built around a central court and surrounded by a moat, over which a chapel projected. Among later additions were a wing for the accommodation of guests, a great hall, and a palace for its Grand Master.

During the thirteenth and fourteenth centuries the free cities of the Rhine and of central Germany, moved by local patriotism, constructed many monumental gates which are still found in these cities. They are high steep-roofed towers with arched openings on the ground level. These gates originally served as entrances to the cities; but as the cities spread, buildings grew up around them. The gate-towers of Freiburg, for instance, dominate busy thoroughfares.

There was great rivalry among German cities for the finest town hall. A *Rathaus,* as it was called, contained at first only a few rooms: one for public meetings, one for the court of justice, and one for executing contracts. Later, as the municipalities grew, other apartments were needed for offices and administrative purposes.

Numerous guildhalls were constructed of wood, tall and narrow, and decorated with the carved and painted emblems of the guilds. There were also many statues of warriors, of the Virtues, and of Justice, with their attributes skilfully depicted. Some German cities still preserve entire sections that have wooden guild houses with the medieval shops of artisans, survivals from the communal life of the Gothic age.

The high façades of these German dwellings usually terminate in a gable. Very often the lower part of the house

The Markt Brunnen in Braunschweig.

is of stone, and where the wall space permits, it is decorated with frescoes from the medieval repertory. Amidst Latin couplets and popular verses in Gothic characters, we find lively representations of vices and virtues, of saints and prophets, with scenes from romances indiscriminately interspersed. Houses entirely of wood have rich adornments of carvings; arcades, pilasters, doors, and windows are bordered with ornamental motifs. Balconies with beautifully carved corbels and railings project over the streets. The emblems of the shops hang out in front, supported by elaborate wrought-iron brackets.

The arrangement of a medieval burgher's house, whether in Cologne, Nuremberg, or Lübeck, is always more or less the same. Back of the part facing on the street is a court with façades similar to the main one, but simpler. The lower floor is composed of the shop, a small back room, and a workshop opening onto the court. The second story, reached by means of

Marienburg, the castle of the Master of the Teutonic Knights.

a small stairway, consists of a kitchen and two bedrooms, one on the street side and the other facing the court. The servants and apprentices occupied the attic rooms, or the stories under the roof, which were poorly lighted by dormer windows.

A characteristic feature of the medieval town was the fountain in the center of the square. It was usually decorated with statues of popular characters from local folklore, local heroes, or even Bible characters. The "Schöne Brunnen" at Nuremberg is a fine example of these fountains, with its lace-like design of Gothic pinnacles and its niches with figures. Meister Heinrich der Balier built it between the years 1385 and 1396. The painted figures on these fountains were clad in the colored garments of the time, and their faces were charming in their frank and sincere expressions. The ideal of beauty seems to have been naïveté and gentle amiability, as set forth in the poems of the Minnesingers.

Beyond the Rhine and the Alps, Gothic art traveled to Bohemia, Poland, and Scandinavia, which was then on the edge of the civilized world. In Bohemia we might mention the Cathedral of Prague, an unusual example of the French Gothic, supposed to have been planned by an architect from Arras. The roof of the nave is raised very high above the aisles, and its thrust is counterbalanced by a remarkably spectacular arrangement of flying buttresses placed one above the other. Poland's principal Gothic buildings date from near the end of the Gothic development, that is, about the end of the fifteenth century.

In the north, on the shores of the Baltic Sea, Gothic art was victorious among the barbarians only recently converted to Christian ideals. To Uppsala, Etienne de Bonneuil, who had been one of the master-builders of France, took the style when he became architect of the cathedral there. In 1287 he went with ten other builders to Sweden to direct this work. It was not until a hundred and fifty years later, in 1435, that the church was sufficiently near completion to be consecrated, and this accounts for the numerous details in German style which crept in. In all Scandinavian countries German brick construction is predominant.

BELGIUM AND HOLLAND

In Belgium, the Cathedral of Antwerp is the most ambitiously planned of all Gothic churches. It has a nave with six side aisles; and the tower, the tallest and most beautiful in Belgium, rises from the right side of the façade to a height of four hundred feet. Its mate planned for the left side was never completed and serves as a foil for the awe-inspiring size of the other. The building itself, however, suffers from the lack of symmetry. The cathedral apse was begun by Jean Appelmans in 1352, and work on the building continued until the end of the fifteenth century.

The Cathedral of Brussels and the Churches of Notre Dame and St. Sauveur at Bruges, show a lack of assimilation of the Gothic style. The tower of St. Sauveur is almost typically Romanesque. In their interior treatment, however, these churches are purely French Gothic. The vaulting ribs are carried down the clustered piers in typical style. There are not many examples of this arrangement in Belgium; plain columns soon took the place of clustered piers. A new spirit came into sculpture which assumed a greater degree of gaiety and cheerfulness in keeping with the character of the Flemish and the Dutch. The fourteenth century marked the loss of rigidity and severity typical of the French Gothic.

The Council Room of the Teutonic Order at Marienburg.

Prophets holding Apostles. At the main portal of the Cathedral of Bamberg.

The most important buildings by this time were of a civic character. As in Germany, they consisted of municipal buildings and guildhalls. Perhaps the finest of these in the Low Countries was the Cloth Hall at Ypres. The plain expanse of its steep roof rose above three profusely arcaded and traceried stories and was surmounted by a heavy square tower with crocketed pinnacles at the corners. The building took from 1200 to 1304 to complete. Weaving was the principal industry of the Low Countries, and this Cloth Hall served as the market to which merchants came from great distances to buy the renowned work of the Flemish looms. Two other cloth markets, far less pretentious than the one at Ypres, were built at Bruges.

The *hôtels de ville* (city halls) of Brussels, Louvain, Bruges, and many of the smaller towns were built on approximately the same plan. Many of them, especially those of the smaller towns, were out of all proportion to the size of the town itself. The usual city hall was a large building several stories high, with a portico extending across the front, which served as a market. A square belfry surmounted the building from which the alarm was rung in times of danger. Sometimes the hôtel de ville was built around a court, but usually it was a solid rectangular

building, with a single roof surmounted by a tower.

In Holland, Gothic art
spread from Tournai, which
has four French Gothic churches of the thirteenth century. In
both Belgium and Holland are
found many private houses of
Gothic style; and, as in Germany, some cities have retained
entire medieval streets which
the centuries have left unchanged. This is true of Bruges,
which was a remarkable center
of commercial activity during
the fifteenth century when her
rich merchants were generous
patrons of the arts. We shall
see in the next chapter how important a part this city took in
forming and spreading the late
Gothic style. Her medieval
streets had long rows of houses
typically Gothic in the style
of the Low Countries, with

Detail of a bronze baptismal font at Goslar.

stepped gable roofs. Painters give us an excellent idea of the luxurious interiors of these Flemish homes, with their elegant furniture, their rich
carpets, and tapestries. The rooms were lighted with large windows of
stained glass, and the woodwork was enriched with Gothic carving.

ENGLAND

In England the Cistercians helped to popularize the pointed style. They
built many fine abbeys there, beginning in 1128 with Waverley Abbey, which
we have already mentioned. Most of their buildings were destroyed during
the Reformation in the sixteenth century, and, unfortunately, only romantic
ruins are left to exemplify the style.

In the late twelfth century the French architect, William of Sens, came
to England to aid in the reconstruction of the Cathedral of Canterbury, and
he brought the early austere Gothic style of the Cathedral of Sens. Westminster Abbey, begun in 1245, was constructed in the best French style. The
independent spirit of the English people resisted this kind of importation,
and even in this, the most French of the English cathedrals, there persists a
certain British feeling.

The English Gothic, which crystallized at the end of the thirteenth cen-

Lincoln Cathedral.

tury, is rather modest in ornament and sculpture. The elegance of the English is due in large measure to the high pointed spires and the long, narrow nave, much longer than the French and narrow in proportion to its length. The English made many additions to their buildings, with little attempt at unity of style. Few of the larger churches are homogeneous. The styles of several periods are included in most of them.

The cathedrals in England were usually well endowed and were built on charming sites with extensive grounds. This setting suggested a handling different from that of the city-built French cathedrals. Since they were enhanced by their beautiful garden surroundings, they did not need to rise to the heights and grandeur of those across the Channel. There the cathedral was a symbol of power and majesty to the countless houses huddled against its very walls.

It is interesting to compare the Cathedrals of Amiens and Salisbury, which were begun in the same year, 1220, and which represent the first phase of the fully developed Gothic in France and England respectively. The two are about the same in length, but the English church has only half the height of the French. Its walls are pierced by simple lancets, and the openings are fewer and less elaborate than those of Amiens. What it loses in decorativeness is offset by the interesting arrangement of the smaller masses of the building and the beauty of the central tower. The west

Salisbury Cathedral as seen from the air.

façade is known as a "screen front," which in English churches takes the place of the French monumental portals. The English flat screen façade is decorated with rows of carved figures, giving an effect far less varied and exciting than the French front with its porches where light and shade play over apertures of different depth, statues, moldings, and tracery.

The Early English Gothic style lasted in England throughout most of

Interior of Lincoln Cathedral. View from the Angel Choir.

the thirteenth century. A new style developing out of this continued to grow in the fourteenth century and was characterized by the employment of richer architectural membering and sculpture, in the attempt to break

Angel Choir of Lincoln Cathedral. In Decorated style.

the dryness of the earlier style. This second English Gothic style is called
Decorated.

Lincoln Cathedral in its vaulting, has the multiple ribs which came to
be a distinguishing characteristic of the English Gothic. Its Angel Choir,
built between 1255 and 1280, is a fine example of the Decorated style. The
beautiful lantern verges on a later development, the Flowing style, which
is seen on the upper stories of the two west towers. The cathedral has a
very striking situation on a high hill above the town; but its appearance
is now less impressive than it was before it lost its three spires, the central
one of which, it is said, reached a height of 525 feet and was the highest
of all medieval towers.

Meanwhile at Gloucester the third of the English styles was being developed. In the years following 1331, the interior of the south transept of
the Norman Abbey Church, which later became the cathedral, was re-
decorated with elaborate carved panels. Arranged in vertical lines, these
panels cover the entire wall surface. From this the new style gets its name,
Perpendicular. The choir was subsequently rebuilt in Perpendicular style;
and it is interesting to note that the Norman ambulatory and apsidal
chapels were destroyed to make way for a square end pierced by a magnificent east window. A beautiful tower, perhaps the finest in England, was
raised over the crossing and was decorated with the same type of panel
work. From Gloucester the style spread all over the island and became the
characteristic style of the fifteenth and sixteenth centuries.

A new type of vaulting also characterizes the Perpendicular style. The

Interior of Gloucester Cathedral, showing fan vaulting of the Perpendicular style.

ribs which formerly divided the vault into four, six, or eight divisions, now become a complicated network which confuses the eye. Sometimes they spread out fanwise from the supporting columns. This form when well handled is beautiful and stately. Such fan vaulting can be seen in King's College Chapel, Cambridge. Sometimes intricate circular bands of tracery are accented at the center with a delicately carved boss into which the radial lines seem to converge; sometimes the patterning is more simple and produces merely a weblike appearance.

Even these innovations did not satisfy the English builders. In daring work they pushed forward the ribbings from the transverse arches and gave the vault the appearance of resting on pendants. Such a vault has to be cut out of stone in all its details; but it is not considered a Gothic vault, since it is merely decorative and does not perform a structural function.

During all this time, charming parish churches and private residences of the Perpendicular style were being built in England. Many are roofed with carved open trusses and paneling, effectively managed in as monumental a form as the trusswork in civil buildings.

The English house differs a great deal in plan from the Continental, as a result of its origin. In its rude beginnings it was a simple roofed hall with a hearth. With increasing wealth, the various functions of the household were given separate compartments. The lord and lady had private apartments (the term drawing-room comes from withdrawing room, a place apart from the hall which was used by retainers and servants). The *bower* (boudoir) was added for the lady. As ideas of comfort and manners improved, the kitchen and dining room, then the servants' quarters, were built as separate parts of the house. The result is that the hall in a modern house has retained only its function as an entrance and is commonly a mere passageway. In Gothic times it still had considerable dignity.

We have only a few paintings on wood of the Gothic time in England, but there is extant a considerable number of illustrated books in the style of illumination peculiar to Gothic England. The colors are lighter and more refined than those of the French and the Italians of the same period. We find the same unobtrusive colors in the few stained-glass windows which escaped destruction by the Puritan reformers.

There are no notable examples of medieval English architectural sculpture, except perhaps the figures on the façade of the Cathedral at Wells. Here flourished a strong local school of sculpture. Some tombs with admirable examples of the sculpture of this period are still in existence, as, for instance, the fine recumbent royal figures in gilded bronze in Westminster Abbey. During the fourteenth century a school of artists who carved in alabaster produced much interesting work, which was eagerly bought by the wealthy art patrons. The range of subjects found in these alabasters seems to be limited to a few religious themes as the Ascension and the Coronation of the Virgin. English embroidery was in great demand during this period, and examples of it are still to be seen among the treasures of cathedrals on the Continent.

CYPRUS AND THE NEAR EAST

We have spoken of the establishment of the Frankish Kingdom at Jerusalem as a result of the Crusades, and of the Romanesque character of the first buildings of the Crusaders. At the time of the development of the Gothic style in Europe and its spread to the Holy Land, Jerusalem was in a precarious situation and was threatened by a Moslem attack. In spite of the danger, however, some excellent Gothic architecture was created in Jerusalem, remains of which are still found. There are two Gothic cathedrals in Palestine: one at Sebaste, or Samaria, where tradition places the tomb of John the Baptist; and the other at Tortosa near the sea. There

Trinity College, Oxford. Perpendicular style.

appears to have been also a Gothic church at St. Jean d'Acre, which was built when this city was the last one left in the hands of the Crusaders. The name of its French architect is known to be Corneille de Bruyn. When Sultan Kalaum captured the city, he carried away with him as a trophy one of the doors of this church, and it can still be seen on his tomb at Cairo.

There are many Crusaders' castles in Palestine, which were built to defend the Frankish Kingdom and were used by the Templars in their desperate resistance against the Moslems. The largest one, the famous Krak des Chevaliers, has ramparts on different levels, approached by ramps. Probably from a strategic point of view it was the most important of all the castles erected in this part of the world during that period.

The Lusignans, the noble and devout French family who governed Cyprus, erected on the island two cathedrals that vie with the largest of France: one at Famagusta, and the other at Nicosia, seat of the archbishop. The latter was built in 1193, under the direction of a French architect.

Miniature from an English manuscript of the fourteenth
century. British Museum.

Hooded figures on the tomb of Marguerite of Bourbon. Church of Brou in Burgundy.

FLAMBOYANT GOTHIC

THE FIFTEENTH CENTURY for all Europe was a period of adventure, discovery, and exploration. New mechanical devices, notably the printing press, were invented; new geographical conquests, like the voyages to the Far East and the preliminary sailings to America as far as the Azores, were accomplished; a new spirit was infused into intellectual life. These forces were plainly manifested in Milan, Florence, and Naples, where an effort was made in a spectacular way toward a new kind of culture, which happened to take the form of a "return to the antique." In the next volume, we shall see the attempts of the Medicis, the Viscontis, and Alfonso of Aragon to live in a freer and more civilized way than did their ancestors.

Books are full of descriptions of their Courts at Rome, Naples, Milan, and at Florence, where the circle of the Medicis deserves the name of Court. There the Renaissance had its beginning. We are quite satisfied that it started in Italy in the fourteenth century, and by the fifteenth century

Porch in Flamboyant style. Cathedral of Albi, Provence.

it was already in full swing. However, we generally ignore the fact that the same spirit of discovery and the same endeavor to readjust life to the new intellectual surroundings was made also in the more western and northern countries of Europe. The difference was that instead of taking a definite turn toward the Roman and Greek art and culture, France, Spain, and England developed as their national style the Gothic, which they had been using for two centuries. Now it became imbued with a new freedom, independence, courage, and daring, comparable to the adventurous work done by the Renaissance artists in Italy.

This late development of the Gothic style was given the name of *Flamboyant,* from the French word *flamme* (meaning flame), because the forms gave the impression of a flame-like movement. Ribbings in vaults lost their original structural meaning and intermingled in a sort of embrace entirely unrelated to their purpose. Vaults radiated in starlike fashion into many points, or losing all semblance of a vault they seemed to become embroidery or stone lace. This was a different expression of the same state of mind that produced the Renaissance in Italy. What counted most in the fifteenth century was no longer piety and humility, but daring and efficiency. The architects were seeking the spectacular.

Long before Italian translations of the Greek Classics reached them, these more northern nations had already investigated ancient times and made interpretations of them from the Latin versions in their vernacular. Perhaps never was there so much talk about Greek and Roman heroes as in the fifteenth century in northwestern Europe. Ovid, Vergil, Quintus Curtius, and Valerius Maximus were read in picturesque medieval French and Spanish; Lucretia and Tarquin, Alexander and Roxanna were dressed in Gothic garb. We can hardly call them faithful transcriptions of the Classics, but they served the purpose! Troy became a Gothic city with dungeons and battlemented walls; Hector and Achilles were fearless knights of chivalry, protected by heavenly angels instead of being guided by Olympian gods; the women of the Greek tragedies were represented with the manners of European court ladies.

The inventories of the powerful rulers of the time prove their interest in the ideas as well as the objects of ancient times. In their libraries we find books of Augustine,

Tomb of Marguerite of Austria. Church of Brou in Burgundy.

Boethius, Orotius, and Isidore, as well as of pagan writers. The writers on scholastic theology seem to have been read and esteemed not for what they tell of church history, but for what they recall of pagan legend and ancient life. Classical subjects also appeared in tapestries and jewels, with a preference for religious themes. Lives of saints and allegorical battles of virtues and sins were still popular, but they had a new secular accent. We see, therefore, that what was revolutionary in the earlier Renaissance in Italy was also found in France and Spain. In Italy, however, the ruins of buildings and fragments of Classical art were still visible, and there the attempt to revive Roman life was easier than it was in Paris, Salamanca, or Cologne.

The Flamboyant appeared almost simultaneously in all the countries of western Europe, and it was taken up so enthusiastically that it delayed for a century the importation of Classic styles from Italy. It is wrong to pass judgment on these nations for their spiritual slowness in developing the Italian style. Their alertness was just as great as that of their southern neighbors, but it was differently directed.

Chancel screen in Flamboyant Gothic style. Church of Brou in Burgundy.

The origin of this flamelike style with its intricate, crowded decoration is still an enigma. According to some scholars, England was the first to move in the new direction. The Perpendicular style is a manifestation of the Flamboyant, but the most outstanding works of the style were not produced in England. It is in Burgundy that its most excellent examples, if not its earliest, are to be found.

Burgundy was united with Flanders by the marriage ties of the two rulers; and it would have been entirely possible for the style to go first from England to the Low Countries, and from there to be carried to Burgundy. It could also have happened the other way around, as it certainly happened in Spain, where the Flamboyant was imported into Castile from Burgundy. It is, therefore, easy to imagine that it also reached England from Burgundy. Moreover, we know that it was from Burgundy that a little of that last Gothic infiltrated into Italy. And what of Germany? There the Flamboyant had been employed for two centuries. Again it is hard to believe that the influence was received from England and the Rhine. That there was no close relation between England and Germany at that time is one of the arguments made against the theory of the English

Detail of a tomb in Flamboyant Gothic style. Dijon.

origin of the Flamboyant style. Another is found in sculpture and painting.

No Flamboyant sculpture is to be found in England. The illumination of books in France and Burgundy in the fifteenth century shows the same characteristics of the Flamboyant style used in architecture, but nothing like it is to be found in the English illumination of any time. The coincidence of the Perpendicular in England and the Flamboyant on the Continent may be due to that fact so often observed in history, that the very same thing is invented in different places at the same time. It seems that the spiritual atmosphere becomes saturated with similar ideas and the similar inventions are conceived and introduced by different people who know nothing of each other. This is certainly true of the printing press; and it is probably true of the greatest invention in painting at that time, the use of linseed oil.

Such a style as the Gothic could not die without fighting. It necessarily had to finish with some kind of convulsion similar to the Baroque. We can think of the Flamboyant as the Baroque development of the Gothic. In it we find the Gothic elements employed with the same license with which the Baroque architects abused the Classical two centuries later. When the furore and mystical enthusiasm of the thirteenth century had cooled off, such cathedrals as Amiens and Chartres must have looked quite stale

Moses and David. From the "Well of Moses" by Claus Sluter. Chartreuse of Dijon.

and old-fashioned. The alternative then was either to develop still further the Gothic or to build in the Roman style. For this latter choice the Western nations were not ready. They did not know how to use the Roman, nor did they want to. The experiments of the Italians were the efforts of a small *cénacle;* in the west, the monarchs and the aristocracy had the responsibility of giving a new art to much larger groups.

The pointed arches of the early Gothic style are structurally correct; but in the Flamboyant they are bent from this structural correctness as if they were of bamboo or rubber. They intersect as if they were fighting to render a service which none succeeds in rendering. In the Flamboyant style the piers are no longer comparatively simple rectangular or circular supports; it is as if the stone, usually impenetrable, has consented to the interpenetration of shafts and capitals. The Flamboyant sculptors and architects have the same taste for giving to stone a living and animated quality as have the Baroque. Moldings come out from within the mass of stone

Daniel and Zacharias. Detail from the "Well of Moses" by Claus Sluter.

until the complexity of pilasters, of which the clustered pier is composed, forces itself on our attention. The whole building seems to be made of lace, piers, arches; everywhere are introduced minutely carved flowers, leaves, angels, and birds. Little statues personifying the virtues of Christians and pagans alike are stuck wherever there is a place for them. Courage, Beauty, Nobility, Generosity, Temperance, and Chastity are shown; but they are treated rather like heroes than saints. The saint of the past generation is superseded by the hero in the new. St. George at this

Angel of the Annunciation, and the Madonna receiving the Message. Burgundian School.
Metropolitan Museum of Art.

time would have had better chances of being chosen for depiction than would St. Alexis. The fighter takes the place of the monk.

At the end of the fourteenth century when the royal domain of France became the scene of a civil conflict, Burgundy was the only safe refuge for French artists; and its capital, Dijon, became the most important center of a new Gothic style. Here toward the end of the century the dukes of Flanders and Burgundy built a Carthusian monastery, which was to contain the tombs of the reigning family. The site chosen was the meadow of Champmol just outside the city gate. The structure was begun in 1385, but the work on it continued well into the fifteenth century. Artists were summoned from Flanders, and the Dijon masters, before they started their work, went for instructions to Paris schools and to artists employed by the Duc de Berry at Mehun. Little of the monastery remains today, but we are fortunate in having intact the portal with the statues of the dukes of Burgundy and their patron saints. These famous works were made by Claus Sluter. Little of his life is known, and nothing of his early

Madonna in polychromed limestone. Burgundian school. Metropolitan Museum of Art, New York.

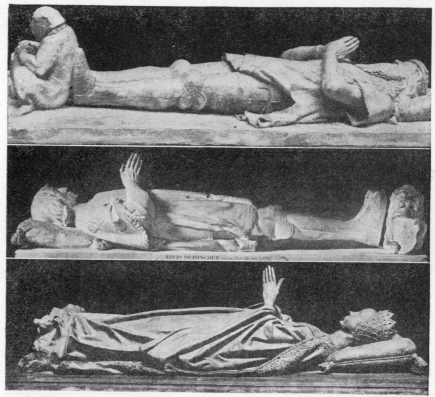

Tomb statues of Jean II of Vienne (Long Beard); Louis de Poncher, Counselor of the King of France; and Marie, Duchess of Burgundy. Louvre.

works. According to documents, he was a native of Holland, entered the service of the Duke of Burgundy in 1393, and from that time on he remained in Dijon working on the monastery sculpture.

After he had finished his work on the façade, he undertook the execution of a "Calvary," which seems to have occupied the center of the cloistered court. The base of this great work, which is all that remains, is known as the "Well of Moses," for it has the shape of a wellhead, and the most important figure on it is that of Moses. It is hexagonal and is decorated with figures of angels and prophets who foresaw the coming of the Redeemer. Moses is an imposing figure dressed in a full mantle; his long, parted beard is like a mane, and two horns project from his forehead. At his side stands David, with a crown upon his head; his noble face is pensive and sorrowful. The other prophets are Jeremiah, Zachariah, Daniel, and Isaiah. Each representation is characteristic in posture and expression. The conception and execution of the work are marvelous. Very important is the

Details from tomb statues of Anne de Montmorency and Madeleine de Savoie. Louvre.

early date of its execution. A work of art does not depend for its beauty on belonging to any period, and the "Well" of Claus Sluter would bring renown to any school at any time. Our admiration is all the greater when we realize that this "Moses" was carved in the year 1400, more than a century before Michelangelo created his great statue of Moses and his paintings of the Prophets in the Sistine Chapel. The "Well of Moses" was painted

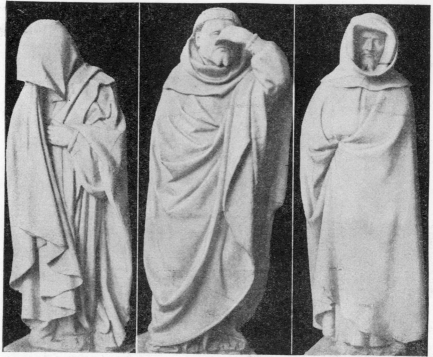

Three mourners from the tomb of Phillippe le Beau. Museum of Dijon.

and gilded. The colors certainly added to its beauty; they probably added to its meaning, as it is supposed that the colors were symbolical. The artists of the last Gothic period enjoyed immensely interpreting anew the old themes of the Christian faith. The Well of Life was an old Scholastic subject. The *Fountain of Life* by the Spanish Jew, Avicebron, or Ibn Gabirol, was one of the most influential books in the preceding centuries. Everything about the book was clothed in mystery to the people of that time. The author used an alias, and the text was circulated first in an Arabic translation from the original Hebrew, and later in Latin. The "Well" of Sluter represents the "Fountain of Life" of Avicebron, but the spring of living water has become the blood. Without the cross surmounting the well, the Prophets around the sides lose their meaning. The beauty of the work is so great that even in its present mutilated state it is one of the greatest masterpieces of all times.

The tombs of the Flamboyant period in France and Spain are so costly and so decorated that it seems an extravagant sacrilege for them to be placed in the chapels of the churches. Altars play a minor part in these chapels; small statues of saints do honor to the large statue of the deceased, instead

Three cowled mourners from a Burgundian tomb. Metropolitan Museum of Art, New York.

of the deceased looking to the saints for help. This has been explained as a natural development of the old idea of the resurrection of the flesh on the Judgment Day. Since the body is only in part subject to corruption, it ought to be preserved as much as possible; the soul will enter it again to remain forever. The words of St. Paul in regard to spiritual bodies were by this time entirely forgotten.

The desire to preserve the shell in which we must live again may be an excuse for some of the richly ornamented mausoleums; but they are also the result of the new ideas of glorification of the great outstanding men and women, who were powerful, learned, and beautiful. Life is no longer a hard lot, and flesh is no longer an enemy. Death has to be appeased with commemorative monuments, the largest possible. Sometimes the entrails of the dead were buried in another place far from the tomb where the embalmed body was interred. The funerals lasted for many days, and the deceased were carried in a procession of mourners to the place they had selected in life for burial. The mourners are often represented on the sarcophagus. There are little hooded figurines of the servants, friends, and clients of the deceased, who came for the funeral procession. The executors of the testament generally provided them with dark woolen robes. The cowled figurines of the marble coffin became a popular theme for the decoration of tombs not only in Flamboyant France, but also in England and Spain. They were for the late Gothic sarcophagus, what the classic subjects of the battles with the Amazons and with barbarians were for the Roman carvers.

The sculptors of the late Gothic period produced their greatest works in carving the recumbent statues of the lords to be buried in the sarcophagi. The statues lay in state as on the day of the funeral. At their feet is the faithful dog who feels the death of the master probably more keenly than the relatives. On the tombs of great lords the lion takes the place of the dog, as a symbol of supreme command and strength. On some there are angels holding the arms of the deceased or guarding him in death. These death figures appear still, but not utterly dead; they only sleep, waiting to come to life and to perform great deeds on the Resurrection Day.

Portrait of Jeanne d'Armagnac, wife of Jean, Duc de Berry. Poitiers.

Old Arabic inscription on ivory, framed with modern border.
Thirteenth century. From Egypt.

ISLAMIC ART

WE KNOW LITTLE OF ARABIA before the coming of Mohammed except what we learn from a few isolated accounts that have come down to us. Some writers of antiquity tell marvelous tales of the Land of Sheba and the visit of its fabulously wealthy queen to the Court of King Solomon. As yet, however, there is no real tangible evidence of the culture or the artistic style of Arabia before the seventh century. Recent explorations in the peninsula have brought to light only a few tombstones and alabaster figures.

The Nabataeans in the Syrian Desert were the only Arabs who possessed a writing system of their own. The half-ruined rock tombs with carved façades can still be seen in Petra. We also know that they carved figures in the round; but Petra, like Baalbek, Palmyra, and other Arab cities of the desert has long since fallen into decay.

For centuries there had been in Mecca a shrine called the Kaaba. It was a simple building sheltering the sacred Black Stone which had fallen from heaven. In Mohammed's time, the Kaaba, then in ruins, was rebuilt into a small square structure without windows and with no decoration of any kind. To make a pilgrimage to Mecca and to kiss this stone has been

Two alabaster figures of Pre-Islamic Arabs, with inscriptions. University of
Pennsylvania Museum, Philadelphia.

the duty of all Mohammedans. The first mosque built in Medina, which
is the earliest Mohammedan building on record, like the Kaaba, was
severely plain and unadorned. It consisted simply of a square court enclosed
by porticoes with palm trunks used for columns.

Since the Moslems had inherited no traditional art forms, it was natural
that they should borrow them from the people they conquered. The first
lands to come under their domination were the two rich provinces of
Mesopotamia and Syria, which were then part of the Byzantine Empire,
and full of creations in the Byzantine style. From these provinces artists
were summoned to help with the work on the Mosque of Omar in Jerusalem, and they left indelible marks of their own tradition. It is interesting
to note in passing that this mosque was built on Mount Moriah, the

Decoration from a wall in the Omayyad Castle of Mshatta in the Syrian Desert. Berlin.

former site of the Temple of Jerusalem. The plan is octagonal. It has two concentric aisles, and a dome over the center of the building. The Sacred Rock occupies a place beneath the dome. This rock is more sacred to the Arabs of Syria than the stone of the Kaaba, for on Mount Moriah took place the sacrifice of Abraham and from there the Prophet was carried to heaven. The building for this reason does not face Mecca, as do all

Mosque of Omar. Seventh century. Mount Moriah, Jerusalem.

other mosques, since its people do not recognize as of superior importance the other great Moslem centers. The dome was started in 687 A.D., and the building has been restored and added to a number of times since its completion, even down to the time of Suleiman; but some of its original mosaics are still preserved. Those were the work of Syrian and Byzantine artists.

With this one exception, all the early Mohammedan mosques consisted simply of a court, or open-air temple. We have already seen that in all Semitic temples, even that of Jerusalem, the court was the most important part of the building, the holy place to which worshipers were not admitted. The temple of Byblos, or Jebeil, in Phoenicia, consisted mainly of a sacred court; and the famous sanctuary at Baalbek in Syria was a magnificent enclosure surrounded by temples and shrines.

In the first mosques there was a colonnade only on the side of the court toward Mecca, the direction in which worshipers offered their prayers. In the center of this wall was a niche called the *mihrab,* which contained neither statue nor idol, but was simply a symbol of the Kaaba. The early Mosques of Almutasin and Abu Dolaf on the Mesopotamian desert, which

Mosque of Ibn-Tulun. Eighth century. Cairo.

exemplify the primitive type, are only rectangular courts having a single row of columns on the side toward Mecca. Later, the number of rows of columns on this side was increased, and the other three sides were enriched with the addition of a simple arcade. The additional rows of columns gave the entire mosque a very different aspect. It became a temple composed of many aisles divided by parallel lines of columns, in front of which was a court that served as a sort of vestibule.

In the Mosque of Ibn-Tulun at Cairo, for example, there were five rows of columns on the side of the mihrab; at Kairwan in Tunis there were still more, but the court was still an important feature. Finally in the Mosque of Cordova we find aisle after aisle, a veritable forest of columns, with the court merely an accessory feature. In seeing this mosque, it is hard to realize that the court was originally the principal part of the sanctuary.

The conquest of Syria was followed by that of Egypt; and here, particularly at Cairo, the new capital, the caliphs erected many handsome mosques. Cairo is still the most characteristic Mohammedan city in existence and contains examples of Moslem art of every period, from early

Mosque of El-Azhar. Ninth century. Cairo.

mosques, like the one of Ibn-Tulun, to those of modern times still in Arab style. In all these Egyptian monuments, we note one predominant element, the raised, or pointed arch which the Saracens borrowed from the Coptic structures. We find in the later mosques of Cairo a cruciform plan consisting of a court or hall with four aisles for the four rites of the Mohammedan religion. Out of the main aisles opens the mihrab, and to one side is the small pulpit, or *mimbar*, which is always the most elaborately decorated piece of furniture in the mosque. There is also the tribune, or *dikkeh*, for the reading of the *Koran*, raised on eight columns and set toward the center of the main aisle.

Some of the mosques of Cairo are incorporated in a vast mass of buildings containing hospitals, schools, apartments for the accommodation of strangers, and the tomb of the sultan who founded the establishment. The Mosque of Hassan is typical of this sort and is one of the most interesting structures at Cairo. There is a central court with a fountain in the middle. Out of the court open the four halls for the four rites. At the corners are the four schools and behind is the square domed hall containing the tomb of the founder. On the outside is a cornice of stalactites, and the great building is flanked by minarets. The doorway is a great arch seventy-five feet high. The entire structure is magnificently decorated and is today an important religious center. Another school-mosque of Cairo is that of El-Azhar which is the seat of a university.

After seizing Egypt, the Arabs overran Cyrenaica, Tunis, and Algeria. A number of the ancient mosques which they built are still standing; those of Sfax and Tunis probably date from the eighth century. The most important is that of Sidi Okba at Kairwan. It was originally built by Okba-ben-Nafi in 670, but it did not take on its present appearance until the beginning of the ninth century when it was rebuilt. In front is the great colonnaded court; and down the center from the door to the mihrab runs a central aisle wider than the side aisles. The latter are separated by antique columns with capitals supporting a simple construction of arches and beams, above which is a wooden ceiling. The mihrab of the Kairwan Mosque is faced with tiles and wooden panels which are said to have been imported

Court of the Mosque of Hassan. Cairo.

Mosque of Abd-er-Rahman. Eighth century. Cordova.

from the Orient and are among the most beautiful of Moslem decorative art.

We have seen that the Arabs who overran the Near East learned much from the Byzantine styles there. The same thing was bound to occur in Spain. In the first buildings which the Arabs erected on the Iberian peninsula, there is evidence not only of the materials, but also of the architectural technique of the Visigothic monuments. At least, we note a great difference between the buildings they erected immediately after the conquest and those erected centuries later.

It is possible that these same Arabs who built structures of a Visigothic character also learned in Spain how to construct the horseshoe arch so typical of the Moslem monuments found in Mediterranean lands. The Cordova Mosque was begun in 786 by Abd-er-Rahman I, who utilized the walls and columns of the Visigothic church; the central nave leading to the mihrab is somewhat wider than the others, as at Kairwan. Hisham I added a number of lateral aisles, built the minaret, and beautified the court with a magnificent fountain of purification. Hisham II constructed eleven more aisles with as many rows of columns; and in Almanzor's time, when the Berber immigration made more space desirable, still more aisles were added to the mosque.

"Court of the Lions" of the Alhambra, the palace of the Moorish kings of Granada.
Granada.

This multiplication of the aisles raised the new problem of a proper roof for so great a structure. As long as there was only a single arcade on the side of the mihrab, or at most a series of three to five columned aisles, a wooden roof was quite sufficient. But when, as in the Mosque at Cordova, the aisles became more numerous, the great space enclosed made it necessary to raise the ceiling. Otherwise the monument would have seemed excessively low. The Moslem architects depended on the ancient buildings for their columns and capitals, and they found it difficult, if not impossible, to obtain enough marble shafts of the size necessary to give the proper proportions to the new temple. They overcame the difficulty by setting one arcade on top of another. Above the lower columns they put a second series surmounted by arches. Sometimes there was even a third series of arches and columns to raise the ceiling still higher.

About the year 1171 Almanzor began the Mosque at Seville on the site of the present Gothic cathedral. The mosque entirely disappeared except for its famous minaret, now called the Giralda, but even this has been much restored and added to. Today the Giralda is the most highly prized monument of the city and is the belfry of the cathedral. It has the simple outline of a square tower with a Renaissance superstructure rising from its upper

"Court of the Myrtles" of the Alhambra. Granada.

platform. Its form is characteristic of the Moslem architecture of Spain and northern Africa. Indeed, the minarets of the mosques at Rabat, Marrakesh, and Oran follow the same type.

Among the Arabs, as among all Oriental peoples, the most important civil building was the residence of the monarch. Originally a nomadic people, the Arabs had no antecedents for this type of structure. Consequently, they were obliged to learn from the nations they conquered. The light and complicated character of Persian construction appealed to the tastes of the Mohammedan builders and became the prototype of the most charming Oriental palaces, with broad pools bordered with myrtles and rosebushes. Their gardens were watered by the play of fountains. Rare plants bloomed in secluded spots, and in the center rose a graceful kiosk. Within the pavilions were richly colored and gilded reliefs of alabaster, the only decoration of the walls; while the ceilings were covered with ingenious patterns of gleaming gold and enamel. After the eleventh century all the Arab palaces followed the same type. In Sicily, in the outskirts of Palermo, we still find the remains of palaces constructed by the Saracen princes and later enlarged by the Norman kings who occupied them. These differ little from the Moslem palaces of Spain.

Decorations from the walls of the "Mirador de Lindaraxa" and "Court of the Lions."
The Alhambra, Granada.

Decoration on the upper wall of the "Tower of the Infantas." The Alhambra, Granada

At Granada rose the Alhambra, perhaps the most famous Moorish royal palace in the world, the residence of the kings of Granada. It was built by Sultan Mohammed El-Amhar on the hill overlooking the Valley of Assabica. Its name, Alhambra, meaning red, was derived from its red brick walls. Here at the most western point of the Islamic world, the Alhambra, a shred of the Orient, made no concession to the West but rose in an attitude of defiance to the Latin peoples who imposed their manner of living and their artistic tastes upon the Eastern world at the time of the Romans. The Alhambra, a marvelous collection of halls and patios decorated with bright colors, stalactite vaults, delicate marquetry, rich reliefs, and arabesques, had very little planning for a general effect. The design of the palace called for no one monumental façade. The Court of the Myrtles, the Hall of the Ambassadors, the Hall of the Two Sisters, the Hall of Justice, the Baths, and the Dressing Rooms were all planned to be of equal importance. In the structural scheme of the palace the Moors reflected the tradi-

Wall decoration in Western Mohammedan (geometric) style. Hall of the Two Sisters. The Alhambra, Granada.

tions of their people. Underneath the light vaults and graceful walls they built the framework of a desert tent. The panels, merely plaster forms, in spite of their profuse and highly colored ornamentation, took on the appearance of hanging tapestries, very beautiful, but unsubstantial.

The Arabs built other palaces in Spain, and we find also in Morocco structures of the same character. In Andalusia the apartments of private houses open onto a central court and are without windows on the outside. These Andalusian styles are still preserved in Morocco today.

We started the description of Islamic art with the West because there the Moslems remained entirely orthodox, faithful to the idea that Mohammed was the sole prophet; that he and only he had received the Revelation, or the *Koran*. East of the Euphrates there developed another notion, one that had great consequences for art. The worship centered around Ali, the cousin and son-in-law of Mohammed, who was elected caliph only after Abu Bekr, Omar, and Othman had first succeeded to the caliphate. To his followers, Ali was the incarnation of the mind of God and was superior to the Prophet. His divinity was not revealed during his lifetime; for he was stout and boyish-looking, not at all impassioned, but modest, sincere, and humble; and he had accepted without rebellion the precedence of the other three caliphs.

Casket in Eastern Mohammedan style from the Cathedral of Palencia. Archaeological Museum, Madrid.

After Ali died as a martyr, he came to be looked upon by a few as the mind of Allah incarnate.

Since then, millions of Mohammedans in the Near and Far East have believed Ali to be the supreme expression of Wisdom and Good. He is not worshiped; for Islam did not accept the idea of saints, priests, relics, images, or any other symbol of devotion except prayers to Allah. He was rather a manifestation of God, because his great humility made him willing to be ignored by the world. Under the guidance of Ali, the *Koran* loses its character as the sole revelation and may be interpreted as permitting the exact opposite of what it prescribes.

While Western Islamic art remained strict to the letter of the *Koran,* which forbade the representation of living forms, in the East every animate thing was a creation of God, manifesting His beauty, and therefore good to represent. Being orthodox, the art of the Islamic West is chiefly geometric; while the art of less literal Islamic Persia and India is largely made up of figures and flowers.

Mohammed had laid down with finality that any "people of a book"— namely, a people who had a sacred book—were to be tolerated; and Mohammedans lived with them without trying to reform or to impose upon them the new book, the *Koran.* The "people of a book," in the simple knowledge of Mohammed, were only the Jews and the Christians, whom he had found in Arabia and Syria where he traveled. Mohammed did not know of any other sacred book and consequently did not include in this category the Persians who were Zoroastrians and had a sacred book, the ZEND-AVESTA. So it happened that when the Arabs conquered Persia in the seventh century, they compelled the whole Persian nation to become Mohammedan. Since the alternative was Islam or death, only the few thousand Parsis who migrated to India remained Zoroastrian.

As a result of this coercion in Persia, Mohammedanism was not so pure and sincere as it was among the converts of the West. Most of the Persian poets reflect an Epicurean belief rather than the spirit of the real Koranic faith. They persisted in their heathen ways of living, drinking wine, and declaring death to be the end of all. We see the consequences very plainly in their art. For example, in Hispano-Moresque and Egyptian-Islamic designs the geometric patterns are very seldom varied with the conventionalized forms of running deer or of birds, which could be accused of representing reality. Most of the decorations in the Western Islamic style are letters which repeat one or two verses of the *Koran*. On occasions, whole walls with complicated systems of friezes and panels are entirely covered with letters without producing any sensation of monotony because several different alphabets are employed. The old Coptic alphabet which is predominantly vertical is combined with more horizontal characters and with the cursive hand which

Interior of the Taj Mahal with the sarcophagus of the Sultana, Mumtez Mahal.

Seljuk Mosque at Konya.

is quite flexible. The combination rather looks like a puzzle, but it gives a very pleasing and dignified effect. Indeed, when we look at those Islamic-Egyptian and Hispano-Moresque decorations, we are so engaged by their traceries that we do not feel the loss of the images of the Islamic-Persian and Indian decorations, in which the followers of Ali indulge all kinds of visionary phantasy.

In Persia the designs have a multitude of colors displaying forms of the animal and vegetable kingdoms. They picture hunts, love scenes, drinking parties, and games—all displayed on their beautiful pottery. The decorations of the Eastern Islamic buildings are very similar. In contrast, the tiles in the Hispano-Moresque ceramics have designs of latticed and interwoven straps making polygonal subdivisions in different colors. Tiles that cover the façade of the Western mosques have representations of cypress trees and flowers. The textiles of the West show great imagination in combining geometric patterns, and it is very seldom that we find in their designs representations of persons or of any living thing. In Persia, Turkestan, and India, however, the pattern is frequently composed of a group of persons in a landscape.

The Moslem architects of the West were rather sparing in their use of vaults and domes; they contented themselves with a structural beam, and when they used anything resembling a vault it was more like a combination of arches than a simple dome. In the Mosque of Cordova, the dome over the mihrab is a single stone. Other vaults there are formed by the crossing of many arches with very little space left between. In Persia and Turkestan, on the contrary, vaults and domes are employed in great profusion. This has been attributed to the Sassanid traditions which remained alive even after the Mohammedans had conquered the land. It was, however, more than

merely a case of borrowing, as
the Arabs in the West had borrowed from the Copts and Visigoths. In Persia there was no
division between conquered
and conqueror. All had to be
Mohammedan; and the Persian
architects worked for the new
masters without restraint in
their own style. In the West,
although the Christians lived
side by side in peaceful relations
with the Mohammedans, there
remained two separate and distinct groups of society. It sometimes happened that a Christian architect worked on a
mosque; and we have records
showing that Moorish architects under unusual circumstances worked for Christians.
In Persia all were of one faith,
and all kept building domes
and arches for their mosques in
the Sassanid tradition.

The entrance to a Persian or
Turkestan mosque is an enormous arch, generally decorated
with shiny glass tile, opening
onto a court, with a fountain in
the center. Some of the mosques
take their names from the color
predominating in these tiles.
The minarets are also decorated
with bright colored tiles. Although tall, they are smaller
than the ones of the West and
are generally cylindrical or
slightly conical in shape. The
Persian tiles are not flat like

Laranda Mosque at Konya.

the Western ones, and their patterns in relief sparkle when reflecting the
sun. Dilapidated as their mosques are today—many of them stripped of their
decorations—the old cities of Bokhara, Samarkand, and Khiva in the desert
still look like fairy towns with their colored domes and minarets.

In the sixteenth century, the Moguls conquered India and took with

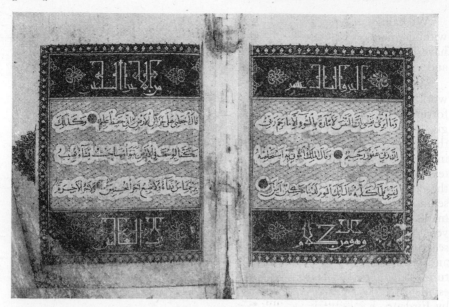

Frontispiece in a "Koran" written at Maragha sometime between the years 739 and 1339 A.D. by Abdallah Ibn-Ahmad Ibn-Fazallah Ibn-Abdallah. Museum of Fine Arts, Boston.

them the styles of Persia. It is hardly necessary to say that in the land where Buddhism had flourished and where the world was thought to be merely an illusion of the mind, the Islamic forms were adopted and became even more imaginative. The Mogul dynasty was founded by Baber, who was a descendant of the great Tamerlane. A brilliant line of emperors succeeded him, many of whom were writers and artists. Baber began the beautification of Agra and this work was continued by his son Akbar, one of the most interesting figures in Oriental history. Jahangir succeeded Akbar and was followed by Shah Jehan, famous as the builder of the Taj Mahal in memory of his favorite wife Mumtez Mahal.

The Taj Mahal was started in 1632 under the direction, it is believed, of a French architect from Bordeaux. It is a large octagonal building set upon a platform that is over eight hundred feet wide and has minarets at the corners. A splendid environment of pools and gardens surrounds it and helps to set off its classic white splendor. Beautifully arched niches and door ways cast shadows which add to the effect. In spite of a certain European flavor and a great deal of minute detail, the Taj Mahal has a sort of lovely aloofness; and it ranks as one of the wonders of the world.

Double and triple walls with formidable gateways, moats, and towers were built to defend the Mogul cities of India. Some of these ramparts are of extraordinary size and beauty, as are the walls of Benares, the holy city on the Ganges, the towers and gates of Delhi, and the fortress of Gwalior.

We cannot leave the subject of Mohammedan architecture in the East without mentioning the monuments of the Seljuk Turks in Brusa, which have been greatly admired, and the mosques at Istanbul (Constantinople) and Adrianople, which have never received the appreciation they deserve.

We find very little mosaic in Islamic buildings, and even less fresco work. Painting was almost entirely confined to manuscript miniatures, and fortunately a great many of the Moslem manuscripts are still in existence to give us examples of this art. In copies of the sacred book of Islam, the *Koran*, there is usually a handsome frontispiece decorated with interlaced bandings in a pattern something like a conventionalized rose. No illustration of the text was permitted. Themes of the *Koran* did not lend themselves as did those of the Bible to representation; and there was the restriction on representative forms. There are a few pictures in other books describing Mohammed's ascension to heaven, but the Prophet's face is always covered with a veil. There is not a single real or imaginary portrait of Mohammed to be seen in all the Islamic world; nor is there any of Ali. Islamic books of history and poetry from the twelfth century on were often illustrated with miniatures. The largest number and the best of these were made in Persia, Turkestan, and India. The great Persian epic, the SHAH-NAMAH (Book of Kings), by Firdausi, has been illustrated more than any other. Some of the manuscripts are very large and of supreme beauty. Miniatures cover full pages of great size. The grand style of Firdausi really demands for suitable illus-

Miniature from a manuscript of Dioscorides' MATERIA MEDICA, translated into Arabic about 1222 in Mesopotamia by Hunain Ibn Ishaq. Museum of Fine Arts, Boston.

Funeral of Rustam and Zawara. Miniature from a manuscript of Firdausi's SHAH-NAMAH. Painted at Tabriz in the fourteenth century.

tration wall painting instead of miniature; but although these miniatures are reduced to the service of decorating a volume, nevertheless they have the spirit and style of monumental painting.

We obtain a better conception of the refinement of Persian society with its poets, musicians, and philosophers from these miniatures than we do from the monuments. Many of the artists were princes and were proud to sign the manuscripts they worked on. The portraits of the owners of the books and of the authors of the texts are frequently painted on the first page. The Persian artists made a sort of frame around the page with floral motives in color and a great deal of gold, to set off their painted scenes. Many of the miniaturists were equally famous as calligraphers in the Near East, where writing was the supreme art.

Provincial schools of Persian miniature art developed in Bokhara and Samarkand, where the Moguls established their capitals at that time. In these schools, the mixture of Tatar-Mogul gave an added charm to the Persian. We find Mongolian types of faces on the heroes of Persian legends. The Mogul of India liked the SHAH-NAMAH of Firdausi and the quatrains of Omar Khayyam as much as he did their Persian and Turkestan counterparts. The Indian bibliophiles of Agra developed a school of miniature that still produces great masterpieces. The artists are fond of scenes of hunting and court life and of other details characteristic of Indian life, as, for example, elephant fights, one of the Rajah's favorite sports.

The latest development of the school of India are the illustrations of the exploits of Krishna, an important figure in one of the branches of the neo-Brahman sects. He is the boy god, a cow herder, a beautiful lad, and a great

Above: Portrait of a Persian poet.
Left: Portrait of Shah Tahmasp by Shah
Muhammad. Museum of Fine Arts, Boston.

flute player. There are many legends about his mischievous playfulness, and
Hindu women never tire of reading about him. His escapades have been
much illustrated in present time, and in many of these late Indian miniatures
there is piquant eroticism.

Islamic ivory carvings were unrivaled, particularly the caskets ornamented
with flat reliefs that we find in many Spanish cathedrals. The largest of these
caskets is the one in the Cathedral of Pamplona, Spain. It is rectangular and
covered with reliefs. Around the four sides runs a prayer imploring the
blessing of God, happiness, and a long life for Almanzor. It also bears the

Portrait of an amir. Probably painted at Bokhara in the sixteenth century.
Museum of Fine Arts, Boston.

Funeral of Murad III, Sultan of Turkey, who died in 1595. Museum of Fine Arts, Boston.

Colored glass bottle with Arabic inscription. From Egypt. University of Pennsylvania Museum, Philadelphia.

name of the artist who directed the work, a eunuch by the name of Nomeir-ben-Mohammed, who seems to have been the head of the Caliph's own workshop. Other names engraved on the medallions are probably those of the artists who carved the various reliefs. There is a similar casket in the Cathedral of Braga in Portugal. Some of the Moslem caskets are of cylindrical form and have either a flat or a rounded cover, like that of Almuqueira, the son of Abd-er-Rahman II.

All Mohammedan peoples display marvelous imagination and technical skill in the art of ceramics, which we have already mentioned in connection with building tiles. In Mesopotamia the traditions of the ancient schools of Babylonia and Assyria had never been completely forgotten, and along the Euphrates River and in Persia the Sassanian architects had continued to use the glazed tiles characteristic of the earlier times. The Mohammedan craftsmen of Mesopotamia and Persia taught their art to their neighbors in Egypt, and from there it passed with all its many forms to the potters of northern Africa and Spain. The art of the Persians is the finest, however. Their plates are exquisitely decorated with patterns in which blue, green, and gold predominate.

To the factories of Rhages in Persia can be assigned an entire series of vases and tiles in shades of blue and green, which show an incomparable forcefulness of design. Rhages was destroyed in 1220, so that we know its beautiful faïence work antedates the thirteenth century. In Mesopotamia the pottery of Rakka, near Aleppo, can be similarly dated because that city was destroyed in 1259 by the Tatar, Khulagu Khan. For other pottery factories we have no dates at all. We lack any precise information about the Turkish workshops of Kutahiah and those of Damascus and Rhodes; but stylistic evidence seems to show their products to be of the sixteenth century. In Egypt the remains of the kilns of Fostat, or Old Cairo, were discovered a few years ago, and this find was of great assistance in the study of the history of Arabian pottery in Egypt.

That the ceramic art moved from East to West is shown by the fact that the most ancient examples preserved in Spain and northern Africa, like the mihrab in the Mosque at Kairwan, are plainly importations from Baghdad. The Spanish potters, first those of Malaga and later those of Valencia, imitated the colors and forms employed by the craftsmen of Persia and Mesopotamia. In the course of time, however, they developed a technique of their own, which they used alike on their vases and jars ornamented with gold designs and on their characteristic blue tiles.

Even after the industry had been abandoned at Malaga and had been transferred to Valencia, the ware made there continued to be called *Tierra de Malaca,* or *Malica.* Later, it acquired the name of *Majolica,* because it was carried to other lands by Majorcan sailors. So popular did this ware become that the Venetian senate

Hispano-Moresque vase. Hispanic Society of America, New York.

suspended duties on it. Bruges and Cairo became great centers for its distribution to all parts of the Occident and Orient. Famous patrons of the arts, such as René of Anjou and the Medicis of Florence became collectors. In Tuscany inferior imitations began to be made, and we find the Florentine ware of this period a poor reproduction of the blue and gold arabesques and conventionalized leaves of Moslem Spain. During the latter part of the

Mohammedan Syrian textile. Eleventh century. Cooper Union Museum, New York.

fifteenth century Italian influence in its turn began to affect the art of Moresque pottery.

Egypt's special skill was in glass work and copper. Probably never has glass been worked into more beautiful forms and colors than in Egypt at the time of the Fatimid sultans. Jars for oil lamps, and bottles for wine are covered with beautiful transparent enamel glazes. Objects of chiseled and carved brass are equally fine in their workmanship and taste, and Egypt surpassed all other manufacturing centers in her pitchers of bronze.

Detail of an imperial rug. McCormick Collection. The Art Institute of Chicago.

Perhaps the finest craftsmanship of the Moslems is to be found in their carpets and textiles. The first principles of their craft had come from the Copts, Byzantines, and Sassanians. To these they added Arabic characters as a decoration. It is probable that the Egyptians of early times had used carpets.

In the tomb of Cyrus, according to Arrianus, there was a magnificent Babylonian carpet spread on the ground, while another covered the sarcophagus. The Greeks greatly admired the carpets of the Persians. "Persian cloths covering the space where the guests walked" are mentioned by Athenaeus. Pliny also mentions Babylonian woven cloths of diverse colors. Carpets with figures of monsters from the East are mentioned among the extravagances of Heliogabalus.

During the Middle Ages, Oriental carpets were included almost without exception in the royal inventories and the cathedral treasures. They are mentioned in literature and appear in very ancient pictures as floor and altar coverings. The name *baldachin,* meaning canopy, is derived from Baldak, or Baghdad, for often the covering consisted of an Oriental carpet. We still go to Persia for our finest rugs, and the silks of India are unequaled in the West. Islam is not dead. Turkey and Egypt, modernized as they are, still build some of their edifices in the old Moslem style and free from imitations of the Neoclassical forms of the Occident.

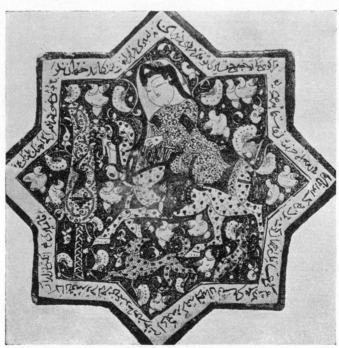

Luster tile. Made in Kashan, Iran, 1206 A.D. Museum of
Fine Arts, Boston.

A Corinthian column, and sea-gods of Greek type. Greco-Buddhist reliefs. From Gandhâra.
Metropolitan Museum of Art, New York.

ART OF THE FAR EAST

INDIA AND CAMBODIA

IRAN (Persia) is divided geographically from India and China by the highest mountains in the world, the Himalayas; and from China, by the most arid desert of Asia, the Gobi. The obstacles in a journey through these regions are so great even today that it is certain the ancients would have known very little or nothing of these distant lands if there had not been routes of travel other than over the mountains or through the desert. We know that sailors and adventurers reached Asia by sea and brought back spices and textiles by way of the Persian Gulf. And there seems to be some evidence that the journey had been made even in very early times over a route from the Caucasus through Mongolia and Siberia. In any event, by the sea route, or perhaps by both routes, art influences from the Far East came West, for there is evidence of such influences in the work of the Egyptian and Hellenic peoples.

The only people of Asia known to the Europe of Greek and Roman times were the inhabitants of India just beyond the high mountains. They were believed to be a mysterious race endowed with super-natural powers; and Alexander's expedition only added to this reputation for mystery. The Greek and Roman commentators speak of the marvels which were seen in the East by scientists in Alexander's army. These men of the fourth century B.C. give us our earliest account of the peoples of India. We are indebted

Flight of Gautama Buddha from his home in search of the "Revelation." The genii of
the forest help him depart. Metropolitan Museum of Art, New York.

also to the narratives of Chinese pilgrims who later came to India to visit
the holy places of Buddhism, but it was not until Portuguese and Dutch
explorers finally reached the distant land that Europe began to have any
complete first hand information about this strange world. The influence
of India is reflected in the late Gothic style of Portugal, in which there
is a certain resemblance to the monuments of India, and in the art of
seventeenth- and eighteenth-century France, in which fabrics and porcelains
imported from eastern Asia played an important part.

It is only during the last few years, however, that excavations in India
have revealed the existence of a civilization more ancient than that of which
we have spoken. We usually think of India as a land of castes which were
the outgrowth of the Arian invasion; but at Mohenjo-daro there have been
brought to light seals and ivory statuettes that indicate the existence of a
people there in contact with the early Babylonians. This is not surprising,
because, as already noted, travel and trade in Asia was being carried on
during the two millenniums before Alexander the Great. Too much importance, however, must not be attached to these Babylonian objects in India,
for up to the present no great artistic consequences seem to be attributable
to them.

The excavation of the ruins of Pataliputra, the capital of northern India
at the time of Alexander's conquest, has resulted in another sensational discovery. According to a description by Megasthenes, a Greek writer and

ambassador of the time, of this city and its buildings, everything was covered with gold. Does this mean gilded wood? That the monuments of Pataliputra in the third century B.C. were of wooden construction is proved by the gigantic foundations of piers and planks which were unearthed. Unfortunately, very little of their original gilded beauty remains.

Of a much later date than the finds at Mohenjo-daro and Pataliputra are the Indian Rock temples. Years ago these were thought to be contemporary with the tombs and temples of early Egypt, or perhaps older. It seemed that India, as the cradle of the white race, must have antedated or at least been contemporary with Egypt in such skilful work. However,

The "Revelation" under the Bo-tree. Metropolitan Museum of Art, New York.

when a systematic study of Indian art was undertaken the imagined hoary antiquity of these temples carved in the rocks of India faded away.

It must be recognized, nevertheless, that some of these cave-temples reflect not only an ancient decorative art native to the country but also the wooden constructions described by Megasthenes. In the caves at Karli, for example, all the elements of a wooden framework are carved from the living rock. In the same manner, we see motifs characteristic of wooden architecture carrying over into ordinary modern construction. We find in these Indian temples not only proof of the accuracy of the descriptions of the Greek writers, but proof also of the influence of Greek taste in this far-off land. Many of the details are reminiscent of Greek ornamentation and moldings. We know that slaves, dancers, and mimes, as well as coins, were imported into India from Ionia in Asiatic Greece. Greek influence is very noticeable in Indian literature, especially in the drama.

Indian coins of Buddhist rulers.

The Greek influence was encouraged by Buddhism. A need was felt for an art expres-

Before the Illumination. Gautama as Prince Sidartha. Metropolitan Museum of Art, New York.

After the Illumination. Gautama as the Buddha, with the *urna,* or mole, in the center of his forehead. Metropolitan Museum of Art, New York.

Buddhist relief. The Buddha stands in the center making the gesture of banishing fear. Metropolitan Museum of Art, New York.

sion different at least in decorative themes from the Brahmanic art, and foreign elements were gladly adopted where it was not possible to develop original Buddhistic elements from traditional Indian forms. Thus, all over the Peninsula and especially in the northwest, a strange new art grew up and spread over a great part of eastern Asia. The myths of Buddha were represented in a manner very different from the Brahmanic epics on the cave reliefs of southern India.

After the death of the founder of the new faith, holy relics associated with his life and ministry were reverently collected and enshrined. The *stupas,* which are found in large numbers in a wide zone extending across northern Hindustan, mark the places where memorable episodes in the life of Buddha occurred. Many of them are also depositaries for the precious caskets containing the relics of Buddha. They are small, moundlike structures, and each is crowned with a stone column decorated with smooth bands or circles.

Since the teachings of Buddhism and the example of its founder are conducive to asceticism, we usually find beside the stupa a *vihara,* or small cell, where lived the anchorite who consecrated his life to the care of the sacred monument. At first the viharas were small rectangular structures of a single small room; but religious veneration inspired the worshipers to decorate more and more elaborately the abodes of these lone monks. In time they became graceful chapels of carved stone, with columns flanking their doorways, moldings, and other architectural ornaments. The gabled canopy over the door gives these buildings an appearance anything but Oriental; the outline resembles rather that of a Greek temple. It is in this particular Indian construction that the influence of Hellenic art is most evident. Even the capitals of the columns are ornamented with volutes and acanthus leaves; and although we find departures from the

Greek models, all the elements of the Corinthian capital are there.

As time went on and Buddhism began to triumph throughout eastern Asia, the stupa and the vihara began to attract pilgrims from many places. Other hermits came and more cells were required. The stupa was finally enclosed by surrounding viharas, the whole group forming a *sangharama,* or monastic cloister, not unlike the European monasteries of the Middle Ages. Later on, the sangharamas with the subsidiary buildings of the religious community were limited in size only by the means at the disposal of the monks; but for a time they were only rectangular enclosures of viharas with the cells opening toward the center of the court where stood the stupa. These monasteries housed not only the living monks, but also an ever increasing population of images, each of which required a shelter in keeping with the veneration in which it was held. The statues gradually crowded the monks out of the inner court, and the viharas were converted into chapels, or shrines. A new cloister was built, plainer than the first, for apartments, which were re-

Statue of Buddha in Greco-Buddhist style, wearing the mantle of a Greek philosopher. Metropolitan Museum of Art, New York.

quired for the monastic life, like the chapter house and the refectory of a Christian monastery.

The structural technique of these great Buddhist monasteries leaves much to be desired. They were usually built of roughly hewn stone blocks and coated with a gypsum stucco, upon which were molded figures in relief. Their walls often bulge or sag.

Vishnu, the Preserver of Heaven and Earth, a member of the trinity to which Brahma and Siva also belong. Metropolitan Museum of Art, New York.

Buddhism gained many converts and spread to other countries; and although today there are no Buddhists in India, communities continue to exist in Tibet, China, and Mongolia, where the monks still practice the traditional activities of the religion. Isolated stupas are found in Cambodia, Burma, Borneo, Sumatra, and Ceylon, and the stupa is an indispensable feature of all Buddhist temples.

Architecture was not so important a vehicle for the spreading of Buddhist art as were carved statues and reliefs. Buildings always had to be adapted to the forms required by the local building material available, but the same sculptural themes could be copied anywhere regardless of material.

Subsequent to Alexander's expedition to India, an independent Greco-Bactrian kingdom was founded in the northwest of India by his followers. The Greek leaders were naturally desirous of maintaining relations with the nations of western Asia, the land of their origin. We find, therefore, among other evidences of their feeling for their native land, that the Bactrian kings had their coins cast according to Greek types. Thus, we have in northwestern India a Hellenistic element which contributed not a little to the development of the sculptures representing the story of Buddha: his flight from home, his penance under the Bo tree, his temptation, his illumination, the discussions with the Brahmans, his death and burial. Even the sending of his relics to distant lands were described in detail.

Taken all together, these reliefs form a series of images comparable with

Base and lower part of a group of three figures, similar to the one on the opposite page. Vishnu is in the center with attendants at his sides. Notice the bracelets and rings on their legs and feet. University of Pennsylvania Museum, Philadelphia.

the Christian series of Gospel subjects. Most important of all was the representation of the figure of the founder himself, standing or seated cross-legged, and wearing a long mantle with narrow folds in imitation of those of Greek statues. This draped Buddha was the means of spreading throughout the Far East the marvelous type of drapery arrangement invented by Hellenic sculptors. Thus, in gigantic rock reliefs along the rivers of China and in the temples of far-off Japan, we find the great reformer standing or seated, immobile, in his eyes the languid expression peculiar to the Asiatic, but always clad in the full mantle of the Occident, the garment of the Greek philosophers so familiar to the student of Hellenic art.

Greek imitations were not confined to coins, portraits, architecture, and statuary; Greek influence on this art was felt perhaps most in purely decorative themes. Bands of garlands supported by cupids, and the division of compositions into square compartments and rectangular niches, were a few of the many decorative ideas introduced from the West. Interpretations of Greek models in the development of Buddhist art are as interesting as the imitations. The pseudo-Greek artists of India in many cases show as great a misunderstanding of forms as we find in provincial schools of Classical art among partly civilized peoples of Europe. At first sight it would be easy to mistake certain Buddhist reliefs for works by artists of Gaul or Thrace during the Greco-Roman period.

Buddhist group of faces in stone. From Cambodia. Metropolitan Museum of Art,
New York.

To the European student this Greco-Buddhist art is more instructive
than Eastern art with its unorganized profusion of decorative elements.
We are interested beyond measure to see in this remote land the decorative
themes of Classical art interpreted in the spirit of the East. From the contrast
thus afforded we perceive how different are our own Western aesthetic
reactions.

So long as Buddhist art flourished in India, the old Brahmanic castes
never ceased to combat it with all the traditions of their race. By the

Bronze cauldron of 1500 B.C. Buckingham Collection, The Art Institute of Chicago.

eighth century, however, the people of India became weary of this never-ending religious struggle, and a reconciliation of the two faiths took place. The people returned to the Brahman priests, who in turn adopted many of the concepts of Buddhism, especially in the north of India. With this compromise, Buddhist art lost its purity in India. To this period of Brahmanic revival belong the great pyramidal pagodas which are, perhaps, the most interesting structures in all India.

Unlike the Buddhist monastery, which is the retreat of a religious community, the Brahman sanctuary is a collection of halls for the accommodation of multitudes of pilgrims, and parks laid out with sacred ponds and open porticoes, crowded with fanciful and complicated sculptural compositions. The richness and profusion of the ornamentation of these temples overpower the Occidental mind, accustomed as it is to beauty of an entirely different type. To its exotic character is added the overwhelming effect produced by its enormous mass. The pagodas, or *gopuras*, are quite high; but their division into horizontal bands of reliefs gives them a still loftier appearance. Some of them are pyramidal piles of spires heaped on spires, rising one above another in incalculable profusion. Some of them date from the invasion of the Arabs, when the Peninsula fell under the sway of Islam. The Arabs, long familiar with the architecture of the Byzantine Empire, introduced the dome into India. Here, however, it is often composed of a solid mass of masonry.

From the invasion of the Arabs also date the great military constructions of India, such as the Gates and Walls of Delhi and Benares. Prior to the

Ritual vessel of bronze. Buckingham Collection, The Art Institute of Chicago.

time of the Mogul conquest, India was not in need of military defenses, protected as she was by her rigid caste system from within and by the sea and the mountains from without. The civil architecture, such as that of the palaces of her princes and rajahs, so famous at every period of her history, also belongs to this Indo-Arabic style; the more ancient examples of wood have long since disappeared.

A school of Brahman art combined with Buddhist themes also developed in Indo-China. In the tropical forests of Cambodia we find the ruins of two magnificent groups of buildings rich with relief sculptures of fantastic monsters and strange mythical characters. They are the work of a people called the Khmers, whose imagination and combination of fanciful themes are beyond what the Occidental mind could even have conceived. The art is Indian beyond all question; and the founders of the kingdom seem to have been invaders from India who were well versed in all the traditions of Brahmanic art. The capital which they built at Angkor covered an immense area, judging by the ruins; and it undoubtedly belonged to the days of the glory of the Khmers.

In the sculpture we see represented military expeditions and court festivals of the unknown Khmer kings. Of the history of Angkor all the definite information we have, is that it was taken twice by the Siamese, once in 1353 and again in 1372, after which the kings moved their capital east to Lovek and later to Pnom-Penh, where a shadow of the old kingdom is still in existence under a French protectorate.

The two groups of buildings at Angkor are Angkor-Thom, which seems to have been the residence of the kings, and Angkor-Vat, apparently a monumental temple. The great wall of Angkor-Thom is still standing; but the rank vegetation of the tropics, which has grown about it for centuries, hides the pyramidal pavilions with their horizontal bands of reliefs. The broad avenues of this Versailles of the Far East may still be followed to artificial ponds, where the steps of boat landings still lead down to the water. One traveler writes of his impressions as he mounted the

Chinese bronze. Early Chou Dynasty. Metropolitan Museum of Art, New York.

terraces and towers at Angkor, saying that as he ascended, the trees seemed
higher and higher, and when he looked out from the topmost tower, nothing
could be seen but an unbroken sea of foliage stretching to the far horizon.

Flying dragon. From an imperial tomb of China. University of Pennsylvania Museum, Philadelphia.

The main building of the great temple is a narrow rectangular hall in the center of a series of superimposed concentric courts. The Khmer architects were not acquainted with the vault system and roofed their buildings by advancing each successive course of stone toward the center. So majestic and imposing is the structure, that it is difficult to believe at first sight that its nucleus is a single narrow hall. The interior is covered with reliefs arranged in horizontal bands or framed by niches and projecting architectural features. Here, in spaces enclosed by moldings and structural work, we see representations of dancers, monsters, and Buddhist ceremonies. The galleries connecting the pavilions are lighted by windows of cut stonework in imitation of wooden lattices. Sometimes this openwork, chastely figured, is used decoratively to separate the reliefs between the windows.

These buildings at Angkor represent the highest achievement of the complicated Brahmanic style. It is an art abounding in exquisite details but lacking the orderly and logical arrangement to which the Western mind is accustomed. Buddhism failed to inculcate the principle of logic in the minds of the people of India, although its almost Hellenic sculptures spread Classical ideas throughout eastern Asia. Only a portion of the technique of the Greek thinking was grafted onto the ancient tradition and mythology. The Oriental spirit was in no wise transformed. The reliefs of Angkor-Vat are perhaps the best example we have of this relapse of Oriental art after its partial acceptance of Classical forms.

Easterners themselves have always possessed a conception of the difference

Scythian plaques in gold. They were used by the Chinese artists as models for their winged lions and griffins. University of Pennsylvania Museum, Philadelphia.

between the Oriental and Occidental mind, and of the unalterable nature of the Eastern art. At the Persian court, which was subject to the influence of both Syria and India, the poet Masnavi imagines the king sending for a Greek and an Oriental artist to compete in the decoration of a wall. The Oriental covered the wall with figures from top to bottom; then the Greek cleaned it off completely and on a white surface left precise lines gleaming in the bright sunlight as his finished work. This story testifies to the opinion that the Western artists, though often weak and uncertain in their handling of color, cannot be excelled in their clear-cut treatment of line and form; while the Oriental is confused, eccentric, and capricious.

With all our prejudices, and accustomed as we are to a totally different type of beauty, we may still appreciate the aesthetic qualities of Asiatic art. Any type of art that is sincere in its work is justified. Beauty has no single standard of taste, nor is it monopolized by a single race.

There also existed in India a school of painting which enriched with color the reliefs of the temples; and there is still to be found in the caves of Ajanta a series of great frescoe, which are the oldest paintings of eastern Asia.

Seventh century Chinese Buddhist bronze, showing the Indian type well preserved. University of Pennsylvania Museum, Philadelphia.

CHINA AND JAPAN

The yellow races of Asia do not display the same taste for the agglomeration that we have seen in India. Although they lie to the east, still farther from Western influences, China and Japan were destined to create an art with clearer ideals and a strength for naturalness superior, perhaps, to that of the Occident. We shall sum up in a few words our knowledge of the

The Lotus of the Good Law. Buddhist memorial stela from China. Dated 575 A.D. University of Pennsylvania Museum, Philadelphia.

spiritual world of the yellow races and discuss briefly the artistic schools of these two countries.

China already had an art antedating the influx of Buddhist influences from India. Certain bronzes, great metal drums and sacred vessels for wine, which are plainly works of primitive artists, with their irregularly interlaced patterns, seem to be contemporary with the first dynasties of China. Indeed, they may even antedate the organization of the monarchy and belong to the period when the country was still divided into clans or independent tribes. A few, at least, are ascribed by Chinese antiquarians to the period of the Hsia dynasty, about 2000 B.C. Others are not so old, their profuse decoration placing them in the Chow dynasty which ruled China from 1100 to 255 B.C. Here we find line decorations, spirals, and conventionalized dragons and birds, which remind us of the decorative motifs of the Maoris and the natives of New Guinea. These bronzes also call to mind the ornaments of the Alaskan Indians and the monuments of Mexico. Some investigators go so far as to believe that there was a prehistoric art common to all the peoples of the Pacific, including China where its principal center may have been, and from where it spread to the islands of the Pacific and to Central America. Besides the bronzes, we have from pre-Buddhistic China engraved stones with innumerable figures outlined in profile. To see the designs clearly, it is necessary to rub them with ink, and then make an imprint. They display an extraordinary clarity of vision in their rep-

Three Chinese figures of Bodhisattvas in bronze. These beings, who have reached Enlightenment, postpone their entrance into Nirvana in order to help the human race. British Museum; University of Pennsylvania Museum, Philadelphia; and The Art Institute of Chicago.

resentation of the movements of animals. Calm and repose are also shown with great naturalness.

Other monuments which likewise bear evidence of a very ancient artistic tradition are the colossal figures of warriors and animals in pairs which

Lohan, one of the sixteen companions of Buddha. Life-size ceramic statue from a holy
cave in China. University of Pennsylvania Museum, Philadelphia.

line the avenue leading to the Imperial Tombs. Some are dragons and
winged creatures, which scholars think may be related to the winged bulls
of Babylonian and Persian art. How did they reach China? It was probably
through the Scythians, who employed similar winged animals in their
decorations.

China with her deeply rooted ancestor-worship would naturally preserve
in the tombs great quantities of material which is important archaeologically.
The tombs themselves are subterranean and consist of vaulted chambers
which are approached from a sacred enclosure by a monumental gateway
and avenue of sculptured beasts. It appears that in earliest times, the de-

A portrait, and the statue of an attendant. Both from a tomb in China. University of Pennsylvania Museum, Philadelphia.

ceased was buried with his slaves, wives, and horses sacrificed to accompany their master beyond the grave. Later, however, the burial of living beings was abolished, and clay figures, which are found today in such quantities, took their place.

About 67 A.D. Buddhism came into China from India. A pious emperor, inspired by a dream of the birth of a divine being, sent emissaries to India, who returned with Buddhist books, relics, and relief carvings. In India, Buddhism had had to combat a religion based on the caste system and rit-

One of the horses of Emperor Tang Taï-Tsong. From his tomb finished in 644 A.D.
University of Pennsylvania Museum, Philadelphia.

uals. But in China the people were more receptive. Confucius, the philosopher of resignation and lover of peaceful compromise, had already prepared
his people for the tenets of the Buddhist faith. It spread rapidly throughout China. Everywhere monasteries sprang up; and in them Buddhist art
and dogma were preserved in all their purity. For this reason the recent
discoveries in China are of great interest; they enable us to follow in detail
the various stages in the development of Buddhist art.

Now that the results of several scientific expeditions have placed the
different schools of Chinese art in their proper chronological setting, it is
possible to hazard an opinion concerning the history of art in the Far
East. In the gigantic sculptures and reliefs found in the mountainous
country of northern China, we see how faithfully China preserved the
Classical traditions of Greco-Buddhist art as well as the principles of the
Indian school down to the sixth century. Many of these enormous figures
are carved on stone walls along which innumerable smaller reliefs of minor
personages are set in niches. There is hardly a noticeable difference between
the reliefs of this Buddhist pantheon of northern China and those of the
semi-Greco-Buddhist art of India. Perhaps the only distinction is in their

Horses and camels from a Chinese tomb. The animals are lamenting the death of their
master. University of Pennsylvania Museum, Philadelphia.

peculiar emanations of serenity and peace so typical of Buddha. In China
there is a deeper abstraction and an even greater gentleness and resignation
to the will of the Infinite.

Until the eighth century there were apparently no artists in China suf-

Portrait of a Buddhist priest. By Chao You. Yuan Dynasty. Freer Gallery of Art, Washington, D. C.

ficiently independent of the Greco-Buddhist tradition to constitute what could be called a genuinely native Chinese school. Their principal work consisted of portraits which were placed in the temples or kept at home to perpetuate the memory of ancestors. Only rarely do we find portraits in early tombs; it was sufficient to represent the deceased by an engraved stone on which was a specimen of his handwriting. Among the Chinese, calligraphy was considered one of the fine arts, just as music is regarded by us as a manifestation of the spirit of greatness. Later on, however, especially during the Tang period, the burial chamber was filled with painted terra-cotta figures of all the household—servants, squires, valets, grooms, musicians, and dancers. The present breakup of China has dissipated respect for the tombs, and archaeological vampires have looted the Chinese necropolises. Thus an enormous number of figurines has become available for study. Some of them are very good; some are worthless commercial products that were purchased for the funeral ceremonies. All of them teach us a great deal about the customs of the Chinese of Tang times. The deceased was carried in pomp in a procession of his servants, concubines, buffoons, and jesters. Some of the figures must have been imported from distant lands, for they have curly hair. Often a clay model of his house was buried with the master. Some of these objects are artistic masterpieces, more than mere ethnographical documents. Some of the horses and camels of the funeral

The household ironing. Chinese painting. Tang Dynasty. Museum of Fine Arts, Boston.

processions, for example, are worthy of comparison with the best objects of this sort in any part of the world.

The buildings of China are of wood, or of stone in imitation of timbered structures. They are ornamented chiefly with gilded dragons and with lacquered panels and terra-cotta tiles. They present an appearance very different from the monumental structures of India with their crowded reliefs. The Imperial Palace at Peking is hardly more than a vast park with bridges and kiosks, but the gates and towers of its great stone wall are decorated with beautiful terra-cotta tiles. The pagodas of China with their many-storied towers and tiled roofs bear a certain resemblance to the stone gopuras of India with their steplike bands of decoration. It seems that some common origin may possibly exist.

Since neither the ancestor cult nor the philosophical religion of Confucius called for the construction of great temples, monumental construction was confined to the walls of the cities and their imposing gates. Beautiful pavilions above the entrances were often built for the guards. One of the most famous military constructions in the world is the Great Wall of China, which extends entirely across the north of China with gates at intervals.

It was not in architecture, however, that the people of the Far East revealed their greatest genius. The speculative philosophy of Confucius led them rather to derive inspiration for their greatest creative impulses from

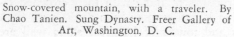

Snow-covered mountain, with a traveler. By   Bamboos. By Chao Chin. Yuan
Chao Tanien. Sung Dynasty. Freer Gallery of   Dynasty. Strehlneek Collection,
Art, Washington, D. C.   Shanghai.

nature itself. The great sage felt an infinite sympathy for all humble
creatures, his brothers in this fugitive world. "One day I dreamed I was
a butterfly," he says, "who knows if today I am not a butterfly dreaming
that I am a man?" The earliest paintings are filled with the spirit of
Confucius. Favorite subjects were: an ascetic sitting beneath a tree contemplating in silent ecstasy the mist rising from the valley; an almond
branch swayed by the spring breeze; a singing bird coyly perched upon a
reed; and the misty atmosphere charmingly suggested by transparent masses
of color. One generation of artists succeeded another under the passing
dynasties. Sometimes even emperors themselves were artists of repute.
Among the painters were also many monks. A Japanese painter-monk
late in the eighth century, wrote of the training he had in China. "The

master," said he, "taught me that the mysteries of the faith cannot be transmitted without the aid of pictures. I, therefore, brought with me sixteen artists and taught them to paint the sacred figures."

From the eighth century on, Chinese Buddhistic art developed rapidly, and during the long centuries of the Middle Ages works of Chinese art were far superior to contemporary European paintings. The Oriental artists seem to have been entirely conscious of their superiority; for when in the eighteenth century two Jesuit painters tried to teach the Chinese the principles of Italian painting, they failed to arouse interest. It is interesting to note the opinion held by Tsu-I-Kuei in his *Observations on Painting*. "The Occidentals," he says "are fond of giving their pictures perspective, and nothing could be more correct than the effect they produce of depth and reality. Figures, houses, and trees cast shadows as in nature itself. Their mural paintings of palaces and houses seem so real that one almost wants to walk into them. While their work shows great skill in draftsmanship and execution, I would hardly go so far as to class it as veritable painting."

What, then, are the fundamental principles of the art of these Chinese painters who refuse even the name of painting to the work of the artists of the Occident? In the first place, it is not realism for which they strive. They seek rather to infuse symbolism into everything they paint. They usually endow nature with the same basic sentiments which govern or inspire mankind. Rocks rise, cliff on cliff, as if aspiring to perfection; trees wave in docile obedience to the wind; water flows as though conscious of its mission to refresh and purify. It is interesting to note, by the way, that a Chinese artist can scarcely conceive of a landscape without water. Curiously enough,

A Japanese painting imitating the Chinese style. By Baitzu Yama.

Two Japanese prints from the "One Hundred Views of Fujiyama" by Hokusai.

the very word *painting* in Chinese is formed by two syllables, one meaning water, and the other land. Animals, too, seem capable of sensing the good and the beautiful. An eagle, lost in deep thought enjoys the coolness of a waterfall; a tiger shows his moral strength; a gracefully swaying swan is conscious of the beauty of the lotus blossoms.

Man, too, is animated by uplifting sentiments. Pilgrims in search of truth approach the hermit's hut with lights gleaming out into the tempestuous night, a pictorial symbol of the tumult within the soul. Although he never loses sight of the moral forces by which mankind is ruled, the Chinese artist also paints domestic scenes.

Chinese art never loses a sympathetic feeling for the humbler beings and plants.

Girl combing her hair. A Japanese print. The Art Institute of Chicago.

The animals of Greek art have an almost human quality—the horses of the Parthenon seem animated with intelligence; but Oriental painting and sculpture, because of the tender understanding of its artists, have found something greater—the divine spark in nature itself. When the Oriental artist paints a plant, every leaf is outlined or painted with an individuality of its own. Long before our modern school of Impressionism, the Chinese artists were satisfied with trying to reproduce the color of a single cloud or the iridescent tones of the mist. In even the most unimportant details they displayed the same care to retain a sense of the harmony of nature.

Hsieh Ho at the end of the fifth century laid down six canons for painting. The first prescribes that a work shall express "the spiritual element of life." From the writer's rather vague language we gather that this element is to be attained by attempting to represent the characteristic movement of every creature and plant. The second canon he calls the "law of the bones," by which he means that the artist must look into the structure of every organism. The third is "conformity to reality," Aristotle's "law of probability;" the fourth, the understanding of generic forms of which individuals are less important manifestations; the fifth, orderly composition; and the sixth, the law of types, or what we call iconography. Thus, the

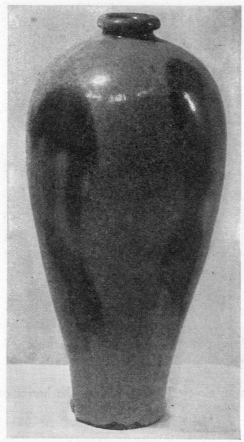

Chiin Yao pot with China's famous blue and lavendar glaze. Sung Dynasty. University of Pennsylvania Museum, Philadelphia.

Asiatic artist is expected to express life as a whole and to look into every living thing, catching the spirit from its movements, and its inner structure through its outer forms.

The history of Chinese painting deserves more space than we can give to it here. Not only is the appreciation of nature in the Orient greater than in the Occidental schools of painting, but the artist of the East is able through his skill to achieve a more refined interpretation of the natural forms than has any artist of the West.

Unlike China, Japan required temples for collective worship. The old Shinto cult of ancestors and deceased emperors became merged with the worship of Buddha, and we find in the Japanese temples huge bronze figures of Buddha, some of colossal size. Japanese architecture in the main follows the Chinese model, although the volcanic nature of the islands has made it necessary to change somewhat the appearance of the temples. They are lower; and their foundation walls are great polygonal blocks of stone, above which rise the upper stories of wood covered with lacquer and gold. Only a few of their great national temples can be compared with the great churches of the Occident. However, they usually have an imposing situation. The complex of gates and sacred enclosures on the mountain's side gain from harmony with its picturesque surroundings what it lacks in massiveness. Characteristic is the fantastic landscape, with surrounding groves and waterfalls with plunge down the mountainside below the temple. The great landscape-architects of Japan, like those of seventeenth-century France and of Renaissance Italy, take joy in commanding nature to obey the caprices of man, but without perverting the laws of nature.

Two Chinese vases. Late Ming Dynasty. University of Pennsylvania Museum, Philadelphia.

Domestic architecture in Japan is extremely simple. Private homes and even royal palaces are composed only of tiled roofs supported by the necessary columns and beams. The walls are of wood, and the interior partitions of paper. Bamboo screens are extensively used.

At a very early period Japan learned from China the art of painting. One of the first Japanese artists, Kanoaka, who lived in the eighth century, enjoyed a reputation as great as that of some of the early artists of the Italian Renaissance. Sesshu, a fifteenth-century painter, was important enough to be called to China to decorate the residence of the Emperor. On one of the ceilings of this great palace he painted the sacred mountain of his own Japan, the volcano Fujiyama, which so often appears in the landscapes of the Japanese artists. Our knowledge of Japanese art which is greater today than formerly, has taught us that it is not second-rate, as we once believed.

We find that every type of Chinese painting, when introduced into

Japanese screens painted with designs of folded and hanging garments.
Museum of Fine Arts, Boston.

Japan, takes on an entirely national character. The Japanese add a dy-
namism and a vivacity of detail that is almost neurotic and is quite foreign
to the original Chinese. Japanese art, however, is in no sense a poor and
unintelligent translation of the Chinese. It excels in certain forms that
were practiced by the Chinese only on a small scale. Their folding screens,
for example, are typically Japanese and compare in beauty with Western
fresco decoration. There are different types of design on these screens:
some have flowers and birds; some have figures in a landscape or a room;
and others have objects in still-life painted on them. The Japanese screens

Japanese Buddhist statues. University of Pennsylvania Museum, Philadelphia, and
Metropolitan Museum of Art, New York.

Actors' masks for the No drama of Japan. Eleventh century. Museum of Fine Arts, Boston.

were painted at first in simple colors; but by the sixteenth century they acquired gilded backgrounds, probably inspired by the figures silhouetted against gold on the Italian altarpieces imported by Jesuits.

Another form of art in which the Japanese excelled was that of theater masks. In the Imperial Collection at Tokyo and in the National Treasure of Nara are amazingly expressive masks carved in wood, which date from the seventh century. Some more modern ones have reached our museums. All of them exhibit the passion and the strange mixture of kindness and ferocity so typical of Japanese drama.

Japanese prints have penetrated our homes and have brought scenes of Japanese life into our midst. Wood-block prints have always been regarded as second-rate, and no skilled artist made a business of making them until about the middle of the eighteenth century, when Hokusai, a great Japanese painter, began to specialize in this type of work. He painted a series of one hundred views of Fujiyama, showing the sacred mountain in each season of the year, at every hour of the day, in the mist, in the falling rain, in light, in shadow, and even through the meshes of a fisherman's net. Hokusai had a marvelous talent, and his ardent creative passion never gave him any rest. He lived to a ripe old age and worked until the day of his death. In his later years he signed himself "an old man whose mania

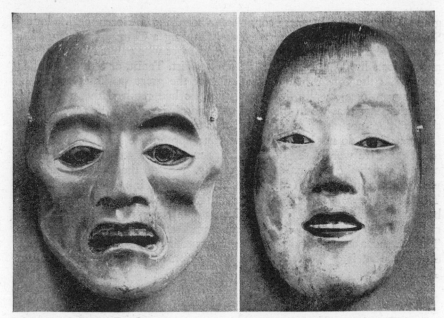

Japanese masks for the No drama. Museum of Fine Arts, Boston.

for painting will not permit him to cease." Indeed, his genius is one of the happiest that has ever blessed a man. We see in the works of Hokusai the latest phase of Oriental painting, a naturalism which turns with preference to everything related to the common people, especially to groups, such as people crossing a bridge, a street quarrel, laborers at work, a shop, or children at play.

Given over wholly to fanciful contemplation of natural forms, Japanese art has accomplished marvels in the production of small ornamental objects decorated profusely with leaves, birds, and butterflies. In the making of exquisite bronze sword-guards we see the inexhaustible imaginative resources of the metalworkers of Japan. Theirs was a famous industry, for the old warrior clans of Japan had a great passion for beautifully decorated weapons. These guards, which were set on the hilts of the swords, could be easily changed, and one man might own a large number of them. The demand was great, and therefore, the artists exerted themselves to create the most graceful patterns to be found in Japanese art. The taste displayed in these guards appears to be so modern that one could easily believe them to be the work of contemporary European artists.

We Westerners have begun only recently to realize our handicaps in appreciating fully the art of the Far East, because, in addition to our mental differences, we do not have complete and accurate translations of the great Oriental books. That we have a different outlook, there is no doubt. Imagine a Chinese or a Japanese connoisseur admiring a Florentine Madonna! Similarly, we are unappreciative when beholding a Chinese landscape. But we suffer also from faulty preparation. The sages who painted those oriental masterpieces lived lives saturated with Buddhist, Taoist, or Shintoist philosophies. At the time when the majority of the great works of art of the Orient were created, all oriental philosophies had resolved themselves into a mystic belief that we in the West call "pantheism." But this word "pantheism" does not satisfy an Oriental; it is too abstract and too precise. Unfortunately we do not have any word more appropriate for it, and this lack of an objective word reveals our inability to convey that relation of man to cosmos, which the Orientals feel so clearly. Nor do the Orientals need, as we do, a precise definition of such sensations. We think of their books—the *Tao,* the *Upanishads,* the *Zen*—as commentaries, as involved and obscure, because we insist upon finding in them organized systems of thought like chains of logical premises. The Orientals smile at our lack of understanding. They consider childish and lowbred our impertinent desire for mathematical order in what is essentially beyond the relation of simple cause and effect.

Netsuke, worn as an object of
identification.

Archaic figurines from the Pedregal region, Mexico.

ART OF THE AMERICAN INDIANS

THE ORIGIN OF THE INDIANS of South, Central, and North America was for a long time a subject of speculation and study on the part of scholars, and of disagreement among them as well. Now it seems quite well established that the aboriginals of these two continents migrated from Asia by way of the Aleutian Islands long before the dawn of history. After their arrival, they lost all close connection with the lands from which they had come and started a civilization of their own, retaining, however, racial characteristics and certain cultural traditions which link them with the East. Scholars find, for example, a resemblance between Chinese and Mayan art forms. The dragon, the plumed serpent, and the animal devouring a man are motifs common to the iconography of both, and it seems plausible that they came from a common origin.

This theory of Oriental influence, especially in connection with the Indians of North America, has been very distasteful to American scholars, and they have been loath to accept it. The author, while he believes in the original migration of the Amerindians from the Asiatic continent, goes further and is convinced that in very early times the Eastern influence continued to be renewed by Chinese merchants and sailors, as well as by zealous

Model of the Temple of Tajin in Veracruz. American Museum of Natural History,
New York.

Buddhist missionaries, who came across the Pacific at great risk and brought
with them at least a few objects of jade and gold, which affected the art
forms of the people of America.

During the centuries that elapsed before the white man's appearance on
these continents, the Indians reached a high point of cultural development.
When the Spaniards came to Mexico and South America in the fifteenth
and sixteenth centuries, they were dazzled by the magnificence of the architecture, sculpture, and minor arts found there. Within this civilization,
however, were already seeds of decadence, and it fell rapidly before the Spanish *Conquistadores*. These conquerors were ruthless in their victory: they
tore down buildings, destroyed the beautiful heathen sculpture which they as
devout Christians believed to be the work of the devil, burned the books,
and reduced the people to slavery. They declared that the religious faith
and the Roman civil law which they brought compensated the people for
the loss of their material civilization and the destruction of their gods.

Finally, after several hundred years of repression, the Indian in Mexico
is beginning to find again the culture trodden down for so long. Mexican
artists are bringing traditional art forms and ideals to the surface again and,
basing their work on what is rooted in the soil, are making a most significant
contribution to contemporary art.

In the Pedregal lava flow near Mexico City have been found what are
believed to be the oldest remains of the Indian civilization in Central

America. A pyramid fifty-two feet high and four hundred and twelve feet in diameter has been excavated there, and this ancient and long-lost temple seems to be the prototype of all the vast pyramidal piles of Mayan and Aztec times. Clay figurines, stone statues, and pottery also were found in large numbers and are comparable to the archaic works of art from which were developed great artistic schools in other parts of the world.

The figurines show a great deal of individuality in their treatment, although they are all of the same archaic style. Some of the figures are nude, some clothed, some of them are seated, others are standing; but the bodies are usually heavy, with tapering limbs, and the features of the faces are crude, either made by bits of clay stuck on or indicated by hollows gouged out. Color is sometimes used to mark tattooing or the textile designs of the clothing. It seems likely that these little figures were intended to represent the deceased in this world, that he might live on in the world of the dead, as did the portrait sculptures of the Egyptians. The nude female figures may have had the magic significance of inducing fertility.

The stone figures of this archaic period are still more primitive than the clay. The explanation for this might lie in the fact that stone is a harder material and more difficult to manipulate than clay. The general type is a rounded oblong stone roughly divided into head and torso, with limbs and features indicated in low relief. These sculptures aim at realism and achieve a certain effect of caricature, which is often clever and humorous. They

A Mayan temple near Rio Bec, Campeche. American Museum of Natural History, New York.

Reconstruction of the Pyramid of Tenayuca, near Mexico, showing the double shrine on the top. American Museum of Natural History, New York.

suggest a tendency toward conventionalization and geometric forms which became common at a later time.

Archaic pottery is heavy and stolid in appearance, with sturdy handles and legs. The decoration consists of simple painted designs or, more frequently, of carved patterns.

The archaic art of Mexico seems to have spread into both North and South America, and its influence is felt throughout the development of North American Indian art. In the Valley of Mexico, where the Pedregal lava flow was found, there is a stratification of cultures covering two thousand years, and an attempt has been made to trace a chronological development from the archaic art to the Toltec and Aztec. In no other place is found material for such a scientific study as here, and although efforts have been made to relate this culture with those farther south—with the Mayan, Mixtecan, and Zapotecan — there have been no very successful results.

The most important of the southern neighbors were the Mayas of Honduras, Guatemala, and Yucatán. The Mayan buildings have a truncated pyramid as a base, like the one we observed at Pedregal; but we are not sure whether the

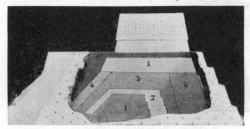

Model of the Pyramid of Tenayuca, showing the five different substructures.

Castillo, the Mayan temple of Kukulcan, at Chichen Itzá in Yucatán.

Mayan objects of jade, showing certain evidence of the influence of Early Chinese styles of decoration. University of Pennsylvania Museum, Philadelphia, and American Museum of Natural History, New York.

idea originated with them or whether they took it from the more northern Mexicans. Low, flat-topped, extinct volcanoes which look like step-pyramids abound in the Central Valley of Mexico and suggest themselves as models which the early builders might have used. On the other hand, it is just as logical to suppose that because of the torrential rains, which made the soil of Honduras for a part of the year like a marshy pond, a heavy superstructure like a pyramid was necessary for the buildings and was developed here out of necessity. We know that in Mesopotamia the step-pyramid was invented to safeguard from floods and tidal waves the shrines which were placed on low ground.

The Mayas first settled in Honduras and Guatemala and developed a great empire, the Old Mayan Empire. Around 600 A.D. the whole nation moved to Yucatán, leaving the cities of the Old Empire to be preyed upon by the jungle. Thus we know when the Empire ended; but scholars are not able to state with equal confidence when it began, nor the exact date at which the buildings were constructed. There are inscriptions in hieroglyphics which have not yet been deciphered completely. The dates, which alone

Mayan vase of jade, with decorations similar to those on Early Chinese bronzes; and a Mayan mask with Oriental features. University of Pennsylvania Museum, Philadelphia.

have been made out, are not very helpful since they can be interpreted according to two different systems of chronology. The inscriptions can be interpreted to place the buildings at the beginning of the Christian Era or several centuries earlier, so that we are left in doubt. The earliest art and culture of the Mayan Empire which has come down to us show signs of great antiquity, but it is sophisticated and complicated, rather than archaic. We cannot estimate how long the empire must have been in existence before it reached this degree of development.

Mayan civilization has been likened to the Greek, and Aztec to the Roman; for, it is said, the Mayas seem to have been originators and men of creative genius, while the Aztecs were organizers and fighters who used borrowed art forms. This generalization is only partly true; the Aztecs did exhibit artistic originality, though of a type different from the Mayas'. Perhaps a better comparison is found if we liken the Mayas to the Byzantines, and the Aztecs to the Nordic invaders, each of which peoples made its own original contribution.

The study of Mayan and Aztec ruins reveals certain definite types of buildings constructed on top of the pyramidal substructure of which we have already spoken. There are the temples and also, fewer in number, dwellings for priests or nobility. It is possible, too, that the towering pyramid temples of Yucatán, called *Castillos* (castles) by the Indians today, were used as strongholds in times of invasion. Sometimes there was a group of rooms at the foot of the pyramid; usually at the top were two shrines, each one sheltering a different deity. The pre-Columbian pyramids, both Mayan and Aztec, are massive and solid, with no rooms inside for religious practices or for tombs like the Egyptian pyramids. They were simply pedestals.

Archway of Labnah, Yucatán, showing a typical Mayan wall made of rubble and faced with stones.

Mayan and Aztec cultures alike had cycles of fifty-two years. At the end of each cycle the tribes broke all their utensils and put out their fires, then they refurnished their houses and renovated their sacred buildings. For the pyramids, this meant putting on a new facing of stone, sometimes several feet thick. The pyramid grew in size with each successive layer. The earlier facings have been brought to light by excavations, and the Pyramid at Tenayuca, as an example, was found to have six smaller pyramids buried within it. The last layer seems to be of the year 1507; so, according to the cycles, the first and original pyramid must have been covered in 1247, and the other facings added in 1299, 1351, 1403, and 1455 respectively.

In one of the pyramids of Chichen Itzá, the shrine on the top, as well as the pyramidal substructure, was built onto each fifty-two years. When modern archaeologists in excavating the top of the present pyramid reached the chamber of the shrine below, they found the old original jaguar-god carved in stone and painted red, his spots indicated with inlays of mother-of-pearl.

The Mayas, and the Aztecs as well, had a taste for planning buildings in a group. It can hardly be called city planning, because the common people lived in thatched huts of which all trace has long since disappeared. But in their monumental buildings they had a sense of grouping that is very rare among the primitive peoples. None of the archaeological sites of Mesopotamia which have been excavated lately, as for instance, Ur of the Chaldees, shows any sign of having been planned in advance. Not even in Delphi or Olympia is there any evidence that a plan for the sanctuary with all its buildings had been made. But the Mayas planned their cities definitely with a square, or civic center, and a castillo on each of the four sides. Larger cities had several such groups of buildings.

The buildings, including the temple and the palace on the level of the ground, were bare inside. The monumental mass of stone was profusely decorated on the exterior, but it enclosed dark, long, narrow rooms, which were divided into still narrower alcoves. A more spacious interior was prevented by construction limitations. The Mayas had not learned to build arches, and the only method of roofing which they knew was that of a tri-angular-shaped arch made by stone beams, each row projecting beyond the row below until the sides met at the top of the arch. A sort of mud-mortar was used as a binding material. The Indian peoples never learned to employ mortar of sand and lime in proportions to make a good, strong cement; and the lack of good building-material compelled the Mayas to build very thick walls to the detriment of the rooms inside. Moreover, because of poor building ma-terials and inadequate methods of putting them together, the buildings disintegrated, great parts of the walls fell, and the vaults collapsed. Very rarely, perhaps only in the Zapotecan region, did the pre-Columbian architects use columns and thus succeed in building rooms of greater width. The best pre-served example of the use of stone shafts is found in the ruins of Mitla.

On occasion the Mayas and Aztecs used wooden lintel structure, which in rotting let the walls cave in. However, be-cause the doors were few and there were no windows at all, a great many façades of Mayan buildings are still standing. The decoration is geometric; each motif is carved on a separate stone in high relief and fastened into the rubble filling of the wall. A rich, harmonious effect is produced by this type of ornamentation. The style of

Decoration of stonework in fret design and mosaic. House of the Governor, at Uxmal, Yucatán.

Restoration of the Temple of Xochicalco, and detail of plumed serpent from the same building.

design suggests two distinct prototypes: one, a wooden building; and the other, an adobe structure faced with cut stone.

The distribution of the reliefs on the Mayan façades is proof of a certain capacity of the American aboriginals for logical reasoning. The decoration is continuous, like the friezes of Classical buildings, and arranged in horizontal bands separated by simple moldings. The lower section of the building is very often entirely plain and unadorned, marked only by the stones in its structure. The undecorated areas help to set off the decorated bands and render them strikingly effective. It is interesting to compare the Classic quality of these Mayan buildings with the highly decorative quality of the Hindu temples, which are covered with reliefs and allow the eye no place to rest. The sense of proportion and fitness characteristic of the early Maya is also in strong contrast with the modern American Indian's aesthetic taste. The sand paintings of the Navajos and the buffalo hunts painted on hides are lacking the logical co-ordination of the much earlier work of the Mayas.

Quetzalcoatl, or the plumed serpent-god, as interpreted by Toltec and Aztec artists. Teotihuacan and Tenotxitlan.

Realism was never attempted in the friezes of the Mayan façades. Geometrical forms, such as curvilinear shapes symbolic of Quetzalcoatl, the plumed serpent, and other animal-gods prevail. Sometimes the animal shape is more clearly represented than at others when it is conventionalized almost beyond recognition. So far from actual appearance does the form of the plumed serpent sometimes

Above: Mayan priest. Museum of Guatemala
of Natural History, New York.

Left: Maize-god throwing the seed into the
earth. Stela from Piedras Negras, Guatemala.
University of Pennsylvania Museum,
Philadelphia.

Two Mayan chiefs. The one on the ground is torturing himself by pulling a
coarse rope through his tongue. From Piedras Negras, Guatemala.

Xochipilli, the Aztec god of spring, with a necklace of buds and flowers. National Museum of Mexico.

become, that it has been taken for an elephant's trunk or a tapir's head; and these forms have been cited as proof of the importation of Mayan decorative motives from the Orient, since neither elephants nor tapirs were known to Pre-Columbian America. This theory of importation created some excitement several years ago; but the Americanists stubbornly continued to believe that the serpent was neither a tapir's head nor an elephant's trunk, but a symbol which originated in America.

The same sort of confusion in understanding the origin and meaning of a symbol occurred in the days of the Spanish conquest in connection with the symbol of the Cross. On one of the most famous Mayan reliefs, the "Tablet of the Cross" from Palenque, we see two Mayan priests worshiping a cruciform symbol which looks like the Christian Cross. It seemed natural to those who came from Christian lands that the Cross should have reached America, since the Apostle Thomas was supposed to have gone to the Indies, and in those days the Indies were believed to be America. We know now, however, beyond doubt that the cross in the Aztec and Mayan reliefs symbolizes the universe reduced to the four corners of the world, the four winds, and the four sides of the starry horizon.

Fresco painting was used a great deal for interior decoration in pre-Columbian America. In the Temple of the Warriors at Chichen Itzá, fragments have been pieced together to make a complete mural about nine feet high and twelve feet long. It pictures a Mayan seacoast village, and, as in the paintings of the Far East, perspective is obtained by placing more distant objects higher in the composition. Men and women go about their daily tasks; houses, boats, and trees are evenly scattered over the whole surface of the picture, as if the artist feared to leave any empty spaces. Many of the tombs in the necropolis of the Zapotecan kings at Monte Alban were painted with frescoes, and traces of the painted decoration are to be seen in the Toltec and Aztec monuments in the Valley of Mexico. These frescoes have not yet been studied as they deserve to be. Their colors are clear and fresh. They include a great variety of reds, ochers, and greens.

Separated from the buildings, but related to them, were often set up sculptured stones, or stelae, upon the surfaces of which were carved representations of gods as well as hieroglyphs. The beautiful stela of the maize-god from Piedras Negras, now at the University of Pennsylvania Museum, Philadelphia, is a splendid example of the best work of this kind. The relief of Piedras Negras has an almost Classic reserve. It is not confused with many details as are other Mayan reliefs. From the top of heaven the maize-god lets fall the seeds which an Indian below is waiting to receive. No effort is wasted on filling every crack and cranny with extraneous ornaments. Some of these stelae are of gigantic size, several yards high. The gods represented are robed in elaborate trappings with fantastic decorations. They wear headdresses of plumes taller than themselves.

Centeotl, Aztec god of maize. The Art Institute of Chicago.

From the hieroglyphics we can estimate the relative ages of these monuments, but we are not able to correlate them with our calendar to determine how old they actually are. Astronomy seems to have been extraordinarily advanced among the Mayas. On one of the stelae we see represented an astronomical congress, in which the squatting scholars seem to be discussing details of the science of the heavens. According to the Mayas the stars were grouped into constellations, some of them having the same names as ours. This would be final proof of the common ancestry of the American Indians and Far Eastern peoples if the constellations were not different; but, unfortunately, the Mayas did not group the constellations like those of

Mayan relief from Piedras Negras, Guatemala. Representing a council of Mayan chiefs. The overlord argues with them from the throne. University of Pennsylvania Museum, Philadelphia.

Babylonia which are still used in the rest of the world, the Far East included.

The Mayan stelae could be put in the rank of highy developed sculpture because they are independent monuments. Besides this, the Mayas, like the Aztecs after them, carved a number of excellent figures of gods and heroes. But the Mayas, as well as the Aztecs, produced the very best of their works by carving masks in hard stone or rock crystal. These are without doubt the best artistic products of America up to the present day. Not even the white races of America that rank high in their contemporary civilization have produced anything in the western hemisphere comparable to the masks of the Mayas and Aztecs of pre-Columbian times. To the reader it may seem sheer exaggeration and delightful extravagance to declare that the obsidian and crystal masks of the Mayas and Aztecs are, from an aesthetic point of view, superior to the great buildings of our cities and the statues which adorn them; but it is a fact that in the humble work of the pre-Columbian Indians we find a superior result. The objects are small; but beauty does not require size. Aztec and Mayan masks were used by the chiefs and the gods, who are represented on the reliefs as wearing them, hanging from their necks like amulets. We do not know whether they were meant to be the portraits of deceased great men. Masks have been found with the dead. The cadavers, tied in a sitting position, wore the masks.

Mayan and Aztec masks are stereotyped, and they repeat well-established types. But they vary in beauty, in size, stone, and color. The characteristics of the Indian races are revealed to perfection by those masks. The faces are still, passive, quiet; but they have a penetrating gaze and an interrogation on their lips, a barely perceptible grimace of transcendental sarcasm.

Many of the masks are carved in granite, obsidian, or jade; and the black, green, or gray polished material seems to take different shapes with the variation of light. Some of the masks change in expression every time they are moved and as the light strikes them from different angles. No artist in Egypt or Greece ever produced a face with such kaleidoscopic possibilities.

In the minor arts the Mayas were skilled workmen. Their pottery was decorated with painting, modeling, engraving, and stamping. As in sculpture, realistic forms are combined with geometric, and hieroglyphs frequently appear. The designs were drawn in black on an

Mayan stone disk, with a carved portrait. American Museum of Natural History, New York.

orange or yellow background, and light washes of color were added to give brilliance to the whole. The surface was polished by rubbing. The work of the lapidary is nothing short of amazing when we remember with what crude tools he worked. Obsidian and jade were carved into fantastic shapes, and semi-precious stones were set in mosaic plaques of great beauty.

Mayan, Zapotecan, and Aztec works in pure gold were made by the lost wax process. Some gold objects have been recovered by dragging the Cenote, or sacred pond, at Chichen Itzá. Many and better articles appeared at the royal Zapotecan tombs of Monte Alban.

Aztec laughing mask. National Museum of Mexico.

Ornamental feather work was general among the peoples of America. Elaborate ceremonial costumes or wall hangings, such as were described in the accounts of the Conquistadores, were made by attaching brightly colored feathers to cloth. The most famous feather-work is the well-known series of mantles presented to Cortés by Montezuma. Cortés presented them to his sovereign, Charles V, who in turn sent them to Archduke Ferdinand. They had long been given up

Toltec mask of greenish basalt. American Museum of Natural History, New York.

for lost when they came to light in the Castle of Ambras in the Tyrol, where they were rescued and sent to the Museum in Vienna.

We have studied Mayan and Aztec art as one, because in spite of the many differences of race and culture they had many traits in common. As a matter of fact, we know very little of the history of either of these two peoples. We have mentioned the fact that the Mayas of the Old Empire left their ancestral settlements in the forestland of Honduras and Guatemala for the dry and barren Yucatán. There they thrived and built the New Empire, and it was there that the Spaniards found them still building cities. Owing to their tribal feuds and the advance of the Aztecs toward the south, the New Empire was doomed when Yucatán was conquered by Montejo and his little band of men.

In the Valley of Mexico after the period of archaic culture which we have already mentioned, the Toltecs were undisputed, except for occasional Mayan raids, for more than a thousand years. Probably most of the great inventions of the Toltecs were adopted and developed by the Aztecs, who were new-comers to Mexico. The record of their migration from the north to the Central Valley is preserved in beautiful drawings. That this people preferred pictorial chronicles to hieroglyphic texts is fortunate for us, since their pictures are comprehensible and tell us something of Aztec history.

The Aztecs had been in the Central Valley only two hundred and fifty

Olmec mask. The Mrs. James Murphy Collection, New York.

years when Cortés arrived. In this short time they had passed from the nomadic Indian culture, such as we still see among the Indians of the United States, to the status of a settled nation, organized, disciplined, and conscious of its strength. They trampled on the old Toltecs and subjected them to servitude, and conquered the other tribes around. The Aztecs needed prisoners for human sacrifice, and this detail of their religion made them very objectionable neighbors and masters. There was no association possible with the Aztecs because their domination meant an exaction of victims for their war-god. The need of prisoners compelled them to make incursions, even into far-away Yucatán. When Cortés came, he found the Mexican nations under the power of the Aztecs very willing to help him.

Since the Aztecs did so much fighting and traveling, and since they were

Front and side view of the Aztec goddess of obstetrics. Brummer Collection, New York.

capable of learning from experience, they were able to develop a political regime which was most like that of the white race up to that time. The cause of their progress—the campaigns for the acquisition of victims—was in time destined to prove fatal, but they attained temporary success at least. Their example is encouraging for the future of the Indian race. While the Aztecs did not reach the high scientific knowledge of Mayan astronomical computations, nevertheless they had all the knowledge they needed. In art they did not produce elaborate reliefs like the "Tablet of the Cross" of Palenque, nor did they create the fantastic decorations of the stelae of the Old Mayan Empire; but their masks are some of the most astonishing carved stones of the Western Hemisphere.

The planning art of the Mayas and Toltecs was carried further by the Aztecs. In the neighborhood of Mexico City is the Aztec citadel of Teotihuacan, a monumental enclosure of walls with altars on top, more imposing than anything in modern architecture. The German fortification in Tannenberg most nearly resembles the Aztec citadel of Teotihuacan, but it is an imitation of a medieval fortress and lacks the authenticity of the more ancient and striking citadel at Teotihuacan.

We have left to the last a brief enumeration of the different peoples of Mexico and Central America, because the differences in their works of art

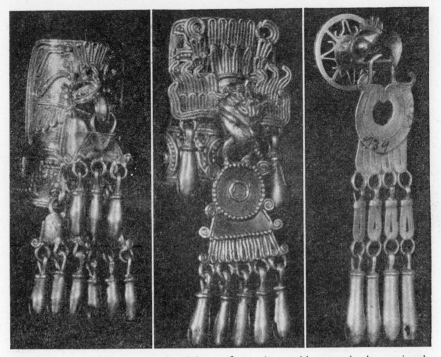

Zapotecan jewels. The two on the right are finger rings, with an eagle that carries the hieroglyphic of jade. The one on the left is an earring. The eagle's head comes out of the sign of the sun and carries the hieroglyphic of the moon. Discovered by Dr. Alfonso Caso in the Royal Tombs at Monte Alban. Oaxaca.

are not great enough to justify separate treatments; and we are not able to classify the styles or establish the relations between them. The Mayan culture can be traced in more degenerate types as far as the Isthmus, and the Aztec culture, considerably diluted, reached the plains of North America.

From Central America let us go to South America and study the cultures there. In the Valley of the Amazon an extraordinary culture grew up in the Maranjó region, producing a great wealth of pottery decorated with animal forms. In Colombia the Quechuas were great metalworkers; large numbers of gold ornaments have been found in their tombs. They also erected monumental statues, some of them as high as five and six yards, stupendous monoliths, cruder than the Mayan stelae, but very impressive in their group arrangement. Next to Colombia is the immense territory of Ecuador and Peru, where the Incas dominated when the Spaniards arrived. The Incas, like the Aztecs, were not original inhabitants, but they drove out the Quechuas who were already established there. These Quechuas were not so cruelly treated as were the peoples later conquered by the Aztecs, for the Incas worshiped the sun and were not so superstitious as the Aztecs.

Two views of a Mayan painted vessel. University of Pennsylvania Museum, Philadelphia.

The Peruvians kept their records by means of knots tied in string, as the earliest Chinese did; and we have not yet found out how to decipher them. No Peruvian hieroglyphics have been found.

The accounts of Spanish writers of the time of the conquest tell us less about Peru than about the early cultures in Mexico and Yucatán. The most important contemporary book of the Incan civilization is the one of Garcilaso, a mestizo, whose father was a Spanish nobleman and his mother an Indian princess. When he was sixteen years old Garcilaso was sent to Spain to study at Salamanca, and he never returned to his native Peru. It was not

Mayan mortuary vessel, with the figure of a man wearing on his head three *cascabel,* snake's rattlers. The bowl is cracked and has a hole in the center, as it was the custom with many primitive peoples to "kill" the vessels. University of Pennsylvania Museum, Philadelphia.

Mayan fresco from the Temple of the Jaguar at Chichen Itzá. American Museum of
Natural History, New York.

Peruvian textile. Requena Collection, New York.

until he was quite old that he wrote his recollections of his native land. His account is full of patriotic pride, and his style is scholarly. He describes the empire of the Incas as an ideal co-operative state, an almost communistic "City of the Sun."

Peru and Ecuador have many relics of the Incan and Pre-Incan cultures. Their buildings are constructed of immense blocks of stone cut in polygonal shapes with uniform angles so that they fit together exactly. They have no decoration of any kind. Their structures are not monumental, but are building efforts that can hardly be given the name of architecture.

To find real Peruvian art we must look in the tombs, which in themselves have no beauty. They were generally made by putting shafts deep into the rock. In rooms constructed underground, the mummies were placed in groups, squatting as if they were sitting in a social gathering. Beside them are their jewels, pots, pans, and precious textiles. Peruvian potters produced vases of great beauty in shape, texture, and color. Some vases are in the shape of a head of an Incan warrior, and some have the shape of the whole human body. Some ware is decorated with geometric designs. It is interesting to observe that, like the Mayas and Aztecs, the Incas prefer in the friezes an organization of lines not straight, vertical, or horizontal, but diagonal, making patterns of forms repeated in a slanting direction. The diagonal motif is the universal note of all aboriginal American art.

Regions of Peru are very dry, and rain is even more rare there than in Egypt. The fertile soil is irrigated by many streams that flow down from the Cordillera. The dryness of the tombs has preserved a wealth of Peruvian

Peruvian pots. Requena Collection, New York.

textiles that are equal in quality to any that have been woven in any part of the world. Since the material used is alpaca wool, their textiles are thicker than the Persian and Chinese textiles, which were largely silk; but the variety of colors used and the beautiful and fantastic shapes in the designs entirely compensate for the roughness and opaqueness of the wool and place them in the category of great works of art.

The earliest aboriginal peoples of the United States (except perhaps a race of unknown men in paleolithic times) were the Basket Makers of Arizona and southern Utah. This name has been given to them because they used baskets of Yucca fibers for every imaginable purpose, even smearing them with mud or pitch to use them for cooking. Some of the rock drawings of the southwest are believed to be the work of these people. The finding of primitive drawings over which others of more skill have been superimposed seems to suggest that the earlier ones may have been done by the Basket Makers.

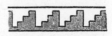

Motifs used in Indian designs.

With the coming of the Pueblo Indians about the beginning of the Christian Era, the Basket Makers' culture disappeared. The newcomers probably absorbed the earlier inhabitants, since we find the Pueblos retaining certain elements of the Basket Makers' culture, as, for example, the sacred kiva, which is believed to

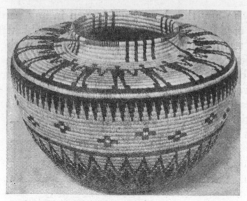

Pomo baskets from California. University of
Pennsylvania Museum, Philadelphia.

be a ritualistic descendant of the circular pit-home in which the earlier people lived.

The Pueblos were forced by the difficulties of the arid country and by their warlike neighbors to live in close co-operation with each other within their own villages, where circumstances enabled them to develop a high civilization. Beneath overhanging cliffs, or on high mesas, where they were protected from marauding bands of nomadic Indians, they built their "apartment-house" towns. The typical communal dwelling was built of stone or adobe brick, with very few openings in the walls and no attempt at decorative sculpture or painting. The homes were built and owned by the women; the efforts of the men went into building the ceremonial kivas, which the women were not allowed to enter.

The women were potters as well as masons. Without any potter's wheel, and with an open fire for a kiln, through remarkable skill they raised pottery-making to a fine art. In earliest prehistoric times the designs seem to have been borrowed from textile weaving and basketry, and such motives as zigzag lines and dots were used.

After the Pueblos were well established, each community developed its own characteristic style of art. The settlements were named after the rivers near which they were situated. The River Mimbres culture produced perhaps the most delightful pottery of all, with both geometric and realistic designs. The geometric designs are remarkable for their mathematical accuracy; and the realistic, for their caricature. All kinds of living things

Totem poles. City Park of Vancouver, British Columbia.

are treated with an inventive wit that is unsurpassed. A rabbit or a fish
is easily recognizable, but the proportions are arbitrarily treated, and
one cannot help wondering what "old master" of ceramic design invented
this style. The fact that many of the abstract motifs have names leads
to the conclusion that every design element has a meaning.

There is profound religious significance of a more definite kind in the
sand paintings of the Navajos. In these strangely beautiful works traditional

symbolism is preserved. There is no more impressive ceremony than that of the making of the painting in the sand and its destruction at the setting of the sun. This was the method the Navajo devised, since he had no written language, to teach his people the tribal beliefs.

The medicine man first prepares the sandy surface, making it smooth and flat. Then with his little pile of colors beside him, he takes up one color after another and lets it trickle through his fingers to form the pattern he wishes. His palette consists of white alkali, ground charcoal, red iron oxide, yellow ocher, and combinations of all these. His design as it takes shape discloses elongated gods, the forms of sacred plants, of corn, beans, squash, and tobacco. The work is skillfully done, entirely freehand. At sunset, pollen is scattered over it, prayers are chanted in a singsong tone, and finally with a gourd rattle the medicine man erases the image.

The most elaborate type of sculpture is the totem pole of the Northwest Indians. Grotesque animals carved on the poles are the geneological records of the family before whose house they stand. Some of the tribal animals are mythological, such as the thunder-bird, the rustling of whose wings produces the thunder.

Peruvian vase in the form of an Inca chief. University of
Pennsylvania Museum, Philadelphia.